THE MIDDLE GAME IN CHESS

Also by Reuben Fine

CHESS THE EASY WAY

BASIC CHESS ENDINGS

THE IDEAS BEHIND THE CHESS OPENINGS

CHESS MARCHES ON!

MODERN CHESS OPENINGS, *Sixth Edition*

PRACTICAL CHESS OPENINGS

THE WORLD'S A CHESSBOARD

*

THE

MIDDLE GAME

IN

CHESS

Reuben Fine

DAVID McKAY COMPANY, INC.

NEW YORK

Contents

THE MIDDLE GAME IN CHESS

I. *A Few Ideas*

THE APPROACH to the middle game is through the analysis of the positions that occur. Unlike the opening, "theoretical" variations are of little value; unlike the end game, precisely analyzed positions are not repeated over and over again. In the middle game our main concern must be with the ideas that are used to understand what goes on.

Force (or material), mobility, and King safety are the three basic principles of chess.* Mobility can be further subdivided into Pawn structure (or Pawn mobility) and general freedom of the pieces. Add to these the tactical situation at any moment (combinations), and we have a complete outline for the analysis of any position.

However, not all of these elements are of equal importance. First place must of course be given to the position of the King. When it is endangered, nothing else counts. Hence we must devote a special chapter to the various possibilities of attack against the King, i.e., mating attacks.

Still, even in mating attacks the factor of crucial importance is the combination. In the last analysis every game of chess is decided tactically. The reason why a strong player can give a weaker a handicap is that he "sees" more, i.e., he is more alive to the combinations inherent in the position. Among players of equal strength, it is always the last blunder, and the ability to see it, that determines who will win. At every level of chess skill, including the world championship class, it is still true that tactics is 99 per cent of the game. So the first portion of

* For a fuller elaboration see my *Chess the Easy Way*.

this book is devoted to developing the principles of combination play.

Combinations are generally made for the purpose of winning material. Theoretically, with other things equal, *any material advantage is enough to win.* The strength of a player may in fact be gauged by the amount of material he needs to force a win. For a master a Pawn is usually sufficient. For the average player of club strength it would be a Knight, in all probability.

When there is no material advantage or decisive mating attack, we are in the realm of *position play.* Obviously, the goals of position play must be either the gain of material or the building up of a decisive attack. Its principles are really much simpler than most textbooks have made out; as we shall see, it revolves around the evaluation of a position, and the means of exploiting a superior position. The nature of position play may be paraphrased as the art of winning a won game, or from the defender's point of view, drawing a lost game. Of course, in practice, we are often uncertain about whether a position is clearly won; we speak of superior and inferior positions. These questions will occupy us in the second portion of this book.

II. *The Elements of Combinations*

A COMBINATION is a series of moves, all more or less forced, and frequently involving a material sacrifice, designed to effect some radical change in the position. This change will result in one of the two fundamental tangible advantages— material gain or King attack.

Combinations are what chiefly distinguish chess from other games and put it in a class by itself. They represent what Reti called "the triumph of mind over matter." They are unexpected, begin surprisingly, often consist of a series of pointless moves or even mistakes. They are literally the joining up of moves to form one whole and reach one objective. They are the poetry of the chessboard, and their sheer beauty often blinds us to the merits of position play, which is the prose.

At first sight combinations strike us as a bolt from the blue. The amateur looks at the games of the master, and says in awe and wonderment, "How did he see it?" Yet combinations are based on only two simple principles. If the King is not involved, *all combinations are based on a double attack*. If the King is involved, the combination has a mating threat as the pivot.

In this chapter we shall be concerned only with the elementary combinations, where the King is not involved. For this purpose we explore the combinative powers of the various pieces.

It is clear that each piece will be able to build up double attacks in ways peculiar to its moves. Analysis shows however that there are five basic types of double attack:

1. *Fork* of two undefended units, or two units of higher value—this is a power which all pieces possess.

2. *Check and capture* an undefended piece or one of higher value—all pieces but the King.

3. *Pin* an undefended piece or one of higher value—Bishop, Rook, and Queen.

4. *Capture and threaten mate*—Rook and Queen usually, though in rare cases this is possible with any piece.

5. *Capture or advance*—the Pawn.

Let us examine these combinative possibilities in greater detail for each individual piece.

1. The Queen

This is by far the most powerful piece, and the one that lends itself most readily to combining.

The first pattern for Queen combinations is the fork. In *Diagram 1* we have a typical example. Black has just mistakenly played his P to QKt3, White replied with Q to K4. Now the Rook and Knight are both attacked; one must go. Here we see the Queen operating in both directions as a Bishop. In *Diagram 2* we see the Queen attacking the Knight as a Bishop, and the Bishop as a Rook; again equally effective, of course. Naturally the Queen can also threaten in both directions as a Rook; this is seen in *Diagram 3*. Note that in all these Queen combinations the pieces attacked are of lower value. Furthermore, it is essential that the pieces should not be able to defend themselves. E.g., in *Diagram 3* if the White Knight were at QR4 rather than at QKt4 White could hold everything with Kt - QB3.

The second pattern for Queen combinations is check and capture. A typical example is *Diagram 4*. Here the Queen checks diagonally (i.e., as a Bishop) and captures Black's Kt at QR4 horizontally (i.e., as a Rook). In *Diagram 5* both check and capture are performed diagonally (i.e., as a Bishop). After

DIAGRAM 1

FORK

DIAGRAM 2

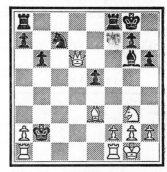

FORK

DIAGRAM 3

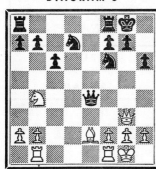

FORK

DIAGRAM 4

CHECK AND CAPTURE

the King moves, the White Queen's Rook goes. In some positions of this kind the Black Queen could be bottled up and captured, but that is not the case here.

The third pattern is the pin. In this respect the Queen is paradoxically somewhat less effective than the other pieces. Typical is *Diagram 6*. Here the White Knight has no moves and is soon gone. Note that a Bishop at Q3 would have done just as well. And also that the Bishop in such cases could pin a Queen, but the Queen could not pin a Bishop diagonally (it could pin a Rook).

Less frequent but quite possible is a position where the pin involves two pieces, rather than a piece and the King. This is seen in *Diagram 7*. Here Black's Bishop at Q5 is under attack; if it moves the other Bishop at KKt5 is lost.

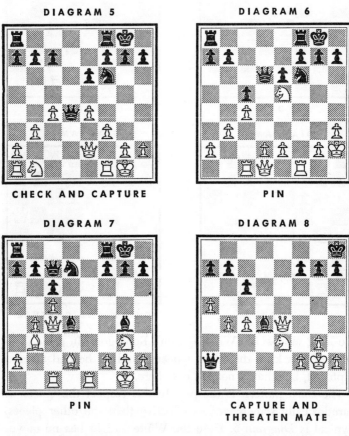

DIAGRAM 5

CHECK AND CAPTURE

DIAGRAM 6

PIN

DIAGRAM 7

PIN

DIAGRAM 8

CAPTURE AND
THREATEN MATE

The fourth pattern for Queen combinations is a mate threat and capture. In *Diagram 8* Black's immediate concern must be to defend against the mate threat; after some Pawn move such as . . . P - KR3, White captures the Bishop. Note that in this sort of position, if the Black King were at KKt1, and the

DIAGRAM 9

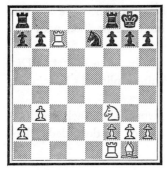

FORK

DIAGRAM 10

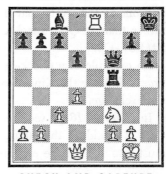

CHECK AND CAPTURE

White Pawn were not at QKt4, Black would have the defensive resources of . . . B - QB4, for if then Q - K8 ch, B - B1.

2. The Rook

As with the Queen, there are four combinatory patterns for the Rook. First of course comes the fork. This accounts for the great effectiveness of a Rook on the seventh rank (a "pig in a poke"). E.g., in *Diagram 9* Black's Kt must be defended, when the QKtP goes. A typical check and capture position is seen in *Diagram 10.* Here the King must move, and then White plays R x B. Note that if Black's Rook were at KB2 here, it could be interposed at KB1 and save the piece.

A somewhat different situation is that in *Diagram 11.* Here the King must move, and then White replies R x Kt.

The pin with the Rook is illustrated in *Diagram 12.* The Black Bishop at K1 simply cannot be defended.

Finally, a mate threat and capture is seen in *Diagram 13.* Again Black's immediate concern is to stop mate at Q8; on any adequate defensive move there follows R x B.

3. The Bishop

For the Bishop we have three types of combination—the fork, check and capture, and pin. In *Diagram 14* we see a common instance of a fork. The two Knights cannot defend one another, and one is lost. Note that if the Black Knight were at QKt2 rather than at QB3, Black could hold the position with . . . Kt(K5) - Q3.

An example of a check-capture combination is that in *Diagram 15*. After the King moves, White replies B x R, winning the exchange.

In *Diagram 16* we see the pin at work. The Black Knight at QB2 is shielding the Rook, and cannot be defended. Black must lose at least the exchange.

4. The Knight

With the Knight there are only two combinative possibilities, the fork and the check-capture. In *Diagram 17* we see the fork —one of the two Black Rooks must go. Naturally, the Knight must fork either two undefended pieces or two units of higher value, as here.

Three common examples of a check-capture combination are illustrated in the next few diagrams. In *Diagram 18* the King must move, and then the Rook goes. In *Diagram 19* the Bishop is lost. Note here that if Black's QKtP were at QKt3 instead of QKt4, after . . . K - K2; Kt x B, Q - B2 White's Knight could not get out.

DIAGRAM 11

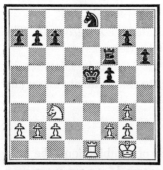

CHECK AND CAPTURE

DIAGRAM 12

PIN

DIAGRAM 13

**CAPTURE AND
THREATEN MATE**

DIAGRAM 14

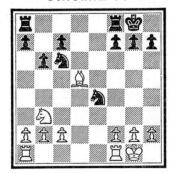

FORK

DIAGRAM 15

CHECK AND CAPTURE

DIAGRAM 16

PIN

DIAGRAM 17

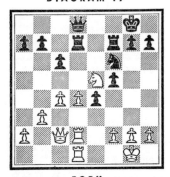

FORK

DIAGRAM 18

CHECK AND CAPTURE

Both of the above combinations are against the uncastled King. A typical combination against the castled King is seen in *Diagram 20*. Again the King must move, and the Bishop is lost.

DIAGRAM 19

CHECK AND CAPTURE

DIAGRAM 20

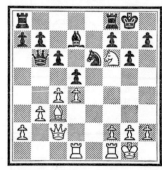

CHECK AND CAPTURE

DIAGRAM 21

FORK

DIAGRAM 22

CHECK AND CAPTURE

5. The Pawn

With the Pawn there are three combinative possibilities— fork, check and capture, and capture or advance. A typical example of a fork in the opening is seen in *Diagram 21*. White has just give up a Knight (opening moves: *1*. P - K4, P - K4; *2*.

Kt - KB3,   Kt - QB3;   3. B - Kt5,   B - B4;   4. Kt x P,   Kt x Kt; 5. P - Q4), which is now regained. A check-capture position is seen in *Diagram 22*. This has come out of a sacrificial attack against the White King. Black now regains his piece.

The capture or promote type of combination is unique to the Pawn, and is possible only because of the special power of the Pawn to promote. This usually comes up only in the end game. In *Diagram 22A* if the Kt at Kt2 moves, P - R7 queens, while if the other Knight moves, P x Kt leads to queening. This combination is possible only on the Rook file. In *Diagram 23* a similar situation prevails: White queens either by capturing or advancing. Such combinations with the Pawn unsupported by other pieces are possible only against the Knights; against other pieces the Pawn needs support.

6. The King

With His Majesty only one type of combination is feasible— the fork. Even this is limited, since the King cannot fork any piece that is checking it; thus, e.g., the King can never attack a Queen. Usually the King forks two Pawns or a Pawn and a minor piece. Typical is *Diagram 24*. Here either the BP or the KP must go.

One comment may be made about combinations in general. Since they are based on double attacks, the question arises, when are such attacks feasible? The answer is that they are feasible only when there are weaknesses in the enemy position. These weaknesses necessarily involve *exposure* of some kind—either there are undefended pieces hanging around loose, or the King is exposed, or both. In such cases the air is full of combinations; something, we think, is bound to turn up.

Compound Combinations

WE HAVE systematically gone through all possible combinations with a single piece. Now we come to those combinations that involve only two pieces. Here there are four possibilities; the pin, discovered check, discoveries in general, and isolated attacks.

A. The Pin

Pins are of course a basic combinative form for every piece except the Pawn and King. What we are concerned with here are those pins where one piece holds the enemy, while the other delivers the knockout blow.

In one type of position, the pin is *absolute*, i.e., the piece

DIAGRAM 22A

CAPTURE OR PROMOTE

DIAGRAM 23

CAPTURE OR PROMOTE

DIAGRAM 24

FORK

DIAGRAM 25

ABSOLUTE PIN

DIAGRAM 26

ABSOLUTE PIN

screens the King and any move with it is illegal. A common instance from the opening is seen in *Diagram 25*. Black's Knight must not move, and is lost to the White Pawn. An example where the pinned piece is attacked by more pieces than can be brought to defend it is shown in *Diagram 26*. The White Bishop at Q1 is defended twice, attacked three times; it is lost. Note that if the White King were closer by, the Bishop could be held.

A second type of pin is a *relative* one, where the pinned piece may move, but by so doing exposes the player to a greater loss. A typical case is that where a piece screens the Queen from a Rook. A frequently seen instance is that in *Diagram 27*. Here if the Bishop moves the Queen is lost. The only rule is that the pinned piece must be screening one of higher value. Thus in *Diagram 28* the Knight is screening the Rook.

B. Discovered Check

This is one of the most destructive devices available to the player—it is the hydrogen bomb of the chessboard. For the piece that moves out of the way may go anywhere, attack anything, capture anything with impunity. In effect the player may make two moves in a row. An amusing instance is that in

Diagram 29. Despite Black's enormous material advantage, White can win everything in and out of sight and leave Black as helpless as a baby. There would follow: *1.* R x R dis ch, K - Kt1; *2.* R - Kt7 ch, K - R1; *3.* R x Kt dis ch, K - Kt1; *4.* R - Kt7 ch, K - R1; *5.* R x B dis ch, K - Kt1; *6.* R - Kt7 ch, K - R1; *7.* R x P dis ch, K - Kt1; *8.* R - Kt7 ch, K - R1; *9.* R x P dis ch, K - Kt1; *10.* R - Kt7 ch, K - R1; *11.* R x P dis ch, K - Kt1; *12.* R x Q and Black is gone. A mating situation would arise here if Black's KR2 were blocked. Thus if Black's Pawn were at KR2, White could continue with *1.* R x R dis ch, K - Kt1; *2.* R - Kt7 ch, K - R1; *3.* R - Kt6 dis ch and mate.

Ordinarily discovered checks are not quite so destructive, but they do enough damage. A position from Petroff's Defense is shown in *Diagram 30.* Here *1.* Kt - B6 dis ch wins Black's Queen.

The *double check* is a special case of the discovered check where the discovering piece gives check as well. Since it eliminates the possibilities of interposition, and capture of the checking piece, the only defense left open is to move the King; frequently this defense is not available, so mate results. An example is seen in *Diagram 31. 1.* . . . Kt - R5 is double check and mate, even though either check alone could easily be parried.

A special case of double check is that shown in *Diagram 32,* the famous Philidor's Legacy. Here White mates in three with *1.* Kt - R6 dbl ch, K - R1; *2.* Q - Kt8 ch, R x Q; *3.* Kt - B7 mate.

C. Discoveries in General

The same principles apply here as in the case of discovered check—but the threat to a Queen or Rook is not so compelling as that to a King, so that such discoveries are somewhat less effective. A common example is that in *Diagram 33.* After *1.* P - Q4 Black's Bishop and Queen are both attacked; a piece is lost.

DIAGRAM 27

RELATIVE PIN

DIAGRAM 28

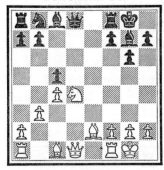

RELATIVE PIN

DIAGRAM 29

DISCOVERED CHECK
WINS

DIAGRAM 30

DISCOVERED CHECK
WINS

DIAGRAM 31

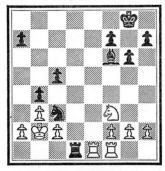

DOUBLE CHECK WINS

DIAGRAM 32

DOUBLE CHECK WINS
PHILIDOR'S LEGACY

D. Isolated Attacks

These occur when there are two separate attacks at two different spots. They may arise as a result of a discovery (as in Diagram 33) or because of an oversight. In *Diagram 34* Black mistakenly played *1. . . .* Q x P ch ?. After *2.* K - Kt1, both Queen and Bishop are under attack, and he loses a piece.

DIAGRAM 33

DIAGRAM 34

In order to complete the examination of the basic combinatory possibilities of the chess pieces we must still examine the mating attack, which obeys its own rules. For this we turn to the next chapter.

III. *The Mating Attack*

WHILE THE MATING ATTACK generally involves all the various combinations described in the preceding chapter, there is the special consideration of mate, which puts it in a class by itself. Because of this, questions of material are frequently secondary. Instead, the central issue is the *exposure of the King*. In all cases we have to decide whether this exposure is sufficient compensation for the material sacrificed. By and large this is a tactical matter that differs for each position, but there are certain general principles and typical positions knowledge of which is of help in the way through the maze.

The Uncastled King

WHEN the King remains in the center too long, the pressure of the opposing pieces often becomes overwhelming. It is for this reason that the expert generally prefers to castle early, and bring his King to safety.

In order to get at the principles governing combinations against the uncastled King let us begin with two famous Anderssen brilliancies, among the most celebrated on record.

Diagram 35 is taken from the game Anderssen-Kieseritzky, London, 1851. White is already one piece behind, but stakes everything on the attack. The game continued:

1. B - Q6 ‼   B x R

DIAGRAM 35

It is essential to calculate the mating combinations with absolute precision. If here, e.g., *1. . . .* Q x R ch; *2.* K - K2, Q x R; then *3.* Kt x P ch, K - Q1; *4.* B - B7 mate.

2. P - K5 ‼

Threatening Kt x P ch and B - B7 mate, as before.

2. . . .   Q x R ch

There is no defense.

3. K - K2   Kt - QR3

At any rate stopping the mate at QB7.

4. Kt x P ch   K - Q1

DIAGRAM 36

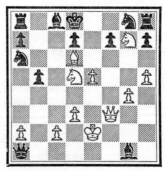

5. Q - B6 ch

This part of the combination, while pretty, is unnecessary. 5. Q x P also leads to mate in short order.

5. . . .   Kt x Q
6. B - K7 mate

The second Anderssen brilliancy is from his game against Dufresne at Berlin, 1853. In *Diagram 37* it is not readily apparent how White will win. The continuation was:

DIAGRAM 37

1. R x Kt ch !   Kt x R

As happens so often in mating attacks, Black could have warded off the mate by piece sacrifices, but the end result would have been no different. The best defense was *1.* . . . K - Q1; 2. R x P ch !!, K - B1 (if 2. . . . K x R; 3. B - B5 dbl ch, K - K1; 4. R - K1 ch, K - Q1; 5. B - K7 ch, Kt x B; 6. Q - Q7 mate); 3. R - Q8 ch !!, K x R (if now 3. . . . Kt x R; 4. Q - Q7 ch, K x Q; 5. B - B5 dbl ch, K - B3; 6. B - Q7 mate); 4. B - B5 dis ch, Q x R ch; 5. Q x Q ch, Kt - Q5; 6. P x Kt and wins because the Black pieces are too disorganized.

DIAGRAM 38

    2. Q x P ch !!   K x Q

Or 2. . . . K - B1; 3. Q x Kt mate.

    3. B - B5 dbl ch   K - K1

If instead 3. . . . K - B3; 4. B - Q7 mate.

    4. B - Q7 ch   K - Q1

Or 4. . . . K - B1; 5. B x Kt mate.

    5. B x Kt mate

If we analyze the above two games we find several points in common. First of all, *in a mating attack material is of secondary importance.* In several cases Black was a Rook or Queen or more ahead; he still could not prevent mate. Second, *the essential idea is to expose the King.* Nothing else really counts. The King must be stripped of defenders, and must be kept stripped. Third, and crucial, *all combinations must be calculated with precision.* It is not enough to sacrifice on "general principles" that the exposed King position will automatically lead to mate. This is the mistake most commonly made by the amateur—he sacrifices for "mating threats" without a clear idea of what he is up to.

Mating attacks against the uncastled King are of a number

of varieties. There are of course what we might call "oversight mates" such as *1.* P - KB3 ?, P - K4; *2.* P - KKt4, Q - R5 mate. Or the other famous "Fool's Mate": *1.* P - K4, P - K4; *2.* B - B4, B - B4; *3.* Q - R5, Kt - QB3 ??; *4.* Q x BP mate.

Apart from these oversights, we have first of all the *double check* leading to mate. The simplest example is that in *Diagram 39.* After *1.* Kt - B6 dbl ch, K any; *2.* Q - K8 is mate. Note that Kt x B dbl ch here would not be as strong as Kt - B6 dbl ch. Another type case is that in *Diagram 40.* Here White continues with *1.* B - Kt5 dbl ch, K any; *2.* R - K8 mate.

An interesting case where a double check leads to a King

DIAGRAM 39

DIAGRAM 40

DIAGRAM 41

DIAGRAM 42

hunt or quick mate is that shown in *Diagram 41*. Here the sequel is: *1*. B - B7 ch !, K x B; *2*. Kt - K5 dbl ch, K - K2 (or *2*. . . . K - B1; *3*. Q - B7 mate); *3*. Q - B7 ch, K - Q3; *4*. Kt - B4 ch, K - B4; *5*. Q - Q5 ch, K - Kt5; *6*. B - Q2 ch, K - R5; *7*. P - Kt3 mate. The double check is followed up by a King hunt.

The next type of combination is that involving *material gain or mate*. A classical example of this has come down as Legal's Legacy. In *Diagram 42* Black has just made a mistake (opening moves: *1*. P - K4, P - K4; *2*. Kt - KB3, P - Q3; *3*. B - B4, B - Kt5; *4*. Kt - B3, P - KKt3 ?), which is punished by *5*. Kt x P !!. For if now *5*. . . . B x Q; *6*. B x P ch, K - K2; *7*. Kt - Q5 mate.

There are many variants on the Legal idea. We give a few. In *Diagram 43* after *1*. Kt x Kt !, B x Q; *2*. B x P ch, K - K2; *3*. Kt - Q5 is mate because Black's Knight is pinned.

Sometimes the mate can be administered by another piece. This is seen in *Diagram 44*. After *1*. . . . Kt x P !; *2*. B x Q ?, B x P ch; *3*. K - K2, B - Kt5 ch is mate. Here, as in so many cases with Legal's Legacy, White can play *2*. Q - K2 and content himself with the loss of a Pawn.

DIAGRAM 43

DIAGRAM 44

A somewhat more complicated line is shown in *Diagram 45*. After *1*. Kt x P !, B x Q; *2*. B x P ch, Q x B; *3*. R - Q8 is mate.

DIAGRAM 45

This is really a combination of Legal's Legacy with a deflection sacrifice.

DIAGRAM 46

Another type of position in which mate or loss of material are the alternatives is shown in *Diagram 46*. The continuation here is:

1. B x P ch !	K x B

If *1.* . . . K - B1; 2. Kt - K6 ch.

2. Kt - K6 !!	Q - K1

On 2. . . . K x Kt there follows 3. Q - Q5 ch, K - B3; 4. Q - B5 mate.

3. Kt x BP   Q - Q1

After 3. . . . Q - B1 the variations are similar.

DIAGRAM 47

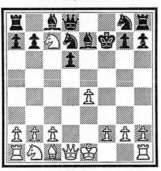

4. Q - Q5 ch

The quickest, but White also has an adequate alternative in 4. Q - R5 ch, P - Kt3; 5. Q - Q5 ch, K - B3; 6. B - Kt5 ch, K - Kt2; 7. Kt - K6 ch winning the Queen.

4. . . .   K - B1

On 4. . . . K - B3 or 4. . . . K - Kt3; 5. Q - B5 ch is mate.

5. Kt - K6 ch   K - K1
6. Kt x P ch

Leads to mate. 6. Kt x Q is of course also good enough.

6. . . .   K - B1
7. Kt - K6 ch   K - B2
8. Q - R5 ch   K x Kt
9. Q - B5 mate

The next type of combination that we encounter is the *clearance sacrifice*. As the name implies, in this type of sacrifice lines are cleared to permit mating threats. A classic example is taken from the game Morphy-Duke of Brunswick, Paris, 1858. From *Diagram 48* the continuation was:

DIAGRAM 48

1. Kt x P !	P x Kt
2. B x KtP ch	QKt - Q2
3. O - O - O !	R - Q1
4. R x Kt !	R x R
5. R - Q1	Q - K3
6. B x R ch	Kt x B

DIAGRAM 49

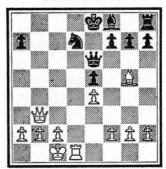

    7. Q - Kt8 ch !!   Kt x Q
    8. R - Q8 mate

Another type of clearance sacrifice is seen in *Diagram 50*, taken from a game Fine-Landau, Ostende, 1937. The continuation was:

DIAGRAM 50

    1. Kt - B5 !!   B x B

If instead 1. . . . Kt - K3; 2. Q x Kt ch !!, BP x Q; 3. Kt - Q6 ch wins a piece.

    2. Kt x P ch   K - Q1

DIAGRAM 51

3. P - K6 !!

The clearance maneuver.

3. . . .	Kt x P
4. R x Kt !	Kt - R3

Desperation. If 4. . . . BP x R; 5. Kt x P ch, K - B1; 6. Q - B8
mate.

5. R x Kt

and Black soon resigned.

Examination of *Diagram 52* reveals how the deflection com-
bination can take place. If the White Queen did not cover the
K3 square, Black could play . . . Q - K6 ch and mates after
B - K2, Q x B mate. Hence the job is to deflect the White

DIAGRAM 52

Queen. This is done by

1. . . .	R - Kt6 !!
2. Q x R	

Or 2. P x R, Q - K6 ch.

2. . . .	B - R5 !!

and wins.

The last type of combination under consideration here is the *King hunt*. Once the King is forced out into the open in the early part of the game disaster is almost certain to follow. Examples are both instructive and delightful.

DIAGRAM 53

Odds games often yield a rich harvest of such combinations because the odds player is not sufficiently familiar with the principles of sound chess. Here is a position from a Rook-odds game that was won successively by Walker, Morphy, and Steinitz, and most likely by countless others since. From *Diagram 53:*

1. P x B !!	Kt x Q

With *1. . . .* BP x P Black can hold out a little longer, but the ending would not be as pretty.

2. P x P dbl ch	K - Q2
3. B - K6 ch	K - B3
4. Kt - K5 ch	K - Kt4
5. B - B4 ch	K - R4
6. B - Kt4 ch	K - R5
7. P x Kt mate	

Even when there is no immediate mate in sight, a King out in the open spells trouble. In *Diagram 54*, at first sight White looks relatively safe, yet he cannot escape the net. There followed:

DIAGRAM 54

1. . . .	B - B7 ch
2. K - R3	P - Q3 dis ch
3. P - K6	

On *3.* P - Kt4, Kt - B5 ch is mate. Even if White tries to give up the Queen with *3.* Q - Kt4, Kt - B5 ch is still mate!

3. . . .	Kt - B5 ch
4. K - Kt4	Kt x KP

The threats are all too many. Besides a discovery with the Knight Black also has . . . R - B5 ch and . . . R - R5 mate.

5. P - Kt3	Kt x Kt dis ch
6. K - Kt5	

There is no escape. If *6.* K - R4, R - B5 ch forces the same position.

6. . . .	R - B4 ch
7. K - R4	R - B5 ch
8. K - Kt5	

Another pretty mating variation is 8. K - R5, P - Kt3 ch; 9. K - R6, Kt - B2 mate.

8. . . .	Kt - K3 ch
9. K - R5	P - Kt3 ch
10. K - R6	R - R5 ch !
11. P x R	B - K6 mate

It should not be assumed that a sacrifice which drives the King out into the open automatically wins; there are many exceptions to the rule. A well-known one is the so-called Fried Liver Attack in the Two Knights' Defense, which arises after 1. P - K4, P - K4; 2. Kt - KB3, Kt - QB3; 3. B - B4, Kt - B3; 4. Kt - Kt5, P - Q4; 5. P x P, Kt x P; 6. Kt x BP ! ?, K x Kt; 7. Q - B3 ch, K - K3 (*Diagram 55*). It would take us too far afield

DIAGRAM 55

to go into an exhaustive analysis of this position, which has shown that Black's game is preferable. The main variation runs as follows:

8. Kt - B3	Kt(B3) - Kt5 !
9. Q - K4	P - B3 !
10. P - Q4	K - Q2 !

This kind of maneuver is known as "castling by hand."

11. Kt x Kt	P x Kt
12. B x P	Kt x B
13. Q x Kt ch	K - B2

Black's King is now comparatively safe. If *14.* Q x KP ch, B - Q3; *15.* Q x P ch, B - Q2 Black's attack is stronger than White's.

The Castled King

CASTLING is undertaken with the double purpose of bringing the King to safety and increasing the communication between the pieces. In general, as we shall discuss in more detail later, it is best not to move the Pawns guarding the King. Yet, both with Pawns unmoved and moved there are certain typical sacrificial positions that occur time and again.

When the King has not castled, the most vulnerable point in the defense is KB2. *When he has castled on the K-side, the weakest link in the defensive chain is KR2.* It is against this point that the majority of sacrificial combinations are directed.

The type position is shown in *Diagram 55A.* White continues:

1. B x P ch !	K x B
2. Kt - Kt5 ch	K - Kt3

DIAGRAM 55A

WHITE TO PLAY WINS

Black has only a choice of evils, If here 2. . . . K - Kt1; 3. Q - R5 and mate next move at KR7.

3. Q - Kt4   P - B4

On other moves Black loses his Queen to a discovered check.

4. Q - R3   any
5. Q - R7 mate

Clearly this sacrifice is feasible only when Black cannot defend his KR2 square. When he can, the attack may easily fail. E.g., in *Diagram 56* the sacrifice is unsound:

DIAGRAM 56

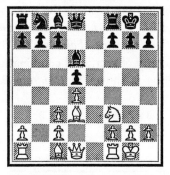

1. B x P ch ?   K x B
2. Kt - Kt5 ch   K - Kt1
3. Q - R5   B - KB4

and White is lost.

Often the sacrifice of the KB is combined with action along the King's Rook file. An example of this is seen in *Diagram 57.* After

1. B x P ch !	K x B
2. Kt - Kt5 ch	

there are three possible continuations:

A.	2. . . .	**B x Kt**
	3. P x B dis ch	**K - Kt1**

Or 3. . . . K - Kt3; 4. Q - R5 ch, K - B4; 5. Q - R3 ch, K - Kt3; 6. Q - R7 mate.

	4. Q - R5	**P - B3**
	5. P - Kt6	

And mate next.

B.	2. . . .	**K - Kt1**
	3. Q - R5	**R - K1**

With 3. . . . B x Kt Black can transpose to Variation A.

	4. Q - R7 ch	**K - B1**
	5. Q - R8 mate	
C.	2. . . .	**K - Kt3**
	3. P - R5 ch	**K - R3**
	4. Kt x BP dbl ch	**K - R2**
	5. Kt x Q	

with an easy win.

In most cases in practical play the sacrifice does not crash through immediately, but depends on the bringing up of reserves. Thus in *Diagram 58* the continuation is:

1. B x P ch !   K x B
2. Q - R5 ch   K - Kt1

DIAGRAM 58

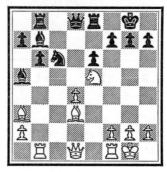

3. Q x P ch   K - R1
4. R - Kt3

and Black must give up his Queen to hold off mate for a while.

Frequently one sacrifice is followed by others, all made possible by the imminence of mate. *Diagram 59* is taken from the celebrated game Colle-O'Hanlon, Nice, 1930. It continued:

DIAGRAM 59

> *1.* B x P ch !!   K x B
> 2. Kt - Kt5 ch   K - Kt3

Another pretty offer comes up after the alternative 2. . . ,
K - Kt1; 3. Q - R5, Kt - B3; 4. Q x P ch, K - R1; 5. R - K4 !!,
Kt x R; 6. Q - R5 ch, K - Kt1; 7. Q - R7 ch, K - B1; 8. Q - R8 ch,
K - K2; 9. Q x P mate.

> *3.* P - KR4 !

Threatening P - R5 ch.

> *3.* . . . .   R - R1

DIAGRAM 60

> 4. R x P ch !!   Kt - B3

Black finds that he must either lose his Queen or be mated.
After 4. . . . P x R there would follow 5. Q - Q3 ch, K - B3 (on
5. . . . K - R3 or R4 the variations are similiar); 6. Q - B3 ch,
K - Kt3; 7. Q - B7 ch, K - R3; 8. Kt x P dis ch with mate shortly.

> 5. P - R5 ch !   K - R3

Or 5. . . . R x P; 6. Q - Q3 ch, K - R3; 7. Kt x P mate.

> *6.* R x B

Naturally 6. Kt x P dbl ch is also good enough.

6. . . .	Q - R4
7. Kt x P dbl ch	K - R2
8. Kt - Kt5 ch	K - Kt1
9. Q - Kt3 ch !	Resigns

For he must give up still more material, and then be mated into the bargain !

The position in *Diagram 61* has an amusing history. It first came up in a game Janowski-Chajes, New York, 1916. Janow-

DIAGRAM 61

ski continued:

1. B x P ch !	K x B
2. Q - R5 ch	K - Kt1
3. Q x P ch	

Exactly the same position occurred fifteen years later in the game Mikenas-Kashdan, Prague, 1931. Mikenas took the draw by perpetual check. Instead Janowski won as follows:

4. Kt - Q7	Kt x Kt

Forced.

5. R x Kt

Threatening both R x B and Q x B

> 5. . . .   B - B3
> 6. Kt - K4 !!

An elegant move: if 6. . . . B x R; 7. Kt x B ch leads to mate, while if 6. . . . B x Kt taking the pressure off White's Rook, 7. Q x B is crushing.

> 6. . . .   B x P
> 7. Kt - Kt5 ch   K - R3
> 8. P - Kt4 !   P - Kt3

The King has no place to go. On 8. . . . K x Kt; 9. Q - R5 ch, K - B3; 10. R - B7 ch is mate.

> 9. P - KR4   R - R1

DIAGRAM 61A

> 10. Q - R7 ch !

And after 10. . . . R x Q; 11. R x R ch is mate.

Sometimes this sacrifice can be advantageously refused. E.g., in *Diagram 62*, from Marshall-Burn, Ostende, 1907, White played:

> 1. B x P ch   K x B ?

DIAGRAM 62

After this he is lost. With *1. . . . K - B1* he could have refuted the previous sacrifices, which Marshall described as "a
little on the wild side."

2. Kt - Kt5 ch   K - Kt3

On *2. . . . K - Kt1* White's Rook eventually comes in with
devastating effect: *3. Q x P, Kt - B3; 4. Q x P ch, K - R1; 5.
0 - 0 - 0* and wins.

3. Kt(Q2) - B3	P - K4
4. Kt - R4 ch	K - B3
5. Kt - R7 ch	K - K2
6. Kt - B5 ch	K - K3
7. Kt x B ch	K - K2
8. Kt - B5 ch	K - K3
9. P - Q5 ch	K x Kt
10. Q x P ch	K - K5
11. O - O - O	

Now there is no defense to *P - B3* mate.

As we have seen, frequently the follow-up of the sacrifice at
KR7 involves shifting the Rook to the KR file. Thus in *Diagram 63* White wins as follows:

| 1. B x Kt | B x B |

It makes no difference if Black captures with the Pawn—the same sacrifice wins.

| 2. B x P ch | K x B |
| 3. R - R3 ch | K - Kt1 |

Or 3. . . . B - R5; 4. Q - R5 ch.

| 4. Q - R5 | |

To stop mate Black now must play 4. . . . B - R5 and give up Bishop and Queen.

A somewhat similar idea is illustrated in *Diagram 64*, from Keres-Fine, Ostende, 1937. White continued:

| 1. Kt x RP ! | Kt x Kt |
| 2. R - R3 | |

Now the Knight must not move because of the mate at KR8. He tried a desperate maneuver, but without success.

2. . . .	Q - B8
3. Q x Kt ch	K - B1
4. R(R3) - K3	P - Q5
5. Q - R8 ch	K - K2
6. Q x P	

Threatening Q x P mate.

6. . . .	R - B1
7. Q - B6 ch	K - K1
8. P - K6 !	

With the King so exposed Black's game falls apart. There might have followed: 8. . . . P x R; 9. P x P ch, K - Q2; *10.* B - K6 ch, K - Q3; *11.* B x R dis ch, K - B2; *12.* R x Q ch, etc. Black resigned.

DIAGRAM 64

Another combinative sequence that tears open the defenses of the enemy King is the *two-Bishop sacrifice*. This was first seen in the classic Lasker-Bauer, Amsterdam, 1889. From *Diagram 65* Lasker continued:

DIAGRAM 65

1.	B x P ch !	K x B
2.	Q x Kt ch	K - Kt1

What now?

3.	B x P !!!

The offer of the second Bishop is decisive.

3. . . .		K x B

Black has no choice. If *3.* . . . P - B3; *4.* R - B3 leads to a quick mate.

4.	Q - Kt4 ch !	K - R2

Not *4.* . . . K - B3; *5.* Q - Kt5 mate.

5.	R - B3	P - K4

Black can just manage to stave off mate by giving up his Queen. If the Black Queen were at QB2 mate would be forced.

6.	R - R3 ch	Q - R3
7.	R x Q ch	K x R
8.	Q - Q7	

Winning one of the Bishops.

8. . . .		B - KB3
9.	Q x B	K - Kt2
10.	R - KB1	QR - Kt1
11.	Q - Q7	KR - Q1
12.	Q - Kt4 ch	K - B1
13.	P x P	B - Kt2

If *13.* . . . B x P; *14.* Q - K6 ! wins the Bishop.

14.	P - K6	R - Kt2
15.	Q - Kt6	P - B3
16.	R x P ch !	

Not necessary, but effective.

16. . . .	B x R
17. Q x B ch	K - K1
18. Q - R8 ch	K - K2
19. Q - Kt7 ch	Resigns

Twenty-five years later, at St. Petersburg in 1914, Tarrasch played the same sacrifice against his archcritic Nimzovitch. The critical position is shown in *Diagram 66*. Here Tarrasch continued:

DIAGRAM 66

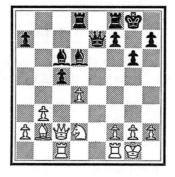

1. . . .	B x P ch !!
2. K x B	Q - R5 ch
3. K - Kt1	B x P !!

As in the Lasker-Bauer game. And again as in that game White can stave off mate by sacrificing his Queen, but then loses a piece. Thus on *4. K x B*, there would follow *4. . . .* Q - Kt5 ch; *5.* K - R2, R - Q4; *6.* Q x BP, Q - B5 ch; *7.* K - Kt2, R x Q; *8.* R x R, Q x Kt. Nimzovitch tries a different defense.

| 4. P - B3 | KR - K1 ! |

Threatening . . . Q - Kt6 and if then Kt - K4, R x Kt.

    5. Kt - K4

Again the Bishop may not be taken: if 5. K x B, R - K7 ch.

5. . . .	Q - R8 ch
6. K - B2	B x R

White must already resort to desperate measures. On 7. R x B, Q - R7 ch wins White's Queen.

    7. P - Q5

Trying to conjure up a threat.

7. . . .	P - B4 !
8. Q - B3	

It is there—mate. Black of course has an easy way out.

8. . . .	Q - Kt7 ch
9. K - K3	R x Kt ch
10. P x R	P - B5 ch

The amateur may be consoled—the grand master also misses the quickest way. With 10. . . . Q - Kt6 ch he forces mate in three: 11. K - Q2, Q - B7 ch; 12. K - Q1, Q - K7 mate. Not that it really matters, though.

11. K x P	R - B1 ch
12. K - K5	Q - R7 ch
13. K - K6	R - K1 ch
14. K - Q7	B - Kt4 mate !

The two-Bishop sacrifice comes up every once in a while. Here is another instance, from a game Koltanowski-Defosse, Belgian championship, 1936. In *Diagram 67* Koltanowski (this time looking at the board!) played:

1. B x P ch !	K x B
2. Q - R5 ch	K - Kt1
3. B x P !	K x B

Koltanowski shows that on 3. . . . P - B3; White wins with *4.* Q - R8 ch, K - B2; *5.* B x R, B x B; *6.* Q - R5 ch, K - K2; 7. Q - R7 ch, K - Q3; *8.* R x B ch.

4. Q - Kt5 ch	K - R2
5. R - Q4	

As before Black must give up his Queen to stop mate.

5. . . .	B - R7 ch
6. K - R1	Q - KB5
7. R x Q	B x R
8. Q x B	R - KKt1
9. R - K5	

Even with the Queens off Black finds himself exposed to too many mating threats. E.g., on 9. . . . K - Kt2 there would follow *10.* Q - Kt5 ch, K - R2; *11.* Q - B6 and the threat of R - R5 ch is fatal. Black resigned.

Apart from the sacrifice at KR7, there are few possibilities for breaking through a castled King position when the defending Pawns have not moved. These arise only in certain special instances; no rules about them can really be laid down.

One type of mating combination involves a mate with two Knights. The classical model is a game Marache-Morphy, New Orleans, 1857. In *Diagram 68* Morphy played:

1. . . .	Kt - KKt6 !!!

White resigned, for if *2.* Q x Q, Kt(Q5) - K7 mate. On other moves the Queen is lost.

DIAGRAM 67

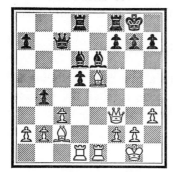

DIAGRAM 68

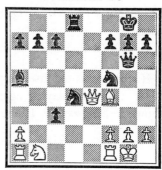

An analogous idea appeared in the celebrated game Lewitzky-Marshall, Breslau, 1912. In *Diagram 69* Marshall played:

DIAGRAM 69

1. . . .   Q - KKt6 !!!!

White resigned, because he is lost in all sensible variations. The possibilities are:

A. 2. RP x Q, Kt - K7 mate

B. 2. Q x Q, Kt - K7 ch; 3. K - R1, Kt x Q ch; 4. K - Kt1, Kt - K7 ch; 5. K - R1, R - QR6 and Black is a healthy piece ahead.

C. 2. BP x Q, Kt - K7 ch; 3. K - R1, R x R mate.

History repeated itself again. In a blindfold exhibition in 1942, Alekhine, playing against Supico, reached the position shown in *Diagram 70*. The same move wins:

1. Q - Kt6 !!

The main variations are:

A. *1.* . . . BP x Q; 2. Kt x P ch, P x Kt; 3. R - R3 ch, Q - R5; 4. R x Q mate.

DIAGRAM 70

B. *1.* . . . RP x Q; 2. R - R3 mate.
C. *1.* . . . B x B; 2. Q x KtP mate.
D. *1.* . . . Q x Kt; 2. Q x KtP mate.

Sometimes the defender's KKt2 square is especially vulnerable to attack. An instance is seen in *Diagram 71* (Spielmann-Grünfeld, Carlsbad, 1929). White played:

DIAGRAM 71

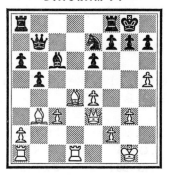

1. B x KtP !	K x B
2. Q - Kt5 ch	Kt - Kt3

Or 2. . . . K - R1; 3. Q - R6 ch, K - Kt1; 4. P - R6 and mates.

3. P - R6 ch

And after 3. . . . K - Kt1; 4. Q - B6 mate is unavoidable.

Another possibility is that seen in *Diagram 72,* from Spielmann-Tartakower, Munich, 1909. Spielmann continued:

1. Kt x KtP !	Q - Q1

DIAGRAM 72

Accepting the sacrifice leads to mate after *1*. . . . K x Kt;
2. Kt - B5 ch, K - Kt1; 3. Q x Kt.

2. Kt(Kt7) - B5

With the King exposed White now has a winning attack.
The immediate threat is B - KKt5.

2. . . .	Kt - Kt3
3. Q - R6	Kt - K1
4. Kt - B3 !	B x B ch
5. P x B	Q - B3
6. Kt - Kt5	Q - R1

Some position!

7. Kt - K7 ch

Mate is forced after 7. . . . Kt x Kt; 8. B x P ch.

With the Bishop focused on the defender's KKt2, sacrificial
possibilities come up. A beautiful example is *Diagram 73*,
from a game Nielsen-Nimzovitch, Copenhagen, 1930 (simultaneous exhibition). Nimzovitch played:

1. R - Q7 !	QR - Q1

Forced.

2. R x B !	R x R
3. Q - B6 !!!	

The brilliant point. On 3. . . . P x Q there follows 4. R - Kt4
ch, K - R1; 5. B x P mate. Black is compelled to sacrifice his
Queen, and therefore resigned.

DIAGRAM 73

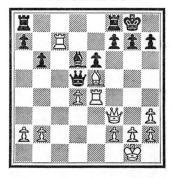

As we saw in an earlier chapter if the Bishop can hold the long diagonal, and the Rook occupy KKt7, a discovered check can be devastating. This idea is made use of in *Diagram 74*, from the game Alekhine-Sterk, Budapest, 1921. Alekhine sprang the surprising

> *1.* B - B6 !!   R(B1) - B1

The classical combination comes in after *1. . . .* R(R1) - B1: **2.** R - Kt4 !!, Q x Q; *3.* R x P ch, K - R1; *4.* R - Kt6 dis ch and mate.

> 2. Q - K5 !!   R - B4

Desperate. On *2. . . .* R x R; *3.* Q - KKt5 leads to mate: *3. . . .* K - B1; *4.* Q x P ch, K - K1; *5.* Kt - K5 !

> 3. Q - Kt3   P - Kt3
> 4. R x Kt

White is a piece ahead and still has mating threats—the rest is simple.

> 4. . . .   Q - Q6
> 5. R - KB1   Q - B4

6. Q - B4		Q - B7
7. Q - R6		

And mates shortly.

DIAGRAM 74

A sacrifice at KB6 to clear the files for Rook and Bishop also appeared in the famous game Paulsen-Morphy, New York, 1857. In *Diagram 75* Morphy continued:

1. . . .	Q x B !!
2. P x Q	R - Kt3 ch
3. K - R1	B - R6

DIAGRAM 75

Threatening mate with . . . B - Kt7 ch and . . . B x P(B6) mate. On 4. R - Kt1, R x R ch; 5. K x R, R - K8 ch leads to mate.

4. R - Q1	B - Kt7 ch
5. K - Kt1	B x P(B6) dis ch
6. K - B1	

Here Morphy played 6. . . . B - Kt7 ch, which also wins. But we give the more precise continuation, which is prettier.

6. . . .	R - Kt7 !
7. Q - Q3	R x P ch
8. K - Kt1	R - Kt7 dbl ch
9. K - R1	R - Kt8 dbl ch and mate

Sacrifices at KB6 may take various forms. Here are some more examples. In *Diagram 76* White plays:

DIAGRAM 76

| 1. Kt - B6 ch ! | P x Kt |

After 1. . . . K - R1; 2. Q - R5, P - R3; 3. B x RP it is also mate.

| 2. B x P | Q - Q2 |

Allows mate. Black's only defense was to give up the Queen immediately with 2. . . . Kt - Kt3.

3. B x P ch !   K x B
4. Q - R5 ch   K - Kt1
5. Q - R8 mate

Another type of sacrifice, which combines the pressure against KKt7 with that along the eighth rank, is shown in *Diagram 77,* from Havasi-Sacconi, Folkestone, 1933. Havasi played:

DIAGRAM 77

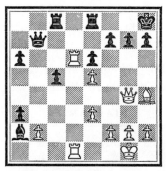

1. B - B6 !   P x B

Actually Black resigned, but we give the finish because it is so instructive. On the alternative *1. . . .* R - KKt1 White mates with *2.* Q x P ch !, R x Q; *3.* R - Q8 ch, R x R; *4.* R x R mate.

2. P x P   R - KKt1
3. R - Q8 !!   R(B1) x R
4. R x R   R x R
5. Q - Kt7 mate.

When the Bishop has command of the long diagonal, a number of interesting combinations may occur. Some have been seen above (Diagrams 71, 73, 74). Another is shown in *Diagram 78.* White mates in four:

DIAGRAM 78

1. R x P ch	K - R1
2. R - Kt8 dbl ch !!	K x R
3. R - Kt1 ch	Q any
4. R x Q mate	

Another pretty combination which is made possible by command of the long diagonal is *Diagram 79*, from Rabinovitch-Goglidze, Moscow, 1939.

DIAGRAM 79

1. Q - R6 !!

Black resigned because mate is unavoidable. On *1. . . .*
P x Q; *2.* Kt x P ch is mate. And if *1. . . .* Q - B3 simply *2.*
B x Q ! with the same threats.

While the safest defensive position for the King is to be
ensconced behind three unmoved Pawns, this entails one danger, mate on the eighth rank. The elementary position is
shown in *Diagram 80.* Here White mates in two with

1. R - K8 ch   R x R
2. R x R mate

In *Diagram 81* the position of *Diagram 80* is set up via a
sacrifice. Here White mates as follows:

DIAGRAM 80

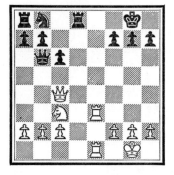

DIAGRAM 81

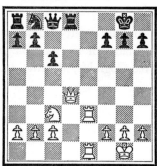

1. Q x R ch !   Q x Q
2. R - K8 ch   Q x R
3. R x Q mate

Obviously when the eighth rank is vulnerable to the heavy
artillery, the road is open for combinations. We give some
examples. *Diagram 82* is similar to the two previous cases.

DIAGRAM 82

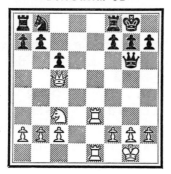

White wins with:

>   *1.* Q x R ch !   K x Q
>   *2.* R - K8 mate

Of course in actual play the combinations are usually more complicated. One of the most dazzlingly beautiful ever seen arose in a game Adams-Torre, New Orleans, 1925. From *Diagram 83* the continuation was:

>   *1.* Q - KKt4 !

The Queen is held by the mate threat: *1.* . . . . Q x Q; 2. R x R ch and mates.

DIAGRAM 83

$1. \ldots$ Q - Kt4

2. Q - QB4 !!

Prettier and prettier. Again the Queen is held both ways by the mate threat, and White continues to threaten.

$2. \ldots$ Q - Q2

3. Q - B7 !!   Q - Kt4

4. P - QR4 !   Q x RP

5. R - K4 !!   Q - Kt4

6. Q x KtP !!!!

The Queen finally has no moves, and he must lose heavily in material to stop mate.

One final type of combination against the King defended by unmoved Pawns remains to be mentioned, and that is the sacrifice at KB2. This involves, as do the others, the collaboration of several pieces and is made possible by the mate threats on the eighth rank. The model position is shown in *Diagram 84*. White mates with:

DIAGRAM 84

DIAGRAM 85

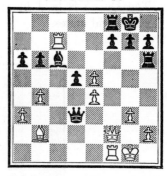

1. Q x P ch !   R x Q

2. R - K8 mate

A similar theme comes up in *Diagram 85*, from a game
Thomas-Marshall, Hamburg, 1930. Thomas surprised his emi-
nent opponent with:

1. Q x P ch !	R x Q
2. R - B8 ch	B - K1
3. R x B ch	R - B1
4. R x R mate	

Two other examples illustrate still different variations of this
sacrifice. *Diagram 86* is taken from a game of Anderssen's.
He won with:

DIAGRAM 86 **DIAGRAM 87**

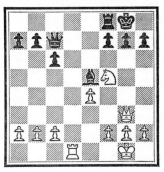

1. Q x P ch !	R x Q
2. R - K8 ch	R - B1
3. R x R ch	K x R
4. R - K8 mate	

Capablanca is the author of our next example; it is taken
from a game Capablanca-Tanerow, New York, 1910. In *Diagram 87* Capablanca played:

1. Kt - R6 ch   K - R1
2. Q x B !!   Q x Q
3. Kt x P ch   R x Kt
4. R - Q8 ch and mates shortly.

Summing up this section, when the defender's King is placed behind three unmoved Pawns, some typical mating combinations are available to the attacker. These are:

1. *Sacrifice at KR7* (Diagrams 55A–67). Usually the Bishop is sacrificed to clear the lines for the Queen supported by other pieces. The attacker follows up on the opened Rook file.

2. *Sacrifice at KKt7* (Diagrams 71–79). Any piece may be offered. The attacker follows up on the opened KKt file. The defending Pawn at KKt2 may be removed by a check or attack at KB6 or KR6.

3. *Sacrifice on the eighth rank* (Diagrams 80–83). This is accomplished by the heavy artillery.

4. *Sacrifice at KB7* (Diagrams 84–87). This is combined with a mate on the eighth rank.

From this enumeration and the examples cited it is readily apparent that it takes an overwhelming mass of enemy pieces to break through the unmoved Pawns directly. This explains why such a setup is by far the safest defensive position.

When the defender's Pawns are at KB2, KKt2, and KR3,

Black's Pawn at KR3 is a natural target. The principle for the attacker is: *mass pieces and sacrifice at the appropriate moment.*

A model position for the sacrifice is shown in *Diagram 88.*

DIAGRAM 88

WHITE TO PLAY WINS

White continues:

> *1.* B x P ! P x B

On *1.* . . . K - Kt1; *2.* B x P leads to mate fairly quickly.

> *2.* Q x P ch K - Kt1
> *3.* Q - R7 mate

If the Rook is at K1 in the above position we have a different model mate (Diagram 55A).

In many cases sacrifices are successful because the attacker has command of the long diagonal. Thus in *Diagram 89* White plays:

> *1.* Kt x P !! K x Kt

Other moves stop mate for a while.

> *2.* Q - Kt4 ch K - R1
> *3.* Q - B5 ! K - Kt1
> *4.* B x Kt B x B
> *5.* Q - R7 mate

DIAGRAM 89

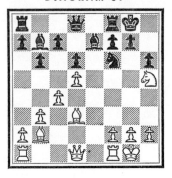

A beautiful Queen sacrifice leads to mate from the position shown in *Diagram 90*, taken from the game Spielmann-L'Hermet, Magdeburg, 1927.

DIAGRAM 90

Spielmann played:

> *1.* Q x P !!   P x Q

The alternative is *1. . . .* P - B3; *2.* P x P, which is no better.

> *2.* P x P dis ch   K - B1
> *3.* R - Kt8 ch !!

A second pretty surprise . . .

3. . . .   K x R
4. P - R7 ch   K - B1
5. P - R8(Q) mate

When the KRP has advanced to KR3, the enemy's command of the diagonal QKt1 - KR7 is thereby strengthened. A model position for the attack is then seen in *Diagram 91*. Here Black must give up material to stop mate. On

DIAGRAM 91

1. . . .

DIAGRAM 92

P - B5 ?

there could follow

2. Q - R7 ch   K - B1
3. Q - R8 mate

After 1. . . . P - Kt3, which is forced to stop mate, 2. P x P is decisive.

A pretty illustration of this idea is shown in *Diagram 92*, from the game Tylor-Winter, Hastings, 1933. Tylor mated in four:

1. Q - R7 ch   K - B1
2. Q - R8 ch   K - K2
3. Kt - B5 ch !   P x Kt
4. B - B5 dbl ch and mate

Often the mate threat can be parried only by the loss of a piece. This is seen in *Diagram 93*. With

1. Q - B5 !

White wins a piece, for the only move to stop mate is *1.* . . . P - Kt3, when *2.* Q x B follows.

DIAGRAM 93

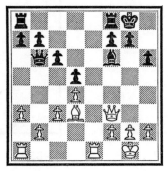

Some elegant break-throughs via Knight checks may be possible if the defender's position becomes too cramped. *Diagram 94* is taken from the game Keres-Candolin, Helsingfors, 1936. Keres continued:

1. Kt - B6 ch !!   P x Kt

The offer cannot be refused: if *1.* . . . K - Kt3; *2.* Q - Kt4 ch, K x Kt; *3.* R - K6 ch, P x R; *4.* Q x KP mate.

2. Q x P

Threatening Q x BP mate.

2. . . .	K - Kt1
3. R x Kt	R - R2
4. R - R3 !	Resigns

For after 4. . . . Q-KB1; 5. R-Kt3 ch, R-Kt2; 6. B x P
Black has to give up his Queen to hold up mate for a few
moves.

When the defender's KKtP has moved up one square, KKt2
is weakened and should be occupied. When it is not the road
is open for innumerable combinations. The Pawn position we
are discussing is diagramed here:

DIAGRAM 95   DIAGRAM 96

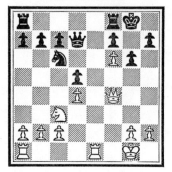

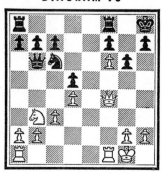

WHITE TO PLAY MATES IN
TWO MOVES

Mating threats of course come up at KKt7. One model position is shown in *Diagram 95*. With

> *1.* Q - R6

mate is forced.

The defender can hold this position by covering his KKt2 square. There is one important case when that cover is inadequate. In *Diagram 96* White to play mates as follows:

> *1.* Q - R6   R - KKt1
> *2.* R - B3

The threat is now Q x RP ch, K x Q; R - R3 mate.

> *2.* . . .   P - Kt4
> *3.* R - R3

and mates next move or the move after if Black prefers to give a spite check.

Even when Black does hold his KKt2 square well, brilliant

combinations may arise. Here are a few. *Diagram 97* arose in a game among the masters traveling to the international team tournament at Buenos Aires in 1939. The Whites continued:

1. Kt - Kt5 !!

and the Blacks gave up. For if *1.* . . . Q x Q; *2.* Kt x P mate. On other moves mate is also forced, e.g., *1.* . . . R - Kt2; *2.* R - Q8 !!, Q x R; *3.* Q x R mate.

Naturally the Bishop may be substituted for the Pawn at KB6. Essentially the same sort of position arises when the Pawn is at KR6 and the Queen at KB6.

DIAGRAM 97

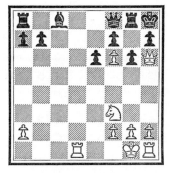

As we have mentioned, the defense in this position must be able to cover the KKt2 square. Here are several more positions where this defense is broken through by force.

In *Diagram 98* White continues:

1. R x B !   Q x R
2. B - Kt5 !!

The point—if *2.* . . . Q x B; *3.* B - B6 and mate.

DIAGRAM 98

2. . . .	Q - B1
3. B x R	Q x B
4. B - B6	Q - B1
5. Q x Q ch	K x Q
6. R - Q1 !	Resigns

Black must now give up a piece to stop mate.

In *Diagram 99* again the first step is to remove the cover for the crucial square.

1. R x B !	R x R
2. Q - Q4	Q - K4

DIAGRAM 99

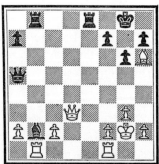

Black seems to have found an adequate defense.

3. R - K1 !!

Not so. If the Queen is taken 4. R x R mate follows.

In conjunction with command of the long diagonal by the Bishop White may build up various types of mating threats. Our first example involves a Knight check at KR6. This comes

DIAGRAM 100

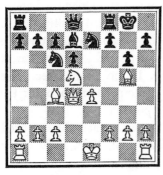

DIAGRAM 101

to pass from *Diagram 100* as follows:

1. Kt - B6 ch   K - R1

Or 1.... K - Kt2; 2. Kt - R5 dbl ch, K - Kt1; 3. Q - Kt7 mate.

2. Kt - Kt4 dis ch !   Kt x Q
3. B - B6 ch   K - Kt1
4. Kt - R6 mate

Fireworks come to the fore in *Diagram 101*. White played:

1. Kt - B5 !!

With a number of pretty variations. If *1.* . . . P x Kt; *2.* Q - Kt4 ch ! and mates on the KKt file. And if *1.* . . . Q - K3; *2.* Kt - R6 mate. So Black tried

1. . . .   Q x R

Thinking that if you take my Queen I'll take yours . . .

2. Q - R5 !!

and Black gave up, for this second sacrifice cannot be met. On *2.* . . . Q x Q; *3.* Kt - K7 ch is mate, on *2.* . . . P x Kt; *3.* Q x Q. Even the countersacrifice *2.* . . . R - Q8 is met by a mate: *3.* Kt - R6.

Apart from a mate at KKt7, command of the long diagonal

**WHITE
MATES**

also suggests a mate at KR8. The strongest threats come up when the Queen is backed up by the Bishop. In such a position Black can avoid mate by a capture of either the Queen or the Bishop, or by occupation of the KKt2 square. If the White pieces are farther back, an interposition to block the diagonal may be possible.

For the mate at KR8, the model position actually occurred once in a game Euwe-Loman, Rotterdam, 1923. In *Diagram 102* Euwe played

DIAGRAM 102   **DIAGRAM 103**

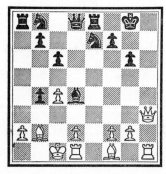

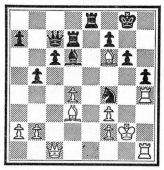

1. Q - R8 ch   B x Q
2. R x B mate

Ordinarily some sacrifices are necessary to break through to the enemy King. We give some examples. In *Diagram 103,* from the game Blackburne-Schwartz, Berlin, 1881, Blackburne crashed through in a surprisingly quick way:

1. Q x Kt !!   B x Q
2. R x P !   P x R
3. R x P

and mates at KR8.

A similar idea occurred in the game Teichmann-Mieses, Carlsbad, 1907. From *Diagram 104* White mates in three:

DIAGRAM 104

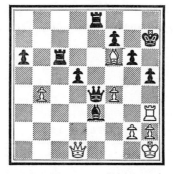

1. R x P ch !   P x R
2. Q x P ch   K - Kt1
3. Q - R8 mate

The great attacking master Spielmann is the author of our next example. In *Diagram 105,* from a game of his against Hönlinger at Vienna, 1929, he played:

DIAGRAM 105

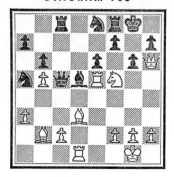

1.	Kt - K7 ch !	Q x Kt
2.	Q x RP ch !!	K x Q
3.	R - R5 ch	K - Kt1
4.	R - R8 mate	

The check that allows the Rook to penetrate to R8 is a potent weapon. *Diagram 106* is another typical example, taken from a game Belitzmann-Rubinstein, Warsaw, 1917. Black played:

1. . . .	Q x RP ch !
2. K x Q	P x P dbl ch
3. K - Kt1	R - R8 mate

DIAGRAM 106

When both Bishops are bearing down on the enemy King, a mate is possible at KR7. This is illustrated in *Diagram 107*. White mates with:

DIAGRAM 107

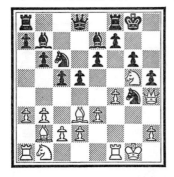

DIAGRAM 108

1. Q x P ! P x Q
2. B - R7 mate

A similar idea occurred in a game Flohr-Pitschak, Bilin, 1930. In *Diagram 108* Pitschak played:

1. . . .	Q x P !
2. Kt(K1) - B3	Kt x Kt ch
3. Kt x Kt	B x Kt
4. P x Q	B - R7 mate

More complicated sacrificial possibilities may come up in various positions when the defender's KKt2 is unguarded. Here are some examples. In *Diagram 109* White mates as follows:

1. R x P ch !!

If now *1. . . .* RP x R; *2.* Q - R8 mate, and if *1. . . .* BP x R; *2.* Kt - K7 dbl ch and mate.

In *Diagram 110* the finish was:

1. . . .	Q x R ch !!
2. K x Q	R x P ch
3. K - Kt1	

Or 3. K - K1, R - K7 ch; 4. K - Q1, R - B8 mate.

DIAGRAM 109   **DIAGRAM 110**

   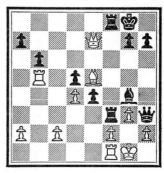

3. . . .	R - B8 ch
4. K - Kt2	R(B1) - B7 mate

The vulnerability of the defender's KB2 square is illustrated in *Diagram 111,* taken from a game Janowski and Soldaten-kov-Lasker and Taubenhaus, Paris, 1909. The White allies played:

DIAGRAM 111

1. B x P ch !	K x B

Prolongs the agony. On *1. . . .* R x B; *2.* R - K8 ch, R - B1;
3. Q x R ch is mate.

2. Q x RP ch	K - B3
3. Q - R4 ch	K - Kt2
4. R - K7 ch	R - B2
5. Q - Q4 ch	K - B1
6. Q - R8 ch !	K x R
7. R - K1 ch	K - Q3
8. Q - Q4 mate	

Diagram 112 at first sight looks perfectly harmless; Black
will consolidate with . . . Q - Q2, . . . R - K3, . . . P - B3
with fairly easy equality. There comes a rude awakening:

1. Q x R ch !!   K x Q

DIAGRAM 112	DIAGRAM 113

2. B - R6 ch   K - Kt1
3. R - K8 mate

Another way to exploit the weakened King position is seen
in *Diagram 113*, a trap that comes out of the Ruy Lopez.
White mates with:

> 1. R - R5 !!   P x R
> 2. Q - B6 mate

When the defender's Pawn at KB2 is missing, mating threats may arise when the attacker has command of the open diagonal. The final mating position is shown here. It is evident that to reach this final position White must force the removal of Black's KRP. This may be done in one of two ways —either by a check at Kt6, or a sacrifice (usually Rook or Queen) at KR7. These two possibilities are seen in *Diagrams*

DIAGRAM 114

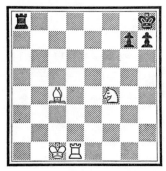

DIAGRAM 115

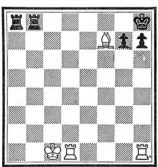

114 and *115*. In *Diagram 114* the mate proceeds as follows:

> 1. Kt - Kt6 ch   P x Kt
> 2. R - R1 mate

While in *Diagram 115* White mates with:

> 1. R x P ch !   K x R
> 2. R - R1 mate

Both these possibilities are frequently seen in practical play. We give a number of examples.

Diagram 116 is given by the Italian writer Greco in his

DIAGRAM 116

DIAGRAM 117

manual written in 1619. White mates with:

>*1.* R x Kt ch   K x R
>*2.* Q - R5 mate

The double check is a device often used to break through the Black defenses. In *Diagram 117* the redoubtable Marshall was toppled by an unknown named Johnston (but then the game was played in 1899, at which time they were both unknowns!). Johnston played:

>*1.* Kt - K7 dbl ch   K - R1
>*2.* Kt - Kt6 ch !   P x Kt
>*3.* RP x Kt ch   Q - R5
>*4.* R x Q mate

Even great masters fall into traps. Here is an "elementary" one from a game Grünfeld-Torre, Baden-Baden, 1925. In *Diagram 118* Torre played:

DIAGRAM 118   DIAGRAM 119

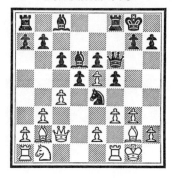   

1. . . .	B - B4 ch
2. K - R1	

He can stave off mate with 2. R - B2.

2. . . .	Kt x P ch
3. P x Kt	Q - R3 ch
4. B - R3	Q x B mate

Through the chess ages sacrificial combinations involving *Diagrams 114* or *115* have come up time and again. Here are a few more pleasing examples: *Diagram 119* is taken from a game Anderssen-Lange, Breslau, 1859. Lange played:

1. . . .	B - B4 ch
2. K - R1	Kt - Kt6 ch !
3. P x Kt	Q - Kt4

Threatening . . . Q - R3 mate.

4. R - B5 !

Apparently an adequate defense.

4. . . .   P - KR4 !!

Not so. If the Queen is taken, . . . P x P dis ch is mate.

5. P x RP   Q x R

Still threatening mate.

6. P - Kt4		Q - B7

Again threatening mate.

7. P - Kt3		Q x KtP
8. Q - B1		Q x KtP

With every move Black threatens a new mate.

9. Q x P ch		

What's this? Just a few spite checks.

9. . . .		K x Q
10. B x P ch		K - K2
11. B - Kt2		Q - R5 ch
12. B - R3		Q x B mate

The latest version is taken from a game Denker-Botvinnik, Radio match, U. S. A.–U. S. S. R., 1945. In *Diagram 120* Botvinnik played:

1. . . .		R x P ch !
2. K x R		R - R1 ch
3. Q - R4		R x Q ch
4. B x R		Q - B5

White resigned because one of the Bishops must go.

DIAGRAM 120

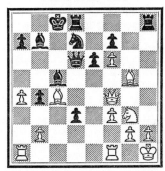

Other mating combinations can be grouped around the Pawn positions that arise. We shall discuss this point more fully later on, but the reader should get into the habit of looking at the structural characteristics (particularly the Pawns) of a position and imagining the combinative possibilities in them.

When the defender has only two Pawns, at KB2 and KR2, holding the King, he has left himself wide open for combinations.

One typical mate that occurs only in this position is seen in *Diagram 121*. Here the procedure is:

DIAGRAM 121

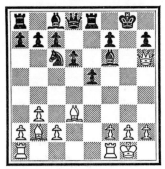

1. B x P ch	K - R1
2. B - Kt6 dis ch	K - Kt1
3. Q - R7 ch	K - B1
4. Q x P mate	

There are of course other possibilities as well, but they adhere to no systematic grouping. Use of the open KKt file will be discussed below.

When the defender's Pawns are at KB2, KB3 and KR2, the coordinating power of the defender's pieces is blocked, which allows for many a pretty mate. Massing of heavy artillery on the KKt and KR files is of course indicated. Thus in the model position in *Diagram 122* White mates in three:

DIAGRAM 122

DIAGRAM 123

1. Q x RP ch !!	K x Q
2. R - B4	any
3. R - R4 mate	

Once the heavy pieces are at hand the defense is usually difficult. *Diagram 123* is taken from a game Kashdan-Steiner, New York, 1942. White, faced by numerous threats, blundered:

1. P - B6 ?

Later analysis showed that *1.* B - K2 was good enough to draw.

1. . . .   Q - R6 !!

And now he must lose his Queen to stop mate.

2. B - K2	R - Kt7
3. Q - Kt1	R x Q ch

4. R x R	R x R ch
5. K x R	Q - B1
6. B - Kt5	Q - B2

and Black won the end game.

Various other mating threats may be built up with command of the open files. *Diagram 123A* is taken from a game of Capablanca's. He played:

1. R - K7 !!	Q x R
2. Kt x B	

DIAGRAM 123A   DIAGRAM 124

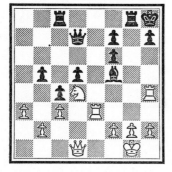 

And now mate is unavoidable: *2.* . . . Q - B1; *3.* R x P ch, K x R; *4.* Q - R5 ch, Q - R3; *5.* Q x Q mate.

Even masters miss forced mates. *Diagram 124* is taken from a game Henneberger-Bernstein, Zurich, 1934, which was drawn. Henneberger overlooked this elegant mate:

1. B - Kt7 ch !	R x B
2. R - B8 ch	R - Kt1
3. Q - Kt4 !!	Q - Q1
4. R x Q	

And mate next—if *4.* . . . B x Kt; *5.* Q x R mate, on other moves, *5.* Q - Kt7 mate.

In conjunction with the Bishop at KR6, a mate can be forced on the KKt file:

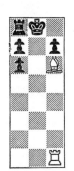

White plays:

1. R - Kt1 ch	K - R1
2. B - Kt7 ch	K - Kt1
3. B x P dis ch and mate.	

WHITE TO PLAY MATES IN THREE

This idea was used by Pillsbury in a trap he devised in the Queen's Gambit. After sixteen moves the position in *Diagram 125* is reached. Pillsbury won with:

1. Q - B3 **!!**

and Black resigned. For if *1.* . . . Q x Q White mates as above with *2.* R - Kt1 ch, while on other moves a full Rook is lost.

Even command of one open file is enough to provide mating threats galore. *Diagram 126* is an example from the Queen's Gambit. White plays:

DIAGRAM 125

DIAGRAM 126

1. B - R7 ch	K - R1
2. B - Kt6 dis ch !	K - Kt1
3. R - R8 ch !	K x R
4. Q - R5 ch	K - Kt1
5. Q - R7 mate	

Often command of the open file is assured artificially. In *Diagram 127*, from a game Menchik-Thomas, London, 1932, White concluded with:

DIAGRAM 127

DIAGRAM 128

1. Q x P ch !	K x Q
2. R - R1 mate	

The King is barred from the KKt file by his own Rook and by the White Pawn.

A not dissimilar idea is seen in *Diagram 128*. Here mate is effected by:

1. Q - Kt8 ch !!	K x Q
2. R - K8 ch	R x R
3. R x R mate	

When the lines are open, sacrifices almost come of themselves. Thus in *Diagram 129* the finish is:

DIAGRAM 129   DIAGRAM 130

1. R - R7 ch !	K x R
2. Q x P ch	K - R1
3. R - R1 ch	R - R3
4. R x R mate	

With a completely exposed King, mate can be warded off only at enormous expense. Thus in *Diagram 130,* from Fine-Grossman, New York, 1933, Black is a Rook and two Knights ahead, yet he can only manage to draw with best play. The game continued:

1. . . .	Kt x P ?
2. R - Kt1 ch	K - R3
3. Q - K3 ch	K - R2
4. Q - K7 ch	K - R3
5. Q - Kt7 ch	K - R4
6. Q - Kt5 mate	

In the diagramed position Black could have drawn with *1. . . .* Kt - K4 !; *2.* R - Kt1 ch, K - R3; *3.* Q x Kt, R - KKt1; *4.* Q - K3 ch, K - R2; *5.* Q - R3 ch, Kt - R4; *6.* Q x Kt ch, Q - R3; *7.* Q - B7 ch, R - Kt2, and White must be satisfied with perpetual check.

When White manages to establish a Pawn at KKt6, various mating threats arise. The schema for the model position is shown here.

White mates with:

1. Q - R4 ch   K - Kt1

2. Q - R7 mate

WHITE TO PLAY MATES IN TWO

There are of course almost innumerable variations on the manner in which the exposed Black King may be exploited. In practice the most important is that where a Rook is sacrificed at R8 to clear the way for the Queen. *Diagram 131* comes out of the Ruy Lopez. Black to play mates as follows:

DIAGRAM 131

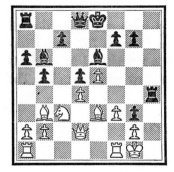

DIAGRAM 132

1.	R - R8 ch
2. K x R	Q - R5 ch
3. K - Kt1	Q - R7 mate

Note that Black cannot afford to wait: if *1.* . . . . K - Q2 (to play . . . Q - R1); *2.* R - K1, Q - R1; *3.* K - B1 and White escapes.

An old application of this idea is seen in *Diagram 132*, from a game Mayet-Anderssen, Berlin, 1859. Black announced mate in five:

1. . . .	B x P ch
2. R x B	Q - Q8 ch
3. Q - K1	Q x Q ch
4. R - B1	R - R8 ch
5. K x R	Q x R mate

One of the most ingenious versions of this theme comes from Alekhine.

DIAGRAM 133

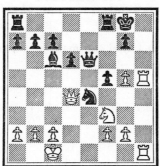

In *Diagram 133* he mated as follows:

1. Kt - K5 !!	P x Kt
2. P - Kt6 !!	Q x P
3. Q - B4 ch	B - Q4
4. Q x B ch	R - B2
5. R - R8 mate	

When the defender's King is confined to the corner, mating possibilities arise on the long diagonal. Here are two pretty examples. *Diagram 134* was reached by Pillsbury in a blindfold exhibition. He mates with:

DIAGRAM 134   DIAGRAM 135

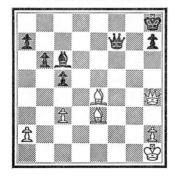   

1. . . .	Q - B8 ch
2. B - Kt1	Q - B6 ch !
3. B x Q	B x B mate

Blackburne also found the mate in *Diagram 135* during a blindfold seance. He played:

| 1. . . . | Q x P ch !! |
| 2. P x Q | B x P mate |

When the seventh rank is exposed, mating threats with Queen and Rook arise. In *Diagram 136,* from a game Taubenhaus-Janowski, Paris, 1903, White breaks through with a sacrifice:

DIAGRAM 136   DIAGRAM 137

   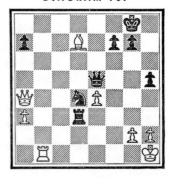

1. R x P ch !	K x R
2. Q - R5 ch	K - Kt1
3. Q - B7 ch	K - R1
4. Q x P mate	

Another sacrificial idea comes to the fore in *Diagram 137,* from the game Stahlberg-Keres, Bad Nauheim, 1936. Keres played:

| *1.* . . . . | Kt - B6 !! |

White resigned. The sequel could be:

2. P x Kt	R - Q7
3. P - B4	Q x P
4. K - Kt1	Q x P ch
5. K - B1	Q - R8 mate

A concealed approach to the seventh rank comes out in *Diagram 138,* from the game Fine-Dake, Detroit, 1933. White

DIAGRAM 138

played:

1. Kt x BP !!	K x Kt
2. Kt - K4 ch	K - Kt2
3. R - QB2 !	Q - R5

He must give up his Queen to hold off the mate.

4.	Q x P ch	B - Kt3
5.	R - B7 ch	K - Kt1
6.	Q x B ch !!	

The point.

6.	. . .	P x Q
7.	Kt - B6 ch	K - R1
8.	R - R7 mate	

An unusual mate with two Knights is demonstrated in *Diagram 139*. Black played:

DIAGRAM 139

DIAGRAM 140

1.	. . .	Q x R ch !!
2.	K x Q	

No worse than 2. R x Q, Kt - B7 mate.

2.	. . .	Kt - K7 ch
3.	K - R1	Kt - B7 mate

A related idea came out in the game Bogoljubow-Monticelli, San Remo, 1930. In *Diagram 140* Black played:

1.	. . .	Kt - K7 ch !
2.	R x Kt	R - B8 ch !

| 3. K x R | Q - R8 ch |
| 4. K - B2 | Kt - Kt5 mate |

The exposed King often permits relatively simple mates. Thus in *Diagram 141*, from a game of Morphy's, White plays:

DIAGRAM 141

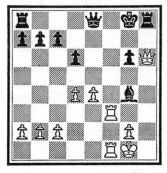

DIAGRAM 142

1. R - B8 ch !	Q x R
2. R x Q ch	R x R
3. Q x P mate	

In *Diagram 142* the force of the double check is again demonstrated. White mates with:

1. Q - R7 ch !	K x Q
2. R - K7 dbl ch	K - R1
3. R - R7 mate	

Unusually cramped positions simply cry for a combinative decision. The one in *Diagram 143* is surprisingly simple. White plays:

1. Q x P ch !!	P x Q
2. P - Kt6 ch	K x P
3. R - Kt1 ch	K - R2
4. R x B mate	

DIAGRAM 143

DIAGRAM 144

And should the reader ask which Rook takes in the above position the answer is: either one !

The power of the discovered check is again demonstrated in *Diagram 144*. White mates with:

1. B - K7 ch	K - K1
2. B - B6 dis ch	K - B1
3. Q - K7 ch	K - Kt1
4. Q x B mate	

When both sides' Kings are exposed, the outcome is determined by who has the first decisive combination. In *Diagram 145*, from Vidmar-Euwe, Carlsbad, 1929, it looks as if White will be mated. The ingenious Vidmar finds a beautiful way out:

| 1. R - K8 ch | B - B1 |

A necessary interposition, for if *1.* . . . K - R2; *2.* Q - Q3 ch wins the Rook.

| 2. R x B ch !! | K x R |

Again forced, for on other moves, R x BP ch wins the Queen. But it is still not clear how White will manage to escape. Maybe he's just giving spite checks?

DIAGRAM 145

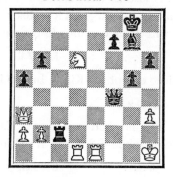

3. Kt - B5 dis ch   K - Kt1
4. Q - B8 ch !!!

Now we see the real point. Black is mated next move, for
if 4. . . . K x Q; 5. R - Q8 mate, and if 4. . . . K - R2; 5. Q - Kt7
mate.

Open lines always raise the question of combinations. In
Diagram 146, from the game Rotlewi-Rubinstein, Lodz, 1907,

DIAGRAM 146

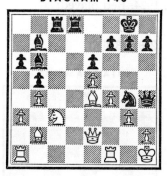

Rubinstein continued:

1. . . .   R x Kt !!
2. P x Q

All other moves lose as well. If 2. B x R, B x B ch; 3. Q x B, Q x P mate. And if 2. B x B, R x KtP tears White's position apart. But how will Black continue in the game variation?

2. . . .   R - Q7 !!

Now every piece except the King's Bishop is en prise.

3. Q x R

Again there was no better defense. E.g., on 3. Q x Kt, B x B ch is decisive, while if 3. B x R, R x Q leads to mate.

3. . . .   B x B ch
4. Q - Kt2   R - R6 !!!

The final beautiful point. Mate is now forced. The last moves might be:

5. B - Q4   B x B
6. R - B3   B x R
7. Q x B   R x P mate

Simpler, but in its own quiet way no less spectacular, is the conclusion in *Diagram 147*, from the game Reti-Bogolju-bow, New York, 1924. Reti played:

1. B - B7 ch   K - R1
2. B - K8 !!!

DIAGRAM 147

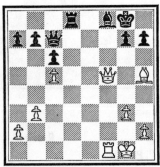

Black resigned because he cannot prevent mate for long.
If 2. . . . R x B; 3. Q x B ch, R x Q; 4. R x R mate. And even 2.
. . . P - R3 does not hold out more than a few moves: 3.
Q x B ch, K - R2; 4. B - Kt6 ch !, K x B; 5. Q - B5 mate.

Advanced attacking Pawns allow many sacrificial dandies.
Diagram 148 shows one from a game Anderssen-Zukertort,

DIAGRAM 148

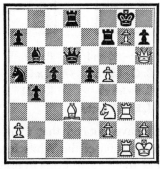

Barmen, 1869. Anderssen played:

1. Q x P ch !!	K x Q
2. P - B6 dis ch	K - Kt1

Capturing the Bishop is no better: there follows 3. R - R3 ch
and *4.* R - R8 mate.

3. B - R7 ch !	K x B
4. R - R3 ch	K - Kt1
5. R - R8 mate	

In *Diagram 149,* from the King's Gambit, a double sacrifice
forces the mate:

DIAGRAM 149

DIAGRAM 150

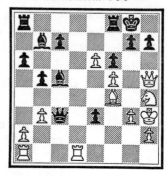

1. Kt - B6 ch !	P x Kt
2. Q - B8 ch !!	K x Q
3. B - R6 ch	K - Kt1
4. R - K8 mate	

The reader will have noticed that in many of the above positions the concentration of the White forces is overwhelming. Such a mass of force again leads to fireworks in *Diagram 150*. White concluded:

1. R - Q7	Q x R
2. R x P ch !	K x R
3. B - R6 ch	K - R1
4. Kt - Kt6 ch !	P x Kt
5. P x P !	

White's calm is amazing; he sees that Black's checks are useless.

5. . . .	Q - B8 ch
6. K - R4	Q - B6
7. B - Kt7 dbl ch !	K x B
8. Q - R7 mate.	

Here is another example of the kind of devastating punishment that can be meted out to an exposed King. *Diagram 151* is taken from the game Reshevsky-Vasconcellos, Boston, 1944. Reshevsky forced mate as follows:

1. R x P ch !!   B - K2

In despair. On *1.* . . . B x R; *2.* Q - Kt4 ch mates after *2.* . . . K - B3; *3.* Q - B3 ch, K - Kt2; *4.* Q - B7 ch, K - R3; *5.* Q - B6 ch, K - R4; *6.* P - Kt4 mate.

2. Q - R5 !   R - B1

DIAGRAM 151

Again *2.* . . . B x R allows mate, this time via *3.* Q - B7 ch, K - R3; *4.* Kt - Kt4 ch, K - Kt4; *5.* Q - Kt7 ch, K - R4; *6.* Q - R6 ch, K x Kt; *7.* P - R3 ch, K - B4; *8.* P - Kt4 mate.

3. Q - Kt5 ch	K - R1
4. Kt - Kt6 ch !!	P x Kt
5. Q - R6 ch	K - Kt1
6. Q x P ch	K - R1
7. R(Kt7) x B	

Mate at Kt7 or R7 can no longer be stopped. Black resigned.

The goal of many a mating attack is to drive the King out into the open, where he is subject to all kinds of mates. The continuation in *Diagram 152* is from a game Ed. Lasker-Thomas, London, 1911, which has become a classic:

DIAGRAM 152

| 1. Q x P ch !!! | K x Q |
| 2. Kt x B dbl ch | K - R3 |

He cannot retreat, for 2. . . . K - R1 is met by 3. Kt - Kt6 mate.

| 3. Kt(K5) - Kt4 ch | K - Kt4 |
| 4. P - R4 ch | K - B5 |

Every Black move is forced.

5. P - Kt3 ch	K - B6
6. B - K2 ch	K - Kt7
7. R - R2 ch	K - Kt8
8. K - Q2 dis ch and mate	

Another elegant example of this idea is shown in *Diagram* 153, from the game Blackburne-Gifford, the Hague, 1874.

DIAGRAM 153   DIAGRAM 154

Blackburne played:

1. Q x Kt(R6) ch !	K x Q
2. Kt - K6 dis ch	K - R4
3. B - K2 ch	K - R5
4. R - B4 ch !	Kt x R
5. P - Kt3 ch	K - R6
6. Kt x Kt mate	

Many attacks that drive the King out into the open have problemlike finales. *Diagram 154* is from a simultaneous exhibition by Kasparyan:

1. Q x B ch !!	K x Q
2. Kt - K5 dbl ch	K - B4
3. Kt - Q3 ch	K - Q5
4. K - Q2 !!!	any
5. P - B3 mate	

Diagram 155, from the game Fine-Shainswit, New York, 1944 leads to an unusual finish. White played:

1. R x P !!	Q x R
2. Q x P ch	K - R3

Forced.

3. Q - B4 ch	Q - Kt4

Mate can be avoided only at the expense of material loss. On 3. . . . P - Kt4 there would follow 4. Q - B6 ch, K - R4; 5. P - R3 !, R - K5; 6. Q - Kt7, P - R3; 7. P - Kt4 ch, R x P ch; 8. P x R ch, K x P; 9. Q x RP with a winning ending. If here 5. . . . Q - K3; 6. P - Kt4 ch, K - R5; 7. Q - B3, Q - Q3; 8. K - Kt2 ! and mate cannot be stopped. A mating situation similar to this is seen in Diagram 156.

4. B - Kt7 ch	K - R4
5. Q - B3 ch	Q - Kt5
6. Q - Q5 ch	Q - B4

The best chance was *6. . . .* Kt - K4; *7.* B x Kt, Q - B4; *8.* Q - Q1 ch, K - R3, though White should still win.

7. Q - Q1 ch	Q - Kt5
8. P - B3 !	Q - K3
9. P - Kt4 ch	K - Kt4
10. K - Kt2 !!!	

The real point to White's combination—Black must give up his Queen to stop mate.

10. . . .	Q x KP
11. P - R4 ch	K x P

Or *11. . . .* K - B5; *12.* B - R6 ch.

12. Q - R1 ch	K - Kt4
13. Q - R6 mate	

DIAGRAM 155   **DIAGRAM 156**

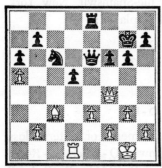 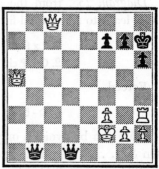

An ending similar to the variation in the note to Black's third move above came out of *Diagram 156*, a game played by Tartakower. It went:

1. . . .	Q - Q5 ch
2. K - Kt3	Q - Kt3 ch
3. Q - Kt4	Q(Kt3) x Q ch

4. P x Q	Q - K6 ch
5. K - R4	P - Kt4 ch !!
6. K - R5	Q - K3
7. Q - B5 ch	

Doesn't White win now?

7. . . .	Q - Kt3 ch !!

No, no, no . . .

8. Q x Q ch	P x Q mate !

Sometimes even when the King is out in the open the mate is not readily apparent. But generally one can be found. *Diagram 157*, from a game won by Maroczy, is a pretty illustration. Black played:

DIAGRAM 157

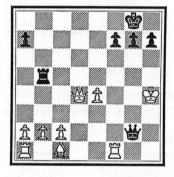

1. . . .	R - R4 ch !
2. K x R	Q - R6 ch
3. K - Kt5	P - R3 ch
4. K - B4	P - Kt4 ch
5. K - K5	Q - K3 mate

When the defender has castled on the Queen's side, the combinational possibilities are by and large of similar charac-

ter to those on the other wing. However, there is one important difference. Since the QRP is undefended, the attacker will
generally have more targets and an easier time.

Several mating combinations that do not occur on the K-side
are worthy of mention. The first occurs when White has control of the diagonal KR2 to QKt8. A typical position would be
that in *Diagram 158*. White mates with:

DIAGRAM 158

1. Q - B6 ch !   P x Q
2. B - R6 mate

A second mating possibility seen primarily on the Q-side is
that shown in *Diagram 159*. Here White mates in six:

DIAGRAM 159   **DIAGRAM 160**

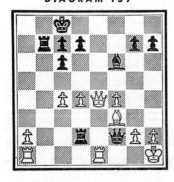   

1. Q - K8 ch	B - Q1
2. Q x P ch !	K x Q
3. B - Kt4 ch	K - Q3
4. R - K6 ch	K - Q2
5. R - K5 dis ch	K - Q3
6. P - B5 mate	

Typical of the mating combinations that the exposed King on the Q-side permits is *Diagram 160,* from the game Pillsbury-Lasker, St. Petersburg, 1895–96. Black played:

1. . . .	R x P !
2. Q - K6 ch	K - R2
3. K x R	

Allows a forced mate, but there is no adequate defense.

3. . . .	Q - B6 ch
4. K - R4	P - Kt4 ch
5. K x P	Q - B5 ch
6. K - R5	B - Q1 ch
7. Q - Kt6	B x Q mate

IV. *The Combinative Art*

THE ELEMENTS of combinative play are the various powers of the pieces, described in Chapter II, and the mating sequences of Chapter III. In this chapter we shall discuss combinations from practical play that make up the core of every game, whether it is played by amateurs or world champions. The emphasis in each case will be an attempt to dissect each combination into its more elementary parts, so that it will not appear to be a "bolt from the blue" as it so often does.

The combinations to be described in this chapter are limited to those in which there is a direct gain of material. There is another type, the positional combination, which aims not at the immediate gain of material, but at a superior position; this will be reserved for the later chapters. Also, since we have already discussed the mating combination, at some length, it will be omitted here except when it is incidental to some other combination.

In *Diagram 161* a combination is suggested by the exposed position of Black's Rook. We know that if the long diagonal were open, and a White B or Q could come to K4, the double threat on QR8 and KR7 would win a Pawn. Hence:

$$1. \text{P - K4 !} \qquad \text{P x P}$$

Black has no choice because of the forking threat P - K5. On $1. \ldots$ Kt - K1; 2. Kt x P wins the QP, while on Queen moves, 2. P - K5 wins the RP.

$$2. \text{Kt x P} \qquad \text{Q - Q1}$$

DIAGRAM 161

The best try. On 2. . . . Kt x Kt; 3. B x Kt, the Rook and KRP are both under attack, and one must go.

| 3. Kt x Kt ch | B x Kt |
| 4. B x P ch | K - R1 |

Black now has two threats of his own: to trap the White Bishop with . . . P - KKt3, and to take the QP. White gets out with a counterthreat.

| 5. B - K4 ! | R - R2 |
| 6. B - K3 | |

White can also give up the Pawn with 6. O - O, for if then 6. . . . B x P; 7. R - Q1. As so often with a material advantage, either way is good enough.

In *Diagram 162*, a position that comes out of the Queen's Gambit Declined, the thought of a combination arises when we look at Black's Queen. It can move only on the diagonal Q1 - QR4. Hence if a Bishop could attack it on that diagonal, it would be lost. So White wins with:

1. Kt x P !

For if 1. . . . P x Kt; 2. B - B7 wins the Queen. This is in effect a mating attack against the Black Queen.

DIAGRAM 162

In *Diagram 163*, from Reshevsky-Fine, Hamilton, 1941, it is clear that there are mating threats on the eighth rank. In fact, Black can hold off mate only because of the interposition at K1. So, we reason, if the square K1 can be weakened in any

DIAGRAM 163

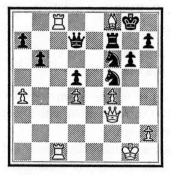

way, mate will follow. This reasoning leads to the winning move (which White missed in a game that has been described as a "comedy of errors"):

1. Q x P!

If now *1.* . . . Q x Q or *1.* . . . Kt x Q; *2.* B - R6 dis ch leads to a quick mate. On other moves Black loses even more material, and his game collapses.

In *Diagram 164*, from Rubinstein-Lasker, St. Petersburg,

DIAGRAM 164

1909, Black has just captured a Kt at K6, and threatens mate. While White can obviously prevent the mate by sacrificing his Rook for the Bishop, it appears that he has to lose two Pawns. But instead he sees a way to set up a new double threat, taking advantage of the fact that Black's Queen is unprotected. Rubinstein played:

1. R x B ch   P x R

2. Q - B1 !

The point—now the Rook is pinned, and the QBP is under attack.

2. . . .   R x P

3. P x R   R - Q2

4. Q x P ch

White has regained his Pawn. He won in a classic ending.

Diagram 165 is a trap that comes out of the center game. The menacing position of the Black pieces is exploited with:

DIAGRAM 165

1. . . .   B x P ch !
2. Q x B

The Queen is lost. If 2. K x B, Kt x P ch.

2. . . .   Kt - Q6 ch

and wins.

The weakened position of the White King, his exposed Queen, and the well-developed Black minor pieces laid the groundwork for this combination.

Even world champions make gross blunders. *Diagram 166,*

DIAGRAM 166

from the sixteenth match game Alekhine-Euwe, in 1937, is a case in point. White is a Pawn ahead, but his position is not easy. He has a chance to win another Pawn and decide immediately with:

1. Q - R8 ch	K x Q
2. Kt x P ch	K - Kt1
3. Kt x Q	

Now the QKtP cannot be taken because Black's QB is en prise. Miraculously both masters and all the expert annotators present overlooked this elementary combination, and it remained for a lowly kibitzer to point it out.

In *Diagram 167*, from Fine-Tartakower, Ostende, 1937, we

DIAGRAM 167

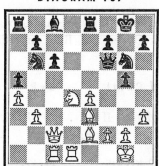

sense that the time is ripe for a combination with the exposed Black Kt at QKt3 and Pawn at KKt4. But two possibilities arise: *1.* Kt x P and *1.* Kt - B3. After *1.* Kt x P, Kt x P !; *2.* Kt x P, Kt - B6; *3.* Q x Kt, Q x Q; *4.* R x Q, R x Kt; *5.* P - B3 White is a healthy Pawn to the good. The same is true of the alternative *1.* Kt - B3. Either way wins. Actually White played:

1. Kt - B3

and won after a few more moves.

This example illustrates the point that when the position

becomes too exposed there are often many ways of deciding.

In *Diagram 168*, from Alekhine-Euwe, sixteenth match

DIAGRAM 168

game, 1937, the combinations are made possible by the discovery on Black's Queen and Rook and the pin of Black's
Knight. Alekhine played:

1. R x Kt !   B x R

There is no defense. If *1. . . .* Q x R; *2.* Kt - K5 wins the
Bishop, while if *1. . . .* Kt x R; *2.* Q x B.

2. Kt - Kt5   Q - Kt1

Other moves are no better.

3. B x R   Q x B
4. Kt x RP

winning a Pawn, which should have won the game. White
blundered later (see Diagram 166) and could only manage to
draw.

Diagram 169, from Capablanca-Spielmann, New York,
1927, shows the power of an advanced Pawn. Capa played:

1. P x P !	Q x B
2. B x P	R - Kt1
3. P x P	R - Kt4

DIAGRAM 169

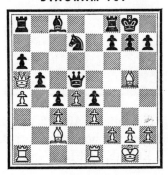

After 3. . . . Q x Q; 4. R x Q the Pawn decides.

4. Q - B7	Kt - Kt3
5. P - R7	B - R6

With a feeble lack of threat. White can now win very simply with P - R8(Q), but why settle for so little?

6. KR - Kt1 !	R x R ch
7. R x R	P - B4
8. B - B3	P - B5
9. P x P	Resigns

A Knight that reaches an advanced rank often cannot get out alive, but the attempt to do so can be decisive. Marshall saw this in a famous game against Tchigorin at Ostende, 1905. From *Diagram 170* he played:

1. Kt(R4) x B	R x Q
2. Kt x B ch	K - K3

DIAGRAM 170

Trying to trap the Knight. After 2. . . . K - Kt1; 3. Kt x R, P - Kt3; 4. P - QB4 gets the horseman out: 4. . . . P - QB4; 5. QP x P, Q x BP; 6. Kt - Kt5, and he is safe.

3. Kt - B8 !	Q - B2
4. B x R	

The first point to White's combination: the Knight is defended indirectly by the check at KKt4.

4. . . .	K - B2

As Marshall shows, 4. . . . P - KKt3 is adequately refuted by 5. KR - K1, e.g., 5. . . . P - KB4 (or 5. . . . K - B2; 6. B - Kt4, P - KB4; 7. B x P !, P x B; 8. R - K7 ch and wins); 6. B - B3 dis ch, K - B3; 7. Kt - K7, Kt - K3; 8. B x P and wins—there's always a surprising sacrificial out.

5. Kt - B5

Again holding the Knight indirectly, this time by a check at Q6.

5. . . .	Kt - K3
6. Kt(B5) - Q6 ch	K - Kt3
7. B - Q3 ch	K - R4

| 8. QR - K1 | Kt - B5 |
| 9. R - K7 | |

In his attempt to get the Knight Tchigorin had to expose himself to a mating attack. The conclusion was:

9. . . .	Q - R4
10. B - Kt1	P - KKt3
11. P - KKt3	Kt - R6 ch
12. K - Kt2	Kt - Kt4
13. B - Q3	R x Kt
14. Kt x R	Q - Q1
15. P - KR4	

Winning handily. The Knight may not move because of R x P mate.

| 15. . . . | Q x Kt |
| 16. P x Kt | Resigns |

A heavy sacrifice of material inevitably demands a combinative sequence. In *Diagram 171*, from Kramer-Drexel,

DIAGRAM 171

New York, 1946, White rises to the occasion, with one of the most splendid attacks on record.

1. B x P ch

White of course had had to foresee this sacrifice when he gave up a Rook.

1. . . .	K - R2

Or *1. . . .* K - Kt1; *2.* Kt - R6 ch, K x B; *3.* Q x P ch and mate next.

2. Q - R6 ch	K - Kt1
3. Kt x B ch	Q x Kt

On *3. . . .* K - B2; *4.* B x P ch, K x Kt; *5.* P - Q6 ch White can win as he pleases.

4. Q - R8 ch	K - B2
5. R x B ch	Kt - B3

It looks as though Black, who is still a Rook ahead, is escaping.

6. B x P ch	

The last sacrifice, and the deciding one.

6. . . .	K x B
7. Q - R6 ch	K - B2
8. R x Kt ch	K - K1
9. R x R ch	K - Q2

At least Black is now threatening mate.

10. Q - K6 ch	

This too had to be foreseen!

10. . . .	Q x Q
11. P x Q ch	K x P
12. R x R	Resigns

The King must be well defended—that is a cardinal rule of the opening. When it is not, we have traps such as that shown in *Diagram 172.* Black wins with

DIAGRAM 172

1. . . .	Kt x Kt
2. B x Q	B - Kt5 ch
3. Q - Q2	

The only legal reply.

3. . . .	B x Q ch
4. K x B	K x B

and Black is a healthy piece ahead.

In a mating attack it is essential to see through right to the very end. Here is one that involves an unusual finish. In *Diagram 173*, from Fine-Steiner, Hollywood, 1945, White played:

DIAGRAM 173

          1. P - Q6 ch   K x P

Forced.

          2. Kt - Kt5 ch   K - K2

Actually Black played 2. . . . Q x Kt and resigned after a few more moves. We give the mating continuation.

          3. R x Kt ch   P x R
          4. B - Kt5 ch   K - K1
          5. Kt - B7 ch   K - Q2

With 5. . . . Q x Kt Black can postpone mate for a few moves.

          6. B - B5 ch   K - Q3
          7. Kt - K8 mate.

The prime rule for the defense is to co-ordinate the pieces. When they are scattered all over the lot, something is bound to go. In *Diagram 174* from the game Fine-Steiner, St. Louis, 1941, White won with:

          1. R - QB1   B - B4

DIAGRAM 174

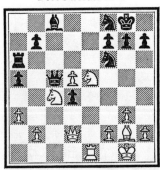

Hoping to make the best of a bad bargain. If *1.* . . . Kt x P;
2. Kt - Q3, Q - Kt4; *3.* P - QR4, Q - Q2; *4.* Kt(B4) - K5, Q - Q1;
5. B x Kt, winning a piece.

2. Kt x BP

With a discovered check on Black's Queen in reply to *2.* . . .
K x Kt.

2. . . .   Kt - K5

There is nothing really adequate.

3. Q - K1   R - KB3
4. Kt(B7) - K5   Q x P

Loses a piece, but the position was hopeless.

5. P - KKt4   P - QKt4
6. P x B   P x Kt
7. Q x Kt   Resigns

Another long diagonal motif comes out in *Diagram 175*,
from Rubinstein-Duras, Vienna, 1908.

DIAGRAM 175

1. Kt(B4) - K5	Kt x Kt
2. Kt x Kt	B x Q
3. B x P ch	Kt - Q2

Black must return much material to avoid mate. On *3. . . .*
K - Q1 there would follow *4.* R x B ch, K - B1; *5.* B - R6 ch,
K - Kt1; *6.* Kt - B6 ch, Q x Kt; *7.* B - K5 ch, Q - Q3; *8.* R - QB1 !
and mates next.

4. B x Kt ch	Q x B

Or *4. . . .* K - Q1; *5.* R x B with decisive threats.

5. Kt x Q	B - R4
6. Kt - K5	

and White's extra Pawn was decisive in the ending.

Another pretty mate against the all-too exposed King is seen
in *Diagram 176*, from Nimzovitch-Alapin, Riga, 1913.

DIAGRAM 176

1. B - B6 !	Q x B

Necessary, for if *1. . . .* P x B; *2.* B x Kt ch and Q - Q8 mate.

2. KR - K1 ch	B - K2

On other moves there are also sacrifices: 2. . . . Kt-K4; 3. R x Kt ch.

3. B x Kt ch   K - B1

Not 3. . . . Q x B; 4. Q - Q8 mate. Now he thinks he has escaped mate, but . . .

4. Q - Q8 ch   B x Q
5. R - K8 mate

Lasker was always an apostle of common sense in chess. In *Diagram 177* from Em. Lasker-Reti, New York, 1924, the common-sense move decides:

1. P - B4

Where can the Black Queen go? Here are the possibilities:
A. 1. . . . Q - B3; 2. Kt - Kt5, Q - K2; 3. Kt - B4 winning a Pawn.

DIAGRAM 177

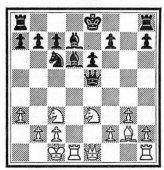

B. 1. . . . Q - KR4; 2. Kt - K4, B - K2; 3. Kt - Q5, winning at least the exchange, for if 3. . . . P x Kt; 4. Kt - B6 ch.
C. 1. . . . Q - QB4; 2. Kt - K4; again a Pawn goes.

D. *1.* . . . Q - QR4; *2.* Kt - B4, Q - QB4; *3.* Kt x B ch, P x Kt; *4.* Kt - K4.

Reti tried:

| *1.* . . . | Q - Kt2 |
| *2.* Kt - Kt5 | O - O |

The Bishop must hold the BP. And if *2.* . . . K - K2; *3.* Kt - B5 ch.

| *3.* Kt x B | P x Kt |
| *4.* R x P | |

and the extra Pawn won handily.

The exposed Queen is invariably a temptation. In *Diagram 178,* from Kan-Fine, Moscow, 1937, Black wins a Pawn simply:

DIAGRAM 178

| *1.* . . . | B - Q2 ! |

with a surprising threat: . . . Kt x KtP winning the Queen. On *2.* Q - Q3, P - K5 wins a piece.

2. P x P	P - K5
3. Kt - K1	Kt x P
4. Q - Kt1	B x P

and Black won easily with the extra Pawn.

As we have seen, the defender's KB2 is often a vulnerable target. In *Diagram 179*, from Dake-Fine, sixth match game, 1933, it cannot be held well:

DIAGRAM 179

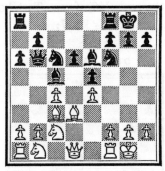

1. . . .	Kt - KKt5
2. Q - B3	

On 2. Q - K2 the combination that takes place can be played at once (2. . . . Kt x P; 3. R x Kt, P - B4).

2. . . .	P - Kt3

It is surprising that there is no defense against the opening of the lines.

3. Kt - Q2	Kt x BP
4. R x Kt	P - B4
5. P x P	

Capitulation. But on 5. R - KB1, P x P; 6. Q x P, B x R ch wins.

5. . . .	B x P
6. B x B	R x B
7. Q - Q5 ch	K - Kt2

| 8. Kt - K4 | B x R ch |
| 9. K - R1 | QR - KB1 |

and Black won easily.

Once a key point in the defense goes, the rest often seems to fall apart. In *Diagram 180*, from Tartakower-Rubinstein, Baden-Baden, 1925, the key is KKt7:

DIAGRAM 180

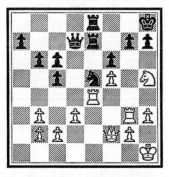

1. R x P	R x R
2. Kt x P	Q - K2
3. Kt x R	Q x Kt

At first sight it looks as though White has nothing, but the "lust to expand" of the passed KBP decides.

| 4. Q - B4 | R - K2 |
| 5. P - B6 | Kt - Kt3 |

Unfortunately forced. On 5. . . . R - K3 the reply is 6. R x Kt, R x R; 7. P - B7.

| 6. R x R | Kt x R |
| 7. P - B7 | Resigns |

For on 7.... Q-B1; 8. Q-B6 ch leads to mate.

Marshall liked to think of his brilliant combinations as "swindles"; we value them more highly. Here is a pretty one from his 1912 match with Janowski. In *Diagram 181:*

DIAGRAM 181

1....	Q x Kt

Naturally the Queen may not be taken because of mate in three: 2. P x Q, B-R6 ch; 3. K-Kt1, R-K8 ch; 4. B-B1, R x B mate.

2. P x B	Kt-B3
3. B-Kt2	Kt x KtP

Really the more difficult combination of the two.

4. B x P ch	K-R1
5. P x Q	B-R6 ch
6. K-Kt1	Kt x Q
7. B x Kt	R-K7
8. R-QB1	

Forced.

| 8.... | QR-K1 |

Threatening mate at K8.

                9. B - B3   R x B

Marshall instead played 9. . . . R(K1) - K6 and also won. But the text, as he points out, is quicker.

                10. R x R   R - K3

and mates next.

As we have seen, a mate threat often is the other half of the double attack. *Diagram 182,* from a game of Blackburne's, is another pretty example.

DIAGRAM 182

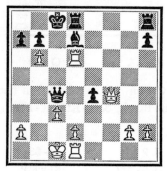

                1. R - B6 ch   Q x R

Forced, for otherwise Q - B7 mate.

                2. P x P

Threatening both Q - Kt8 mate and P queens.

                2. . . .   B - K3
                3. P - R8(Q) ch

and White won quickly.

"One combination leads to another"—this is often the rule in practical play. *Diagram 183* is taken from Botvinnik-Stoltz, match, Leningrad-Stockholm, 1926. Botvinnik has sacrificed a piece for two Pawns, but how to continue?

DIAGRAM 183

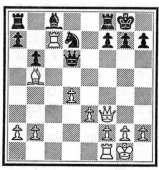

1. Q - B6

Immediately decisive. On *1.* . . . Q x Q; *2.* B x Q attacking both Rook and Knight, regains the piece.

1. . . .	Q - Kt5
2. Q x R	B - R3

Stoltz is hoping for *3.* Q x P, Q x B.

3. Q x R ch

Another surprise.

3. . . .	Kt x Q
4. B x B	P - R4

With his material advantage (two Rooks plus two Pawns for the Queen) White should have no trouble winning. In addition he has command of the vital seventh rank.

5. R x RP	Q x KtP
6. B - B4	Kt - K3
7. B - Kt3	P - R5
8. P - Q5	Kt - Q1

He has no choice, for on 8. . . . Kt - B4; 9. P - Q6 wins:
9. . . . Kt - K3; 10. B x Kt, P x B; 11. P - Q7.

9. R - Q7	Q - B3
10. P - KR3	P - QKt4
11. P - K4	K - R2
12. P - K5	Q - QKt3
13. R - K1	P - Kt5

Note how the Knight is immobilized.

14. P - K6	P x P
15. P x P	Kt x P
16. R x Kt	Resigns

In an attacking position, the defender tries to keep the lines
closed, the attacker tries to keep them open. *Diagram 184*,
from Smyslov-Kotov, Moscow, 1943, shows how a "natural"
attacking move crashes through.

DIAGRAM 184

1. P - B6	Kt x P

On *1. . . .* R x P there would follow *2.* R(Kt1) x B, Kt x R; *3.* Q x P ch and *4.* Q x R.

2. Q x P ch	K - B3
3. R(R7) x B	K - Kt4

The position is lost no matter what he does. Naturally *3. . . .* R x R is refuted by *4.* Q x Kt ch.

4. Kt x P ch	

He is addicted to sacrifices.

4. . . .	K - Kt3

Of course if *4. . . .* Q x Kt; *5.* Q x Q and R x R.

5. P - Kt4	

The most direct.

5. . . .	R - QB1
6. R x R	Q x R
7. Q - Q6 ch	

and White won shortly.

Whenever there is an *overloaded defender* a combination suggests itself. In *Diagram 185,* from Steiner-Fine, Washington, 1944, the White Rook at R7 is defending both the Rook at K7 and the Knight at R5. Hence:

1. . . .	B - Q5
2. R x P ch	K - Kt1

White is lost—he has no check and must give up the defense of one unit.

3. R(B7) - Q7	R x R
4. R x R	

DIAGRAM 185

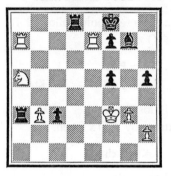

Yet he seems to have found a way out.

    4. . . .   B - Kt3

Also adequate was *4. . . .* P - B7.

    5. Kt - B4   P - B7
    Resigns

It is again the *loose position* of the White pieces that makes the combination possible in *Diagram 186,* from Speyer-Rubinstein, St. Petersburg, 1909.

DIAGRAM 186

$$1. \ldots \qquad B \times Kt$$
$$2. Q \times B$$

Trying to make the best of it. Other moves are refuted by the exposed position of the Queen. If 2. P x Kt, B x P ch; 3. K - Kt2, B - B3; and if 2. B x B, Q x R; 3. R x Q (or 3. P x Kt, Q - Kt4 ch), R x R ch; 4. K - Kt2, B - B3.

$$2. \ldots \qquad R \times B$$
$$3. Q \times Q \qquad R \times Q$$
$$4. P \times Kt \qquad P \times P$$

and with two extra Pawns the ending was easy for Rubinstein.

The danger inherent in a passed Pawn again comes out in *Diagram 187*, a trap from From's Gambit.

DIAGRAM 187

After

$$1. \ldots \qquad Q \times RP$$

White can resign, since he loses a full Rook:

$$2. R \times Q \qquad P \times R$$

and Black gets a Queen all over again.

In *Diagram 188*, from Capablanca-Jaffe, New York, 1910, the Pawn at KB2 is an overloaded defender. Capa concluded neatly:

DIAGRAM 188

| *1.* R x P | Kt - B3 |

For *1. . . .* P x R; *2.* Q x P ch is mate next.

| *2.* Kt - K5 | P - B4 |

To take the Rook would still allow a mate in short order: *2. . . .* P x R; *3.* Q x P ch, K - R1; *4.* Q x P ch, K - Kt1; *5.* Q - Kt6 ch, K - R1; *6.* R - K1, and there is no defense to R - K3 - R3.

| *3.* B x P ch | K x B |
| *4.* Kt x P ch | Resigns |

It is mate soon.

Once the position is opened wide enough something is bound to happen; still, you have to see it. In *Diagram 189*, from Capablanca-Balla, Budapest, 1929, the winning move is simple but none too obvious:

| *1.* R - Q1 | O - O |

DIAGRAM 189

He has no defense. On *1. . . .* P x B; *2.* Kt x B ch, K - B1;
3. Kt x B, Q x Kt; *4.* Kt - R4, R - B1; *5.* R - B1 wins a piece,
while if *1. . . .* B - K2; *2.* Kt x P, Kt x P; *3.* P x Kt, B x B; *4.*
Kt - B7 ch, K - B1; *5.* Q - B4 decides.

2. Kt x B	P x B
3. Kt - R4	Kt - Q1
4. Kt x B	Kt x Kt
5. Q - B6	

And suddenly Black's Knight has no moves.

5. . . .	P x P
6. RP x P	Q - K4
7. Q x QKt	

The rest is simple.

In *Diagram 190,* from Marshall-Wolf, Nuremberg, 1906,
Marshall sees a chance to pull one of our basic mating combinations (Diagram 107).

1. Kt x RP	K x Kt
2. Kt - Kt5 ch	K - Kt1

On *2. . . .* K - R3; *3.* Q - Kt4 wins.

DIAGRAM 190

| 3. Q - R5 | P - B3 |

The only try.

| 4. B x KtP | R - Q2 |
| 5. Kt x P | R - R2 |

A trappy countercombination, of which Marshall says, "A nice try, even though it fails." The variation is 6. Q x Kt?, B x P ch; 7. K - R1, B - K4 ch and draws, since 8. B x R ch ?? would allow a mate after 8. . . . Q x B ch.

6. B x R ch	Q x B
7. Q x Q ch	K x Q
8. Kt x R ch	B x Kt
9. KR - Q1	

With his tremendous material advantage, the rest is easy for White.

Alekhine furnishes a sprightly conclusion in *Diagram 191,* from a game against Asgeirsson, Iceland, 1931.

1. R x Kt ch	B x R
2. Kt - K4	Q - Kt5
3. Kt—Q6 ch	K - B1

He must give up the Queen to stop mate.

> 4. Q - B6 ch   P x Q
> 5. R - B7 mate

Again it is the KB2 square that proves to be the defender's Achilles' heel in *Diagram 192*, from Botvinnik-Vidmar, Nottingham, 1936.

DIAGRAM 192

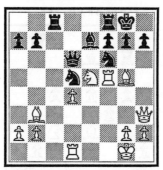

> 1. Kt x P   R x Kt

On *1. . . . K x Kt*; simply 2. B x Kt ch is sufficient, but 2. B x Kt, B x B; 3. R x Kt is even stronger.

2. B(Kt5) x Kt	B x B

There is nothing to be done. On 2. . . . Kt x B; 3. R x Kt, B x R; 4. Q x R ch wins.

3. R x Kt	Q - B3
4. R - Q6	Q - K1
5. R - Q7	Resigns

The Germans have a word for it—they call it the *Zwischenzug*. I have suggested the term in-between move. Whatever you call it, when it's available, it's strong. *Diagram 193* arose in the game Romanovsky-Botvinnik, Moscow, 1945. What is Black to do? On 1. . . . P x R there follows 2. P - B5 with very unclear complications that look good for White. He played.

1. . . .	P x P

The in-between move.

2. R - K7	P x B
3. Kt - K1	R - KB2
4. R x R	K x R

DIAGRAM 193

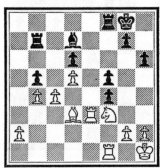

5. Kt x P	B - Kt4
6. R - Q1	B x Kt
7. R x B	R x P

and Black has come out a clear Pawn ahead. The ending he won easily.

How to decide on the right move? That is always the question. The first approach should be to calculate the "normal" sequence of events. Thus in *Diagram 194*, from Mikenas-Sokolsky, Sverdlovsk, 1942, the problem for Black is, which Rook to take? Clearly White's only compensation for the exchange is the strong passed Pawn at Q6. This dictates the winning line:

DIAGRAM 194

| 1. . . . | Q x R ch |
| 2. Q x Q | |

Another possibility is 2. Kt x Q, Kt x Q; 3. P x Kt, R - B8; 4. P - Q7, R x Kt ch; 5. K - Kt2, R - KKt1; 6. K x Kt, R x P and wins.

2. . . .	Kt x Q
3. Kt x Kt	R x P
4. P - Q7	R - KKt1

He must play carefully. On 4. . . . R - Q1 ?; 5. B - K7 wins for White since the Rook must not leave the eighth rank.

5. K - Kt2   Kt - K4

Now Black will win the QP with . . . R - Q5, and the remainder should not be too hard.

In the diagramed position Sokolsky played instead *1. . . . Q x R(Kt7)* and after *2. B x Q, Kt x Q; 3. R x Kt, R x P; 4. P - Q7, R - Q1; 5. R x P, R - B7; 6. R x Kt, R x B; 7. Kt - Q3, R - K7; 8. Kt - B5* the Pawn was held at Q7 and White drew.

The position in *Diagram 195*, from Rubinstein-Capablanca, San Sebastian, 1911, is by no means easy to evaluate. White's KBP is under attack, and his pieces seem to be somewhat dis-

DIAGRAM 195

jointed. Yet Black is weak on the diagonal controlled by the White Bishop. Rubinstein takes advantage of this weakness in a magnificent manner.

1. Kt x P   Q - R3

Let us examine the alternatives:

A. *1. . . . Q x KtP; 2. B x P ch and 3. B x R*
B. *1. . . . P x Kt; 2. Q x P ch*
C. *1. . . . B x P ch; 2. K - Kt2, Q - R3; 3. Kt - B4*

It is clear that Capa had no choice. But it looks as if his rejoinder were more than good enough, for he not only threatens . . . Q x B, but also . . . R - Q1, pinning the White Knight.

2. K - Kt2   R(QB1) - Q1

Suddenly it looks as if Black will win.

3. Q - B1

This is the splendid key to the combination, which Rubinstein must have had in mind when he made his move Kt x P. The same move won against Lasker two years earlier (see Diagram 164) by a remarkable coincidence.

3. . . .   P x Kt

The alternatives are no better: if 3. . . . R x Kt; 4. Q x Q, P x Q; 5. B x P ch and B x R.

4. Q x B   Q - Q7
5. Q - Kt5   Kt - Q5
6. Q - Q3   Q x Q

He cannot play 6. . . . Q x KtP because of QR - Kt1, winning a piece.

7. P x Q

and White won in the ending (but only after some inexact play on both sides!).

The cramped position is responsible for White's loss in *Diagram 196,* from Euwe-Muhring, Hilversum, 1947.

1. . . .   B - Kt5

and White resigned, because he loses a piece. If the Knight moves, 2. . . . P - B6 wins, while on 2. Q - Q1, Kt - Q5; pins the Knight and wins it.

DIAGRAM 196

The exposed King position is responsible for White's downfall in *Diagram 197,* from Thompson-Noteboom, Ramsgate, 1929.

DIAGRAM 197

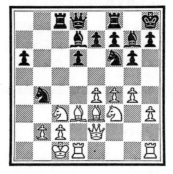

1. . . .	R x Kt
2. P x R	Kt - R7 ch
3. K - Q2	

Hoping to flee to safety. On 3. K - Kt2 there would follow 3. . . . Kt x BP; 4. K x Kt, Kt x P dbl ch; 5. K - Kt3, Q - Kt1 ch and mates shortly.

3. . . .   Kt x P ch

The other brilliancy 3. . . . Kt x BP was of course also possible, since 4. K x Kt tranposes to the above variation. But the
text is naturally strong too: if 4. B x Kt, B x P ch; 5. K - Q3,
B - Kt4 mate.

4. K - K1   Kt(R7) x P
5. Q - Kt2   Kt x R

and with two Pawns to the good Black has no trouble.

After a series of dramatic sacrifices the position shown in
Diagram 198 arose in the game Horowitz-Bisguier, New
York, 1948. The question here is whether Black has enough
for his enormous material lack. Analysis showed that White
could have won by returning two pieces:

DIAGRAM 198

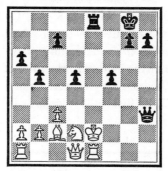

1. B - K4   BP x B

On *1.* . . . QP x B White can escape with *2.* Q - Kt3 ch,
K - Q1, etc.

2. Kt x P   Q - Kt7 ch

Or *2.* . . . R x Kt ch; *3.* K - Q2 and Black will soon be all
checked out.

3. K - K3   R x Kt ch

There is no better continuation: if *3. . . .* Q x Kt ch; *4.* K - Q2, while if *3. . . .* P x Kt; *4.* Q - Q7.

4. K - Q3

and White wins.

In the game White played *1.* Kt - K4 ? and was forced to allow a draw after *1. . . .* Q - R7 ch; *2.* K - B1, Q - R8 ch; *3.* K - B2, Q - R7 ch, etc.

After *1.* Kt - K4, Q - R7 ch there is nothing better than the perpetual for White, for if

A. *2.* K - Q3, QP x Kt ch; *3.* K - Q4, Q - B7 ch; *4.* R - K3, R - Q1 ch winning.

B. *2.* K - B3, QP x Kt ch; *3.* K - K3 and Black mates after *3. . . .* P - B5 ch; *4.* K - Q4, Q - B7 ch; *5.* K - Q5, Q - Kt3.

C. *2.* K - K3, Q - R3 ch; when *3.* K - K2, Q - R7 ch is forced, for if *3.* K - Q4, QP x Kt either mates or wins the Queen.

To draw away the main defending piece (the overloaded defender) is one of the cardinal principles of the attack. This is again seen in *Diagram 199*, from Alekhine-Euwe, eighteenth match game, 1937. At first sight it looks as if White is helpless

DIAGRAM 199

against the threat of check at Q7; if K - R3, then R - KKt2 consolidates. But:

| 1. R - Q4 | Q - K3 |

On 1. . . . Q x R; 2. Q x P ch forces perpetual check: 2. . . . K - R1; 3. Q - K8 ch, K - R2; 4. Q - Kt6 ch, etc. The King may not go to Kt2 because of Kt - B5 ch.

| 2. R x R ch | Kt x R |
| 3. Q x P | |

With only one Pawn to the good in such an open position Black could not win; the game was drawn shortly thereafter.

A potential discovery is the cause of Black's downfall in *Diagram 200,* from Capablanca-Yates, Barcelona, 1929.

DIAGRAM 200

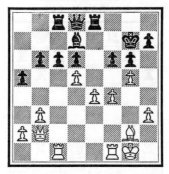

| 1. P x P | R x P |
| 2. P x P ch | |

Winning a Pawn, for if 2. . . . Q x P ?; 3. Q x Q ch, K x Q; 4. P - K5 ch wins the Rook.

| 2. . . . | K - B2 |
| 3. P - K5 | |

and White won quickly.

Diagram 201, a variation from Sokolsky-Botvinnik, Leningrad, 1938, is a position in which Black wins because of the lack of mobility of the White pieces. The correct move is:

| *1. . . .* | B - B6 |
| *2.* P x B | P - Q6 |

Now the White Queen has no moves. If *3.* Q - Q2, or *3.* Q - K1, Kt x P ch forks the King and Queen, while on *3.* Q - Kt2, likewise *3. . . .* Kt x P ch, winning the Queen.

| *3.* R x P | Kt x R |
| *4.* B - Q4 | Kt x R |

An additional finesse—the White Queen is under attack, which decides for Black.

DIAGRAM 201

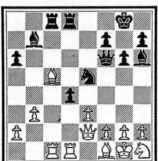

The defender is often faced with the question of deciding whether a certain attack is worth the material sacrificed. In *Diagram 202,* from Christoffel-Steiner, Hastings, 1945–46, the choice is difficult. On *1.* B x R ?, P x B; he is lost, e.g., *2.* P x Kt, R x P; *3.* B x R, B x B; *4.* P - B3, Q x P ch; *5.* K - B2, B - R6 mate. Christoffel found the right way:

| *1.* B x Kt | B x B |

If first *1.. .,*. R x R ch; 2. Q x R, B x B White can afford to
take the piece, e.g. 3. P x B, Q - Kt5; 4. P - B3, B x P dis ch;
5. Q - Kt3, and he is safe.

2. R x R

Again intending to take the piece after *2. . . .* P x R; 3.

DIAGRAM 202

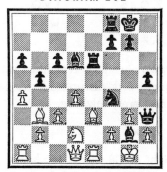

P x B, R x P, since 4. B x P ch, Q x B; 5. K x B then provides
an adequate defense.

2. . . .   B x Kt

Hoping for 3. Q x B, B - B6.

3. P - KB4

Contenting himself with only one extra Pawn: after *3. . . .*
P x R; 4. Q x B, B - Q4; 5. B x B, KP x B; 6. P x P, RP x P; 7.
Q - K3, he should win easily.

3. . . .   B x KBP

No doubt hoping for 4. P x B, P x R.

4. Q - K2

A simple refutation.

4. . . .	B - B6
5. Q x B	P x R
6. R - K1 !	R - B3

He has nothing left. On *6. . . .* B - Q7 White would reply
7. B x P ch, Q x B; 8. Q x R ch.

7. Q x B	R x Q
8. B x P ch	Q x B
9. R x Q	

With a clear Pawn ahead the remainder was easy.

A potential Knight fork disrupts Black's game in *Diagram
203*, from Alekhine-Keres, Salzburg, 1942.

1. B x P

The Black Knight at Q3 carries too heavy a load. If *1. . . .*
Q x B; 2. Q x Q, Kt x Q; 3. Kt - R6 ch, K - R1 (*3. . . .* K - B1;
4. R - B7 mate); *4.* Kt - B7 ch decides.

DIAGRAM 203

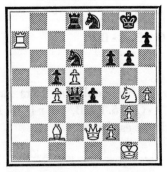

1. . . .	P - B4
2. B x P	

For once Alekhine missed the most forceful continuation: in the game he played 2. Kt - R6 ch, K - R1; 3. B - B2 and also won, but the text is quicker.

| 2. . . . | Kt x B |

Mating threats abound: if 2. . . . P x B; 3. Q - K6 ch, K - R1 (or 3. . . . K - B1; 4. Kt - K5); 4. Q - R6, Kt - Kt2; 5. Kt - B6, and Black has only a few spite checks.

| 3. Q - K6 ch | K - R1 |
| 4. Kt - K5 | Kt(K1) - Q3 |

Should the other Knight go to Q3, then Q - K7 would be conclusive.

5. Q - B6 ch	K - Kt1
6. Q x R ch	Kt - K1
7. Q x Kt mate	

The release of a pin by a counterthreat is the motif of *Diagram 204,* from Tarrasch-Rubinstein, San Sebastian, 1912. Black played:

DIAGRAM 204

1. . . .	Kt x KP
2. B x Q	Kt x Q
3. K x Kt	R x B

Black has regained the Pawn with the better end game; Rubinstein won in a manner that has become a classic for the two Bishops.

At the time he played the game from which *Diagram 205* is taken, Rossetto was only twelve years old. White triumphs with a series of mate threats:

1. B x Kt

The beginning: if in reply *1.* . . . B x Q; *2.* P x Kt, and mate cannot be prevented.

| *1.* . . . . | Kt x B |
| *2.* P - Q5 | P x P |

Again if *2.* . . . B x Q; *3.* P x Kt, followed by mate at QR7.

An alternative combination arises after *2.* . . . Kt - K4; *3.* Q - Q4, P - QB4; *4.* Kt x P, Kt - B6 ch; *5.* R x Kt, B x R; and White has the choice of *6.* Q - B4 ch, P - K4; *7.* Q x B, and *6.* Kt - R6 ch, K x P; *7.* Q x P ch, K - B1; *8.* Q - Kt8 ch, K - Q2; *9.* Q - Kt7 ch, K - K1; *10.* Kt - B7 ch, K - B2; *11.* Kt x P dis ch winning the Queen.

| *3.* P x P | Q - K2 |
| *4.* P x Kt | |

He sacrifices his Queen anyhow.

4. . . .	R x Q ch
5. Kt x R	Q x B
6. Kt x Q	Resigns

He has stopped mate, but finds himself a Rook behind.

Another defensive problem is seen in *Diagram 206,* from Denker-Fine, New York, 1948. Black's Queen must move, when B - B4 wins the exchange. But there is a way out involving a counterattack:

1. . . .	Kt - Kt5 ch

DIAGRAM 206

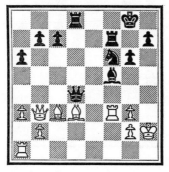

2. K - R1	Q - B4
3. B x B	

He sees that 3. B - B4 would be refuted by 3. . . . B - K3, which hits at the White KB, and threatens a devastating check at KR4; in fact, after 4. B x B, Q - R4 ch it is mate in six: 5. K - Kt1, Q - R7 ch; 6. K - B1, Q - R8 ch; 7. K - K2, Q x P ch; 8. K - K1, Q - R8 ch; 9. K - K2, Q x R ch; 10. K - K1, Q - B8 mate.

3. . . .	P x B
4. R - Q1	R - Q3

Avoiding the trap: *4. . . .* Kt - B7 ch ?; *5.* R x Kt, R x R ch; *6.* Q x R, Q x R; *7.* Q - Q8 ch, and White has at least a draw by perpetual check.

5. R x R	Q x R
6. K - Kt1	Q - R3

White exceeded the time limit here, but it is clear that his game is coming apart.

An artificial pin is created in *Diagram 207*, from Euwe-Alekhine, twenty-fifth match game, 1937. After

DIAGRAM 207

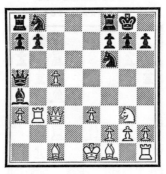

1. . . .	Q - Q1

the White Rook may not move because of the mate threat at Q8. White played:

2. B - B4	Kt - R3
3. B x Kt	P x B
4. O - O	B x R

and Black won the ending.

The theme in *Diagram 208*, from Marshall-Rubinstein, Moscow, 1925, is again *diversion of the defender*. After

DIAGRAM 208

1. Kt(B3) - Q2

the Queen is compelled to keep an eye on the Bishop. There followed:

1. . . .	Q - R7
2. Kt - QB3	Resigns

For the Queen must leave the diagonal.

A *sacrifice for a pin* is the idea in *Diagram 209*, from Zukertort-Anderssen, Berlin, 1865.

DIAGRAM 209

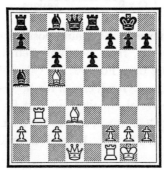

1. B x P ch	K x B
2. R - R3 ch	K - Kt1
3. Q - R5	P - B4
4. R - Q1	B - Q2

Forced, since he has to defend the Rook.

5. Q - R7 ch	K - B2
6. R - Kt3	

Now the natural . . . Q - B3 is not feasible because the Bishop is en prise.

6. . . .	B - B6
7. Q - Kt6 ch	K - Kt1
8. R x B(B3)	P - B5
9. R - KR3	

He plays to continue the attack. 9. R(B3) - Q3 winning a piece is equally effective.

9. . . .	R - K2
10. Q - R7 ch	K - B2
11. Q - R5 ch	K - Kt1
12. B x R	Q x B
13. Q - R8 ch	K - B2
14. Q x R	Resigns

The winning move in a winning position is often not easy to find. *Diagram 210,* from Botvinnik-Petrov, Moscow, 1940, presents a cunning trap. For if 1. Kt - Q6, which seems to win the exchange, 1. . . . R x R ch; 2. R x R, Q - Q1; and Black slips out with material equality, at least for the time being, e.g., 3. Q x Q, R x Q; 4. Kt x P, Kt x P; 5. P x Kt, P x Kt; 6. B - B7, R - Q4; 7. B x P, R x P, etc. Instead a quick decision was reached by

| 1. B x Kt | R x R |

If now *1.... R x B; 2. Kt - Q6* wins at once.

| 2. R x R | Q x B |
| 3. R - K8 ch | R - B1 |

Or *3.... Kt - B1; 4. Kt - R6 ch.*

| 4. Kt - K7 ch | K - B2 |

He has no choice. On *4.... Kt x Kt; 5. R x Kt* forces Black to give up either his King or his Queen.

| 5. Kt x P | Q - Kt2 |
| 6. R - K3 | |

White is a healthy Pawn ahead. The rest is simple.

6....	R - QKt1
7. P - R4	K - B1
8. P - R5	Resigns

After *8.... Kt - R1* White can win in seven different ways, of which the easiest is *9. R - K7.*

Often enough the win of material is bound up with combinations of the basic types. In *Diagram 211,* from Belson-

Fine, Chicago, 1934, Black can afford to take the QP because of a combination involving a mate threat:

DIAGRAM 211

1. . . .	Kt x P
2. Q - R4	B x Kt

He cannot afford to play simply 2. . . . B - QB4; then 3. B - K3 regains the Pawn, since Black must reply 3. . . . B - Q2 to avoid the loss of a piece.

3. Kt x B

Under the impression that he is winning a piece. On 3. P x B, Kt - K7 ch, Black comes out a healthy Pawn to the good.

3. . . .	Kt x Kt
4. P x B	Q - B2

The key move—mate is threatened, and the QBP is under attack.

5. P - Kt3	Q x BP

and Black won in short order.

When a piece gets deep into enemy territory, the danger that it will be trapped is great. The Pawn-chasing Queen is a case in point. In *Diagram 212*, from Steiner-Fine, fifth match game, 1932, the White Queen is lost after

DIAGRAM 212

1. . . .	R - B2

The threat is now 2. . . . P - Kt3 and 3. . . . R - R2. White tried

2. P - QR4	Q - Q3

Threatening now . . . P - QKt4, against which there is no defense.

3. P - K4	P x P
4. B x P	P - QKt4
5. B - Kt7	Q - Q2
6. B - B6	R x Q
7. B x Q	R x B

and White resigned in a few more moves.

In many cases the outcome of a combination can be seen only at the end of a forced sequence of moves. An example of this is the Tarrasch Trap in the Ruy Lopez, *Diagram 213*. White wins a Pawn as follows:

1. B x Kt	B x B
2. P x P	P x P
3. Q x Q	QR x Q

In order to regain the Pawn Black must hold open a mating threat at Q8. On 3. . . . KR x Q White's task is easier, as will be seen below.

4. Kt x P	B x P
5. Kt x B	Kt x Kt
6. Kt - Q3	

Guarding against the mate and threatening to win a piece.

DIAGRAM 213

TARRASCH TRAP: WHITE TO PLAY WINS A PAWN

| *6.* . . . . | P - KB4 |
| *7.* P - KB3 | B - B4 ch |

If the other Rook had recaptured at move 3, so that the Rook now at KB1 were at QR1, White could reply simply 8. K - B1 and win a piece. Now it is not feasible, because on 8. K - B1, B - Kt3; 9. P x Kt, P x P dis ch regains the piece.

| *8.* Kt x B | Kt x Kt |
| *9.* B - Kt5 | R - Q4 |

To hold the Knight; on any other move, B - K7 wins the exchange at once.

10. B - K7

The moves must be played in the right order, otherwise Black has a way out. If *10.* P - QB4, R - Q2; *11.* B - K7, Kt - Q6 saves Black.

10. . . .   R - K1
11. P - QB4 and wins.

Black must give up at least the exchange. One last point: on *11. . . .* Kt - Q6; *12.* P x R, Kt x R; *13.* R x Kt, K - B2, the pin can be released either by *14.* B - R4 or *14.* B - Kt4.

We never tire of the enchanting combinations that mating attacks bring about. *Diagram 214* is from a game Boleslavsky-Ufimtsev, Omsk, 1944. A cursory inspection might lead one to think that Black is worse off than White. Not so!

1. . . .   Kt - K5

Surprise No. 1.

2. Q - R5

DIAGRAM 214

Naturally he avoids the elementary mate involved in 2. B x Q?, Kt x Q; 3. Kt x Kt, R x P ch; 4. K - R1, R x RP dlb ch and 5. . . . R - R8 mate. But, what will Black do now?

2. . . .	KR - Kt1 !

Surprise No. 2. To take the Queen allows a mate in three after 3. B x Q, R x P ch; 4. K - R1, R x P ch; 5. Kt x R, Kt x P dbl ch and mate.

And on the defensive attempt 3. P - KKt3, Blacks tears White apart with 3. . . . Kt x KtP; 4. RP x Kt (if now 4. B x Q, Kt - K7 dbl ch; 5. K - R1, B x Kt mate), R x P ch; 5. P x R, Q x B ch; 6. K - R1, Q - R3 ch; 7. K - Kt2, R x P ch; 8. K - B2, R - Kt7 ch, and mate again !

3. Kt - K1	R x P ch !
4. Kt x R	Kt - Q7 !

Fantastic. There is really only one direct threat, yet White can do nothing about it. On 5. B x Q, R x Kt ch and 6. . . . R x RP dbl ch mates as before while on 5. P - B3, Q x B ch; 6. K - R1, Q - R3 leads to mate.

5. Q - Q5	

Just to stop mate.

5. . . .	B x Q
6. P x B	Q x P

Now it's simple.

7. B x Kt	Q x R
8. B - KB3	B x P ch
Resigns	

Concealed checks and a powerful long diagonal combine to produce the decision in *Diagram 215,* from Zita-Bronstein, match, Prague-Moscow, 1946.

1. . . .   R x B
2. R x R

Naturally, 2. P x Kt loses a Pawn at least.

2. . . .   Kt x BP

The point: control of the two diagonals combines to win for Black. If 3. K x Kt, Kt x KtP and if 3. Q x Kt, Kt - Q6 with an easy win in both cases.

DIAGRAM 215

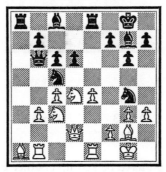

3. R - K3   Kt x P ch

Avoiding unnecessary complications. 3. . . . Kt(B4) x KP; 4. Kt x Kt, B x Kt; 5. R - K1 gives White a little counterplay.

4. K - R2   Kt - B7

He's back! This time it does not even involve a combination—if 5. Q x Kt, B x Kt.

5. R - B3   Kt(B4) x KP

And with so many Pawns for the exchange, not to mention his attack, Black won easily.

A punster would say of *Diagram 216* that Black picks up a

Pawn with a fork. It is taken from Norman-Vidmar, Hastings, 1925–26.

DIAGRAM 216

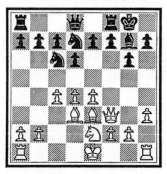

1. . . .	Kt(B3) - K4
2. P x Kt	Kt x P
3. Q - Kt3	Kt x B ch
4. K - B1	

Here Black could have picked up another Pawn with *4.* . . . Kt x P, but preferred

4. . . .	P - QB4
5. P - KR4	Q - Q2
6. P - R5	Q - K3

This takes the sting out of White's attack and concludes quickly.

7. R - R4	Q x BP
8. P x P	BP x P
9. Q - R3	Kt x BP
10. B x Kt	B - Q5
Resigns	

Too many pieces are pinned.

Piece sacrifices with the Queens off the board are unusual. The one in *Diagram 217*, from Takacs-Rubinstein, Rogaska-Slatina, 1929, justifiably earned its author a brilliancy prize.

DIAGRAM 217

1. Kt x KP   BP x Kt

The only chance—if he takes either of the other pieces, Kt - B7 ch, and Kt x R wins.

Since there are no less than three White pieces en prise, moves such as . . . R - R2 or . . . R - QKt1 come into consideration. On *1.* . . . R - R2 White naturally plays 2. B x P. More difficult is *1.* . . . R - QKt1. But still this can be adequately refuted with 2. Kt - B7 ch, K - Q1; 3. B x BP, P x Kt; 4. B - K6, K - K2; 5. B - R3 and White with two Pawns for the piece retains sufficient pressure.

2. B x KP   P x Kt

On 2. . . . K - K2 there would follow 3. B x Kt, B x B; 4. R x B ch, K x R; 5. Kt - Kt6 ch with an easy win.

3. R x B ch   R x R
4. B x Kt ch   K - Q1
5. B - Kt4 dis ch   B - Q3

Or 5. . . . K - B2; 6. R - B1 ch.

6. B x R	K - K2
7. B x P	

and White won the ending with ease.

Some competent critics have considered the game in which this combination was concocted the finest ever played. The crucial position is seen in *Diagram 218;* the game is Grünfeld-Alekhine, Carlsbad, 1923.

DIAGRAM 218

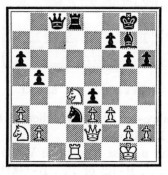

1. . . .	R x Kt

So that if 2. P x R, B x P ch is immediately decisive: 3. K - B1 (or 3. K - R1, Kt - B7 ch), Kt - B5; 4. Q - Q2, Q - B5 ch; 5. K - K1, P - K6 and wins.

2. P x P	Kt - B5
3. P x Kt	

Forced.

3. . . .	Q - B5

A double attack against the Kt at R2 and the Q at K2.

4. Q x Q   R x R ch
5. Q - B1   B - Q5 ch
Resigns

In *Diagram 219*, from Keres-Grau, Warsaw, 1935, the exposed Black QB suggests a combination. One is there, with a series of forks.

1. Kt - Kt6

He must be careful to take the exchange in the right way. If *1.* Kt - B6 ch, R x Kt; *2.* P x R, Kt x P allows Black to come out with two Pawns for it.

DIAGRAM 219

1. . . . .   P x Kt
2. Kt x B   Q - B2
3. Kt x R

and White won.

In an apparently hopeless position, the rule is: look for a counterattack. *Diagram 220* is taken from the game Fine-Capablanca, AVRO tournament, 1938. Black is apparently lost, for on *1.* . . . . B - Q4; simply *2.* P x P. Instead Capa played:

DIAGRAM 220

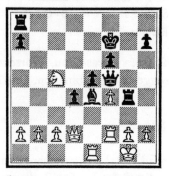

1. . . .	B x KtP
2. R x B	QR - KKt1
3. R - K2	P x P !

And suddenly White finds the tables turned. He just managed to draw with

4. Kt - Kt7	Q - Q4
5. R x R	R x R ch
6. R - Kt2	R x R ch
7. Q x R	P - B6
8. Q - R3	Q - Kt4 ch
9. Q - Kt3	Q - B8 ch
10. K - B2	Q - K6 ch

and Black if he wishes has a draw by perpetual check. He tried instead:

11. K - B1	Q - K7 ch
12. K - Kt1	Q - Q8 ch
13. K - B2	Q x P ch
14. K x P	Q - B3 ch
15. K - K2	Q x Kt
16. P - Kt3	Q - K5 ch
17. K - Q2	

But the Queen ending is drawn.

v. *How to Analyze a Position*

THE PLAYER understandably is always facing us with
the question: What shall I do in this position? Before this
question can be answered intelligently, we must first ask:
How is this position to be evaluated? It is with the second
question that we are concerned now.

The analysis of a position is based on the three fundamental
principles of force, mobility, and King safety. Mobility is
further subdivided into Pawn structure and freedom of the
pieces. Add the tactical situation at any moment, and we have
the five basic questions:

1. Am I ahead, behind, or even in material? (Material)

2. Are my Pawns well placed and how do they compare
with my opponent's? (Pawn structure)

3. How much freedom of action do my pieces have, and is
my degree of mobility greater than my opponent's? (Mobility)

4. Are the Kings safe or exposed to attack? (King safety)

5. What is the threat? (Combinations)

Once these questions are answered, we can evaluate the
position as superior, equal, or inferior, form plans, and proceed
accordingly.

The last question, on combinations, has already been discussed at some length. In those positions where there is a
decisive combination everything else is of secondary importance. In the remaining chapters we shall consider only those
positions where there is no immediate tactical decision, i.e.,
those where strategical considerations are paramount.

The nature of a positional advantage needs some clarification. It can consist either of a superior Pawn structure, greater freedom of the pieces, or a more exposed enemy King. These are of course independent only in theory; in practice one frequently offsets the other, or depends on the other. E.g., we must often decide whether to attack at the expense of a disruption of the Pawn structure.

Advantages are either *permanent* or *temporary*. A permanent advantage is one which is inherent in the structure; it is either a material plus or certain types of superior Pawn structure. A temporary advantage is one which involves greater mobility; since mobility is apt to be dissipated in the course of time, something should be done about it quickly.

The player must often make up his mind whether to stick to the middle game or go into an end game; this latter usually means exchanging Queens. The answer depends on whether his advantage (or disadvantage) is permanent or temporary. With a permanent advantage, or a temporary disadvantage, end-game play is called for, while with a temporary advantage, or permanent disadvantage middle-game play is to be preferred.

In the chapters that follow we shall elaborate all these points more fully; here we wish to give some illustrative positions, and show how they are to be evaluated.

Permanent Advantage

IT WILL be recalled that a permanent advantage consists either of a material plus or certain kinds of Pawn superiority; conversely a permanent disadvantage would consist either of a material minus or certain kinds of Pawn inferiority.

A typical illustration of a material advantage (Pawn) is seen in *Diagram 221*, from Winawer-Lasker, Nuremberg, 1896. It is Black's move. If we go through the five questions, we find: (1) Black is a Pawn ahead; (2) his Pawns are better

placed (White has isolated doubled QB Pawns); (3) freedom
of action is about even; (4) Black's King is not more exposed
per se, but is faced by an immediate concentration of the
heavy pieces; (5) there is an immediate threat in R - R3, for
if then . . . P - R3; B x P with a mating attack.

The over-all question to be answered is whether the White
attack is worth a Pawn; Lasker showed that it was not.

Black thus has a permanent advantage in his extra Pawn.
His ultimate goal is to head for the end game; exchanging
Queens would take the sting out of White's attack and win
easily. White on the other hand has a permanent disadvantage;
he must go all out for the attack.

The immediate threat of R - R3 was met by *1. . . .* Q - B5;
Lasker succeeded in repulsing the enemy pieces and won by
advancing the QRP—the plan which flows logically out of
the analysis of the position.

DIAGRAM 221

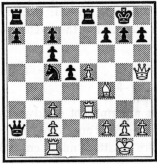

It is instructive to see how short-range plans evolve, and
how Black carried through his major goal.

1. . . .	Q - B5
2. R - B3	

To hold the Bishop; if at once 2. R - R3, Q x B, and White's attack is not worth the piece. Meanwhile White with his last move has created a new threat: 3. B - R6 ! hitting at the Black KBP.

	2. . . .	Kt - K3
	3. B - Q2	R - K2
	4. R - R3	Q - K5

Note that Black's defensive moves have been in response to direct threats.

5. P - B3

Hitting the defending piece. An alternative plan was to block the line with P - KB4 - B5. Black can just manage to find a sufficient reply to this with the following variation: 5. P - KB4, Q - Kt3; 6. Q - R4, R - Q2; 7. P - Kt4, Q - K5; 8. P - B5, Kt - B1; 9. R - K1, Q x QBP; 10. P - K6, P x P; 11. P x P, R - Q3; 12. P - K7, Kt - K3; 13. R(R3) - K3, Q - Kt3; 14. Q - R5 (to take away the defense of the Knight), Q x Q; 15. P x Q, K - B2; 16. R - B3 ch, K x P; 17. B - B4, R - K1; 18. B x R ch, K x B, and Black with three Pawns for the exchange should win the ending.

	5. . . .	Q - Kt3
	6. Q - R4	

Since White has a permanent disadvantage (Pawn minus) naturally he wishes to avoid an ending, and concentrate on the middle game, where his attack might crash through.

	6. . . .	R - Q2
	7. P - KB4	

Threatening R - KB1 followed by P - B5.

	7. . . .	Q - K5
	8. P - Kt4	

White's short-range plans all involve P - KB5, Black's the prevention of this move.

8. . . .   Kt - B1

Again so that if P - B5, Q x KP.

9. Q - B2

In order to have the BP defended, and make P - B5 possible. Black, seeing no direct threat, continues with his major plan: advance of the QRP.

9. . . .	P - QR4
10. R - K3	Q - B5
11. P - B5	P - R5

To capture the KKtP at this stage would merely open another line for White unnecessarily.

12. R - B1

Hereabouts there are also offensive and defensive combinations that must be calculated precisely. If 12. P - K6, P x P; 13. P x P, Kt x P !; 14. R x Kt, Q x P ch and . . . Q x R. With the text White hopes to have some threat on the KB file, but the hopes are still so vague, that Lasker feels no need to do anything.

12. . . .	P - R6 !
13. R(K3) - K1	P - R7
14. P - R3	

White's pieces are now tied to the first rank by the passed QRP, and his attack is at a virtual standstill. Black now forms a new plan: by opening the position up, he will be able either to gain more material or to build up an attack against the White King, which is now somewhat exposed and defended by pieces that are overloaded with tasks.

$$14. \ldots \quad\quad\quad\quad P - B4$$
$$15. K - R2$$

White cannot pursue his attack because of the nasty enemy QRP. If here 15. P - K6, P x P; 16. P x P, Kt x P !; 17. R x Kt, P - R8(Q).

$$15. \ldots \quad\quad\quad\quad P - Q5$$
$$16. Q - B3 \quad\quad\quad\quad P - QB3 !$$

Opening the road for his Rook at Q2. The Pawn is artificially defended: if 16. Q x P, R(Q2) - R2; 17. R - QR1, Q - K7 ch.

$$17. P - K6$$

White becomes impatient, but passive defense was hopeless anyhow.

$$17. \ldots \quad\quad\quad\quad P x P$$
$$18. P x P \quad\quad\quad\quad Kt x P$$
$$19. Q x P \quad\quad\quad\quad R(Q2) - R2$$
$$20. R - QR1 \quad\quad\quad\quad R - KB1 !$$

Now that White's QR is tied down, the attack is switched to the other wing.

$$21. R(B1) - K1 \quad\quad\quad\quad Kt - Q1$$
$$22. Q - Kt6 \quad\quad\quad\quad R(R2) - KB2$$

Black now has a mating attack, and the QRP is of small importance.

$$23. B - Kt5 \quad\quad\quad\quad R - B7 ch$$
$$24. K - Kt3 \quad\quad\quad\quad Q x P ch$$

White resigns. On the natural 25. K - R4, Black has a pretty mate in three with 25. . . . Q x P ch !; 26. K x Q, R(B1) - B6 ch; 27. K - R4, R - R7 mate.

In the above example, the manner in which short-range

plans are merged with the long-range permanent advantage is most illuminating.

The situation in *Diagram 222*, from Fine-Kevitz, New York, 1936, is more complicated. It is Black's move. As we go through the five questions we find: (1) White is a Pawn ahead; (2) his Pawn structure on the Q-side is not as good as Black's, on the K-side better because of the extra Pawn; (3) Black's pieces have more mobility; (4) neither King is exposed, though mating threats might arise along the long diagonal controlled by Black's QB; (5) there is no immediate tactical threat, but White does threaten to improve his position with P - B3, and

DIAGRAM 222

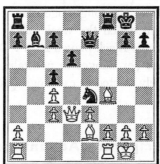

P - K4, which would block the Black QB.

The analysis leads to an evaluation of superiority for White, but the plus is minimal. As might be expected, in what followed the technical problems were quite difficult for White.

In *Diagram 223*, from Boleslavsky-Fine, radio match, U.S.S.R.-U.S.A., 1945, White's permanent advantage lies in the broken Black Pawns on the Q-side.

Let us go through the five questions here: (1) material is even; (2) White's Pawn structure is superior; in effect he is a Pawn ahead; (3) White's pieces have more mobility; (4) Black's King is not entirely safe; (5) there is no immediate

DIAGRAM 223

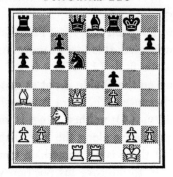

threat. All this adds up to both a permanent and a temporary advantage for White. The long-range plan would be to head for an end game in which the weak Black Pawns could be exploited. In the game Black played *1. . . . Q - B3*, to block at any rate the attack (exchanges to neutralize a command of space). White wisely elected to exchange Queens, and won in the ending.

Temporary Advantage

THIS consists of command of more space, superior mobility.

Diagram 224 is a good illustration; it is from the game Smyslov-Boleslavsky, U.S.S.R. championship, 1941. When we go through the five questions, we see that (1) material is even; (2) White's Pawn structure is superior; (3) White has command of more space; (4) neither King is exposed; (5) there is no immediate threat. Thus the better Pawns and superior development give White the advantage. How should this be made use of? In the end game the Pawn at Q4 is liable to prove weak, and the Pawn structure on Black's K-side is almost impossible to exploit. Hence the correct plan must envisage an attack against the Black King. To do this White must be

DIAGRAM 224

safe. So White played *1.* O - O, continued with an advance of Pawns on the Q-side, and won nicely.

A typical position from the Ruy Lopez is seen in *Diagram 225,* from Kashdan-Reshevsky, fourth match game, 1942.

DIAGRAM 225

Going through the five questions, we find: (1) material is even; (2) White's Pawns are more aggressively placed, but their inherent structure is not better for the end game; (3) White controls more space; (4) neither King is exposed; (5) there is no immediate threat. All this adds up to a temporary advantage for White, which can only be exploited by a K-side attack. Kashdan played *1.* Kt - B5, R - K3; *2.* P - KR4 and won prettily; for the continuation see p. 419.

VI. *Material Advantage*

THEORETICALLY, any material advantage should win. But the problem of how is not so readily answered.

Elementary theory teaches us that with no other pieces or Pawns on the board it takes at least a Rook to checkmate the King. This has an interesting parallel in winning with extra material when the board is full of pieces. *With less than a Rook and a piece to the good, direct mating attacks are as a rule futile.* There are of course ever so many exceptions to this rule, as to all chess rules; yet it holds true by and large. Hence unless the material plus is enormous, an attempt to mate directly is not well advised.

What then is the theoretical method of winning? *The technique for winning with extra material is to increase the material advantage until it is sufficient to mate.* This is the basic principle. The logic behind it is clear. If White is a piece ahead, he cannot force mate. But by attacking a Pawn with two pieces, which the opponent can only defend with one he thereby stands a good chance to increase his material advantage. In time he can queen a Pawn, and then he will have enough to be successful in playing for mate.

A second basic principle is that *the side with a material advantage should exchange pieces but not Pawns.* This again follows logically from our elementary theory. For the only real compensation for a material disadvantage is a counterattack. And the exchange of pieces takes the wind out of an attacker's sails.

Diagram 226, from Fine-Petrov, Semmering-Baden, 1937,

DIAGRAM 226

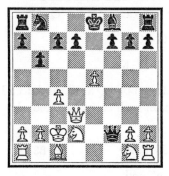

illustrates the winning procedure with an extra piece. As a result of an unsound opening sacrifice, Black has only one Pawn for the piece. He can gain another Pawn (KKt7) only at the cost of an exchange of Queens (*1. . . . Q x P; 2. Q - B3*). Hence he cannot take, but must speculate on the attack. The game continued:

1. . . .	Kt - B3
2. Q - K4	O - O - O

Under ordinary circumstances, a player would not castle into an attack in this manner, but Black is desperate.

3. P - QR3

To safeguard the King—remember that Black's only chance is a counterattack.

3. . . .	R - K1
4. KKt - B3	B - Q3
5. R - K1	

Holding the Pawn by a combination. If now *5. . . .* B x P; *6.* R - K2, Q - B4; *7.* Q - Q5, forcing the exchange of Queens.

5. . . .	Q x P
6. Q - B4	Q - Kt3 ch

7. K - Kt3	B - B4
8. K - R2	Q - B7

To play . . . Q - R5.

9. Kt - Kt3

Now he threatens both Q x BP, and Kt x B, P x Kt; B - K3. Black, as so often in such cases, becomes desperate.

9. . . .	P - KKt4
10. Kt x P	P - B3

For the KP is pinned.

11. Q - K4

The position permits of combinations. If now 11. . . . Q x RP; 12. B - B4, Q - R4; 13. Kt x B, KtP x Kt, and now White can win in two ways: 14. P - K6, P x Kt; 15. P x P ch, K x P; 16. Q - B5 ch, K - Q1; 17. B x P ch and 14. R - R1, Q - Kt3; 15. Q x Q, P x Q; 16. P x P.

11. . . .	Q x Q
12. Kt x Q	R x P
13. B - B4	R - B4

Here we see an example of the principle that a material advantage leads to even more material. The Rook must defend either the B or the BP. To hold both it gets into an uncomfortable position, which costs material later on.

14. R - KB1	B - K2
15. Kt - Kt3	

Now the Rook has no more moves.

15. . . .	R x B
16. R x R	P - KR4
17. R - R4	

Again a Pawn goes; it's two against one at every turn.

17. . . .	P - B4
18. R x P	R - B1
19. R x P	R - R1
20. R - R5	R - Kt1
21. R - Q1	P - R4
22. Kt - Q4	

Exchanges!

22. . . .	Kt - Q1
23. Kt(Q4) - B5	B - Q3
24. R x B	Resigns

More material goes; on 24. . . . P x R; 25. Kt - K7 ch follows. With two Pawns ahead, the same principles hold—exchange pieces, head for the ending, increase the material advantage. *Diagram 227*, from Euwe-Najdorf, Mar del Plata, 1947, is a perfect example. Black's only chance is a counterattack, so he tried:

1. . . .	P - B3
2. Q - Kt3 ch	K - R1
3. P x P	R x P ch

The exchange sacrifice facilitates the attack; on 3. . . . P x P, Black has no attack and his game is hopeless.

4. B x R	Q x B ch
5. K - Kt1	R - KB1
6. R - R3	P - KR3
7. R - KB3	

This return of the exchange is not essential, but it is the quickest way to win—White still has the two extra Pawns.

7. . . .	B x R
8. KP x B	Kt - Q5
9. Q - Q5	Kt - B4
10. Q x P	

To mobilize his extra Pawns; he rightly sees that Black's attack need not be feared.

10. . . .	Kt - K6
11. R - K1	Q - B6

If 11. . . . Q - Q5; 12. Q - K4 forces the exchange of Queens.

12. R - K2	Q - Q5

For now 13. Q - K4 ?? is impossible because of 13. . . . Q x Q; 14. P x Q, R x B ch (although White's position is so strong that even this might win!).

13. P - Kt3	

He sees that the discovered checks do not amount to anything.

13. . . .	R - K1

Threatening . . . Kt x B ch and . . . Q - Q8 ch.

14. Q - R6	R - Q1

With no particular threat.

15. Q - K6	Kt x B ch
16. K x Kt	Q - R8 ch
17. K - Kt2	Q x P
18. Q - B7	

To force another exchange. 18. P - B6 was also sufficient.

18. . . .	Q x P
19. R - K8 ch	

After this White exchanges all the pieces and queens his Pawns: *19.* R x R; *20.* Q x R ch, K - R2; *21.* Q - K4 ch, Q x Q; *22.* P x Q, K - Kt3; *23.* P - B6, and the BP promotes. Black therefore resigned.

DIAGRAM 227

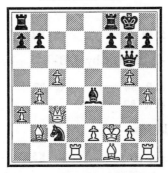

With only one Pawn to the good, the task is usually harder, but exactly the same principal applies: use the extra Pawn to increase the material advantage.

In *Diagram 228,* from Capablanca-Colle, Hastings, 1930–31,

DIAGRAM 228

White must first defend against the mate threat. Capablanca played:

1. P - Kt3

This is unavoidable, though it weakens the long diagonal.

1. . . .   P - B3

He does not have time for *1.* . . . Q - B3; for then *2.* P - KR3 wins a piece.

2. Kt - R4   Kt - K4

Now *2.* . . . Q - B3 is met by *3.* B - B3.

3. P - B4   Q - B3
4. K - B2

An ingenious defense.

4. . . .   Q - K5

Hoping for *5.* P x Kt, P x P dis ch with attacking chances. White chooses a simpler way.

5. Q - Kt1 !

Forces the exchange of Queens.

5. . . .   Q x Q
6. R x Q   B - K5
7. R - Kt3   Kt - Q2
8. R - R3   R - R1
9. R - R5

Pinning the Black pieces down. White will soon win an extra Pawn.

9. . . .   K - B2
10. Kt - B3   K - K2
11. Kt - Q2   B - B3
12. B - B3   B x B
13. K x B   K - Q3

14. Kt - K4 ch	K - B3
15. R - R6 ch	Kt - Kt3
16. Kt x KBP	

The second Pawn.

16. . . .	K - Kt2
17. R - R5	R - QB1
18. Kt - K4	Kt x P
19. R - Kt5 ch	

Avoiding the traps: if *19.* R x P, Kt - Q7 ch, and if *19.* Kt x P ch, K - Kt3. After the text, if *19.* . . . K - R3; *20.* R x P, and *20.* . . . Kt - Q7 ch fails against *21.* K - K2 because Black's Rook is undefended.

Black resigned.

The extra Pawn can of course be used to support an attack against the King, but usually with the idea of gaining extra material rather than mate. *Diagram 229*, from Lasker-Reti,

DIAGRAM 229

New York, 1924, is an example. In this position White is not only a Pawn ahead, he also has a potential attack against the Black King and pressure on the long diagonal. With a Pawn minus such a combination of advantages is by no means unusual, for the Pawn is not only material, but also serves as a defensive barrier. E.g., if in the above position Black had a Pawn at Q4, White's only advantage would lie in the potential attack against the King. The game continued:

1. . . .	KR - Q1
2. Q - Q2	B - K1
3. R - Q1	

White naturally is in favor of exchanges; Black, on the other hand, feels that in avoiding them lies his only chance.

3. . . .	R(Q1) - B1

Lasker now makes use of the dominating position of his pieces to crash through with an attack that yields a conclusive material advantage.

4. P - B5	P - K4
5. P - B6	Q - B1
6. Kt - B5	

Threatening to win the exchange with B x Kt and Kt - K7 ch.

6. . . .	K - R1
7. Q - Kt5	R - B2

Every move loses in its own way.

8. B x Kt	R x B

On 8. . . . B x B the penetration by the Rook also decides.

9. R - Q8	R(B3) - B1
10. Q - Kt7 ch	Q x Q
11. P x Q ch	K - Kt1
12. Kt - K7 ch	Resigns

When the position is locked, the exploitation of an extra Pawn can become a matter of the greatest technical difficulty, but the principles remain the same—exchange pieces, maneuver to increase the material plus. *Diagram 230,* from Tolush-Botvinnik, Moscow, 1945, is a model example.

DIAGRAM 230

Analysis of the position reveals Black's difficulties. While he is a Pawn ahead, his pieces are not co-ordinated. This might be remedied by consistent development, but then White could get control of the diagonal QR3 - KB8 and institute an attack. So Botvinnik devises another scheme, which we shall see unfold as the game progresses.

1. R - K1	B - Q2
2. B - KB1	P - QKt4
3. Q - B3	

This maneuver, which is designed to free the QB, allows a classic refutation. But if White did nothing, Black could break through with . . . Q - Kt3, . . . P - QR4, and . . . P - Kt5.

3. . . .	R - QKt1
4. KR - Kt1	Q - B2
5. B - B1	P - R4
6. B - R3	R - Kt3 !
7. Q - Kt3	Q - Q1

With a positional threat: . . . Q - R5, forcing the exchange of Queens.

8. B - Q6

This stops Black's threat, for if now 8. . . . Q - R5?; 9. R x Kt, but it permits another surprise.

DIAGRAM 231

8. . . .   R x B !

A combination that is all the more remarkable, because it is purely positional—to free Black's game.

9. P x R   B - B3

Again not 9. . . . Q - R5 at once because of 10. R x Kt, P x R; 11. R - Kt8 ch.

10. P - R3

His only chance lies in avoiding the exchange of Queens.

10. . . .   K - Q2

Here the King is quite safe.

11. R - K1	Q - R5
12. Q - K5	Q - B3
13. Q - Kt3	R - R5

Now we see the point to Black's strategy, which of course was hinted at before—to exchange Queens and win the end game. Once the QP goes he will have two Pawns for the exchange, which in such a position is enough to win.

14. R - K3	R - B5

Black must play carefully. If here 14. . . . Q - B5 ?; 15. R - B3 !, Q x Q; 16. P x Q, winning the BP.

15. B - K2	Q - R5
16. B - B3	

Botvinnik's strategy has been successful—he can if he wishes now exchange Queens. But with White's pieces so cramped he tries a more aggressive scheme.

16. . . .	P - Kt5
17. Q x Q	R x Q

Here White has a chance to get rid of the enemy KtP, but Black's Rook then penetrates: 18. P x P, P x P; 19. R - Kt1, R x P; 20. R x P, R - Q7; 21. P - B3, R - B7 and wins still another Pawn.

18. P - Kt3	

Hoping for 18. . . . R x RP; when 19. P x P, P x P; 20. R - Kt1 wins the KtP.

18. . . .	R - R1
19. P x P	P x P
20. R - Kt1	R - QKt1
21. P - R4	R - Kt2

Defending the Rook so as to be able to play . . . Kt - B6.

22. K - R2	K x P
23. P - Kt4	Kt - B6
24. R - QR1	Kt - Kt4

Again—use of a material plus to gain more material.

| 25. R - Q1 | R - R2 |

Threatening to win a Pawn with . . . R - R7.

26. P - R5	P - Kt4
27. K - Kt2	R - R7
Resigns	

For on 28. R - K2, Kt - B6 wins the exchange. Once another Pawn goes, the routine march of the foot soldiers will decide.

VII. *Compensating for a Material Disadvantage*

F ROM THE THEORETICAL DISCUSSION of the procedure for winning with a material advantage, it is clear enough what the nature of the compensation is that the opponent must have to equalize matters. Since the defender is at a permanent disadvantage, he must seek a counterattack. How severe the attack must be depends on the amount of material minus; thus with a Rook down the defender must have mating possibilities, but with only a Pawn down positional pressure may well be a sufficient compensation.

Odds games furnish an excellent illustration of how the side with less material can build up a devastating attack. The odds taker in such games generally makes two kinds of mistakes—he overlooks combinations, and he does not develop properly. Here is a game of Morphy's in which both mistakes are made:

GAME NO. 1

Remove White's QR

New Orleans, 1858

WHITE: *Morphy*   BLACK: *Amateur*

1. P - K4	P - K4
2. Kt - KB3	Kt - QB3
3. B - B4	Kt - B3
4. Kt - Kt5	P - Q4
5. P x P	Kt x P

While this is theoretically correct, to allow the sacrifices at all is to beg for trouble. Black would do better to choose the alternative . . . Kt - QR4.

6. Kt x BP	K x Kt
7. Q - B3 ch	K - K3
8. Kt - B3	Kt - Q5

Not a decisive mistake, but not the best. He violates the first rule of the defense, which is to meet direct threats. The right move is 8. . . . Kt - Kt5, which gives Black the better of it even when White's Rook is on the board.

9. B x Kt ch	K - Q3
10. Q - B7	B - K3

Another weak move, which allows White to drive his King out into the open. With 10. . . . Q - K2 Black can consolidate.

11. B x B	Kt x B
12. Kt - K4 ch	K - Q4

Trying to hold on to his extra material.

13. P - B4 ch	K x Kt
14. Q x Kt	

DIAGRAM 232

14. . . .	Q - Q5 ?

In a difficult position he makes a fatal blunder. *14.* . . .
K - Q5 was the best chance.

15.	Q - Kt4 ch	K - Q6
16.	Q - K2 ch	K - B7
17.	P - Q3 dis ch	K x B

Allows mate. But on *17.* . . . . K - Kt8; *18.* O - O, K x P; *19.*
Q - B2 is decisive.

18.	O - O mate !

Steinitz was once asked how he could consistently give a
certain opponent a Rook. "It is not I who gives him a Rook,"
he replied. "Look at his games and you will see that he never
moves his Queen's Rook and Queen's Knight. He is conceding
me a Knight." In this game of Morphy's Black's two Rooks
and Bishop never moved.

Here is another beautiful and instructive example of odds
play.

GAME NO. 2
Remove White's QKt
Nuremberg, 1890

WHITE: *Tarrasch*   BLACK: *Meiser*

1.	P - K4	P - Q4
2.	P - K5	P - Q5

Many players have the curious idea that just because they
are ahead in material they can violate the rules of sound position play. On the contrary, it is precisely when they are ahead
that those rules are most effective. Here Black needlessly
wastes a move; *2.* . . . . P - QB4 at once was correct.

3.	P - KB4	P - QB4
4.	B - B4	Kt - QB3
5.	Kt - B3	B - Kt5 ?

An elementary blunder which loses a Pawn.

6. B x P ch	K x B
7. Kt - Kt5 ch	K - K1
8. Q x B	Kt - R3
9. Q - R3	Q - Q2
10. Q - QKt3	Kt - R4
11. P - K6	Q - B3
12. Q - KR3	R - Q1 ??

A senseless, pointless move. Why does Black drift into a hopeless position? Because he fails to develop promptly. Correct was 12. . . . P - KKt3 followed by . . . B - Kt2 and . . . O - O. Black could also castle Q-side after 12. . . . Q - Q4.

13. O - O   P - KKt3

Now this is difficult because White has a combinative reply.

14. P - B5 !

The badly placed Rook at Q1 makes it impossible to take the Pawn: if 14. . . . Kt x P ?; 15. R x Kt, P x R; 16. Q - R5 mate.

14. . . .   B - Kt2 ?

Having made one bad move he might as well follow up—after 14. . . . R - Q4; 15. P - KKt4, P x P; 16. P x P, R - Kt1 Black should still win, e.g., 17. Q - R5 ch, K - Q1; 18. P - Q3, R - K4; 19. B - Q2, P - Kt3; 20. QR - K1, Q - Q4, and White still does not have enough for the piece.

15. P x P   R - Q4

He cannot reply 15. . . . P x P because of 16. Q - Q3.

16. Kt - B7	Kt x Kt
17. KtP x Kt ch	K - B1

Forced, for if *17. . . .* K - Q1; *18.* Q - Kt3, B - B1; *19.* Q - Kt8.

    18. P - Q3

With two Pawns for the piece, and such a powerful attack, White already has enough. The finish is pretty.

18. . . .	P - KR3
19. B - Q2	P - Kt3
20. Q - Kt3	Kt - Kt2

He cannot take the KP because of mate with Q - Kt8 ch.

    21. QR - K1   Kt - Q1

Hoping to be able to remove the offending Pawn, but White has something up his sleeve.

    22. R - K4   R - Q3

Not *22. . . .* Kt x KP; *23.* R x Kt, Q x R; *24.* Q - Kt8 ch. After the text Black is finally threatening to take the Pawn.

    23. R - Kt4   Kt x KP

DIAGRAM 233

Allows the beautiful finish, but there is no defense. If *23. . . .* R - R2; *24.* B x P !

> *24.* R x B   Kt x R
> *25.* B x P !!!

The magnificent point—the whole idea is problemlike.

> *25.* . . .   R(R1) x B

Or *25.* . . . R(Q3) x B; *26.* Q - Kt8 ch.

> *26.* Q x Kt ch   K x Q
> *27.* P - B8(Q) ch   K - Kt3
> *28.* Q - B7 ch   K - Kt4
> *29.* Q - B5 ch   K - R5
> *30.* P - Kt3 mate

In tournament play the gambits offer many beautiful examples of attacking play that more than make up for material losses.

Diagram 234 is from the Monte Carlo Tournament of 1904. This tournament was one in which the Rice Gambit was put to a serious test; all the games opened with it.

DIAGRAM 234

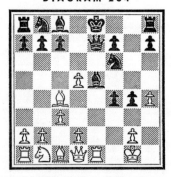

The story of the Rice Gambit is rather amusing. It begins: *1.* P - K4, P - K4; *2.* P - KB4, P x P; *3.* Kt - KB3, P - KKt4; *4.* P - KR4, P - Kt5; *5.* Kt - K5, Kt - KB3; *6.* B - B4, P - Q4; *7.* P x P,

B - Q3. Professor Rice, a New York amateur, had this position once and inadvertently left his Knight en prise; then later he won the game. He was so impressed with his success that he immediately interested a number of the prominent masters in the move, which was easy enough to do because he had a lot of money. For several years the gambit was subjected to extensive analysis by the leading American masters. After 8. O - O, B x Kt; 9. R - K1, Q - K2; 10. P - B3 the diagramed position is reached. The game Marshall-Scheve, one of the finest in the Monte Carlo Tournament, continued:

| 10. . . . | P - B6 |

Subsequent analysis showed that the best for Black was 10. . . . Kt - R4, with a draw as the outcome with best play on both sides.

11. P - Q4	Kt - K5
12. R x Kt	B - R7 ch
13. K x B	Q x R
14. P - KKt3	O - O

Black is now the exchange ahead, but White retains a strong attack.

| 15. B - Q3 |

An excellent continuation of the attack: he gives up another Pawn to hasten development.

15. . . .	Q x P(Q4)
16. P - B4	Q - KR4
17. Kt - B3	P - QB3

Black has troubles. On the more natural 17. . . . Kt - B3 or 17. . . . B - B4; 18. Kt - Q5 is too strong.

18.	Kt - K4	P - KB4
19.	Kt - Q6	P - B5

An attempt to get some counterplay. On the simpler 19. . . . B - K3; 20. B - Kt5, Kt - Q2; 21. Q - Q2 and Black still has a hard time.

20.	Q - K1	P x P ch

Amusing complications come out of 20. . . . P - B7; 21. Q - K7, P x P ch; 22. K - Kt2, B - B4; 23. B - R6, Q x B; 24. Kt x B, Q - B3; 25. Q x KtP and wins.

21.	Q x P	Kt - Q2
22.	B - Kt5	P - B7
23.	B - B5	Kt - Kt3
24.	Kt x B	QR x Kt

Forced return. As Marshall shows, on 24. . . . Kt x Kt White wins with 25. B - K6 ch, K - Kt2; 26. B x P, Q - K1; 27. B x Kt, R x B; 28. B - R6 dbl ch.

25.	B - K6 ch	R - B2

He must already return some of the extra material. On 25. . . . K - Kt2 there follows 26. B x P, Q - K1; 27. B x R, Q x B; 28. B - R6 dbl ch.

26.	R - KB1

Naturally Marshall is in no hurry.

26.	. . . .	R - K1
27.	B x R ch	Q x B
28.	Q x KtP	Q - Kt3

On 28. . . . Kt x P the win is forced with 29. P - R5, K - R1; 30. Q - R4, R - KB1; 31. B - R6.

| 29. R x P | Kt x P |
| 30. P - R5 | R - K5 |

The alternatives are also pretty: *30. . . . Q - Kt2; 31. P - R6, Q - Kt3 (or 31. . . . Kt - K6; 31. Q - B4); 32. R - B6, Q - B7 ch; 33. B - Q2 dis ch and mates.*

DIAGRAM 235

31. B - R6 !!

A splendid finish. Black can capture the Queen but is mated. He must lose at least a piece to begin with and therefore resigned.

When the defender is only one Pawn down, frequently positional compensation is possible. The enemy Pawns may be immobilized, or the enemy pieces may be forced into such awkward positions that the extra material may have to be returned.

Diagram 236, from Nimzovitch-Capablanca, St. Petersburg, 1914, is a model example. Capablanca played the opening carelessly and lost a Pawn. The question is: how can he get any compensation for it? It is clear that he has a temporary advantage in that he controls more space. To convert this into material he must consistently hammer at the enemy position; pressure along the long diagonal is apt to be especially hard to meet. The game continued:

1. . . .   KR - K1

Setting White a problem.

2. Q - Q3 ?

Which he does not solve correctly. To exploit his material advantage White must develop as quickly as possible. Hence

DIAGRAM 236

he should defend the KP with a Pawn, in order to eliminate any further threats against it. After *2.* P - B3 Black cannot shift his Knight to the Q-side, as in the game because the Queen is tied to the defense of the QBP.

2. . . .   Q - K3

3. P - B3

Now he has no choice.

3. . . .   Kt - Q2

To reach QB5.

4. B - Q2 ?

Another mistake that plays right into Black's capable hands. Correct was *4. B - B4 !*, and if then *4. . . . Kt - K4; 5. B x Kt*, or *4. . . . Kt - B4; 5. Q - Q2, R - Kt1; 6. QR - Kt1* (not *6. P - Kt3, Q - B3*), with a winning position, for if now *6. . . . B x Kt ?; 7. Q x B, Q x RP; 8. B - R6.*

| 4. . . . | Kt - K4 |
| 5. Q - K2 | Kt - B5 |

As a result of White's sloppy play Black already has threats. There is first of all . . . Kt x P. On *6. P - QKt3 ?* Black wins the exchange with *6. . . . B - Q5 ch !; 7. K - R1, Kt x B; 8. Q x Kt, Q - B3.*

6. QR - Kt1

Threatening to free himself with P - QKt3.

| 6. . . . | R - R1 |

So that if now *7. P - QKt3, Kt x B; 8. Q x Kt, R - R6* and the RP will go.

| 7. P - QR4 | Kt x B |
| 8. Q x Kt | Q - B5 |

He threatens mainly . . . B x Kt and . . . Q x RP.

9. KR - Q1

Another weak move. The Knight is badly posted, so it should have been shifted by *9. Kt - Q1, Q x RP; 10. Kt - B2.*

| 9. . . . | KR - Kt1 |

Now every Black piece is poised for the kill. In spite of his Pawn plus White cannot even hold the draw.

10. Q - K3

This loses directly, but White's game was already bad. Relatively best was *10. Q - Q3, Q - B4 ch; 11. K - B1* (if *11. K - R1,*

B x Kt; *12.* Q x B, Q x Q; *13.* P x Q, R x R; *14.* R x R, R x P and
should win because White's Rook may not leave the first rank),
R - Kt5 with continued pressure. Black can regain the Pawn as
he pleases.

10. . . .   R - Kt5

With the additional threat of . . . B - Q5.

11. Q - Kt5

Another blunder.

11. . . .   B - Q5 ch
12. K - R1   R(R1) - Kt1

White now loses everything. The immediate threat is to win
a piece with . . . B x Kt. The Knight has no moves, and if
13. R(Kt1) - B1, R x P the Knight is lost. White in desperation
played

13. R x B   Q x R

and Black won.

VIII. *Superior Pawn Structure*

THE PAWNS form the skeleton of the position. Around them the formation of the pieces is centered. It is only by a thorough grasp of the assets and liabilities of any Pawn structure that we can build up adequate plans for a position.

When are Pawns weak and when are they strong? The answer lies in the *principle of mobility. Mobile Pawns are strong, immobile Pawns are weak.* Let us take four simple end-game positions to illustrate this.

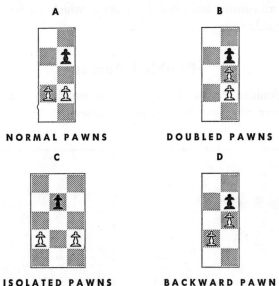

A

NORMAL PAWNS

B

DOUBLED PAWNS

C

ISOLATED PAWNS

D

BACKWARD PAWN

In *Diagram A* White's Pawns are normally mobile. By advancing the unopposed one he can force a Queen; the defender must bring up pieces to hold the Pawns back. In *Diagram B* the Pawns are doubled and are in effect useless—Black is to all intents a Pawn ahead. In *Diagram C* the Pawns are isolated. A Pawn sacrifice, which may or may not be successful, is the only way to force the Pawns through. In *Diagram D* we see the backward Pawn. Again only a sacrifice can lead to promotion.

Thus the ideal position is that shown in *Diagram A;* in all other cases the Pawns are weak.

These considerations, although they apply principally to the end game, furnish the foundation for our understanding of Pawn structure in the middle game.

The *typical Pawn weaknesses* encountered in the middle game are those shown in *Diagrams B-D,* the doubled, isolated, and backward Pawns. For each of these weaknesses, there are countermeasures indicated by theory, which allows the superior side to exploit them.

Doubled Pawns

THE doubled Pawns always limit the mobility of the pieces. However, we must distinguish two cases:

A

B

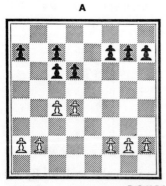
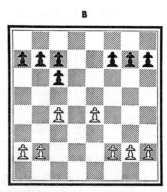

DOUBLED PAWNS
IN A WHITE'S ADVANTAGE IS SMALL;
IN B IT IS MARKED

In the first, *Diagram A*, Black is merely slightly cramped by the doubled Pawn. But in the second, *Diagram B*, Black is in effect a Pawn behind—the three White Pawns on the Q-side hold Black's four, while on the K-side White can force a passed Pawn.

The Pawn position in *Diagram B* is one that can come out of the Exchange Variation of the Ruy Lopez. A game with this variation will help to illustrate the principles involved.

GAME NO. 3

Match, 1908

WHITE: *Lasker*   BLACK: *Tarrasch*

Ruy Lopez

1. P - K4, P - K4; *2.* Kt - KB3, Kt - QB3; *3.* B - Kt5, P - QR3; *4.* B x Kt, QP x B; *5.* P - Q4 (forcing the desirable end-game position), P x P; *6.* Q x P, Q x Q; *7.* Kt x Q (*Diagram 237*).

DIAGRAM 237

Let us examine this position. White has the Pawn majority on the K-side, while Black's only compensation is the two Bishops. The crucial question then is whether the White K-side Pawns can be contained, and the power of the two Bishops make itself felt.

The experience of the masters has generally shown that

Black can hold his own pretty well because of the two Bishops. A model continuation is 7. . . . B - Q2; 8. B - K3, O - O - O; 9. Kt - Q2, Kt - K2; *10.* O - O - O, R - K1; *11.* KR - K1, Kt - Kt3; *12.* Kt - K2, B - Q3; *13.* P - KR3, P - KB4, and Black has the pressure (Petterson-Alekhine, Orebro, 1935).

7. . . .   P - QB4 ?

In terms of the theoretical considerations sketched above, this is clearly a positional blunder. He merely immobilizes his Q-side majority even further, and does nothing about White's Pawns. Yet, in spite of that, the defensive resources inherent in the position are such that it takes several more mistakes to get a lost game. The doubled Pawns lead to an inferior position, not to a definite loss.

8. Kt - K2   B - Q2
9. P - QKt3

Unusual, but not too bad. White frequently has a hard time finding a good spot for the Bishop in this variation.

9. . . .   B - B3
10. P - KB3   B - K2 ?

It is clear that Tarrasch does not understand the positional principles involved. To exchange one of his valuable Bishops is giving away his only counterchance.

11. B - Kt2   B - B3
12. B x B   Kt x B
13. Kt - Q2   O - O - O
14. O - O - O   R - Q2
15. Kt - KB4   R - K1

Black has handled the opening so badly that he can only sit and wait for White to point the way.

| 16. Kt - B4 | P - QKt3 |
| 17. P - QR4 | |

Threatening P - R5.

17. . . .	P - QR4
18. R x R	Kt x R
19. R - Q1	Kt - K4
20. Kt x Kt	R x Kt

DIAGRAM 238

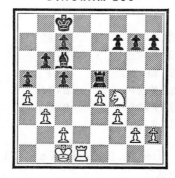

In the ending White has two major advantages—the extra Pawn on the K-side and the possession of a Knight against the Bishop. In such positions Black's Bishop is weak because it is hemmed in by the White Pawns. And yet—there is still one more mistake needed to lose the game.

21. P - B4

Preventing the freeing . . . P - B5.

21. . . .	R - K1
22. Kt - R5	R - Kt1
23. R - Q3	P - B3
24. K - Q2	B - K1
25. Kt - Kt3	B - Q2

To keep the Knight out of B5.

26.	K - K3	R - K1

Note that Black can only mark time, while White consistently increases the scope of his pieces.

27.	Kt - R5	R - K2
28.	P - KKt4	P - B3

A further weakening, but played in the hope that he can free his Q-side.

29.	P - R4	K - B2
30.	P - Kt5	P - B4
31.	Kt - Kt3	P x P
32.	Kt x P	B - B4
33.	P - R5	R - Q2
34.	R - B3	

The only try: after 34. R x R ch, K x R; 35. K - B4, K - K3, the draw is assured.

34.	. . .	R - Q8
35.	K - B4	B - Q2 ?

The decisive mistake. Correct was 35. . . . B x Kt; 36. P x B (forced, for if 36. K x B, R - KR8 wins a Pawn), K - Q3 and Black should be able to draw. The value of this drawing variation also lies in the effect it has on the Pawn structure: White's Pawns are deprived of the cohesive organization they had.

36.	R - K3	R - KR8
37.	Kt - Kt3	R - R5 ch
38.	K - K5	R - R6
39.	P - B4	K - Q1
40.	P - B5	R - R5

There is no longer any defense. If *40. . . . K - K2; 41. P - B6 ch, P x P; 42. P x P ch, K - B2; 43. K - Q6*, and all the Q-side Pawns fall, one by one or many at a time.

41. P - B6

Note how White consistently plays for the passed Pawn.

41. . . .	P x P ch
42. K x P	B - K1
43. Kt - B5 !	

A pretty tactical point: if *43. . . . R x P; 44. Kt - Kt7* wins.

43. . . .	R - B5
44. P - Kt6	P x P
45. P x P	R - Kt5
46. R x B ch	

Also adequate was *46. R - Kt3.*

46. . . .	K x R
47. P - Kt7	K - Q2
48. Kt - R4	

He must still play carefully, for if *48. Kt - R6, R x P; 49. K x R, K - K3* with drawing chances.

48. . . .	R x KtP
49. K x R	K - K3
50. Kt - B3	K - B4
51. K - B7	K - K5
52. K - K6 !	K - Q6

Naturally *52. . . . K x Kt; 53. K - Q6* is hopeless.

53. K - Q6	K - B6
54. K x P	K x P
55. K - Kt5	Resigns

Examination of this game reveals that while Black was on the defensive all the way through, it took several mistakes to lose the game. Thus the doubled Pawns in such a position represent a handicap, but not a losing disadvantage. It is only when the Pawns are both doubled and isolated that they will lose by force.

Since the doubled Pawns are not in themselves a losing disadvantage, except where isolated, under ordinary circumstances it would be desirable for the superior side to create further weaknesses before exploiting his Pawn majority. The following game is an illustration from another opening.

GAME NO. 4

Buenos Aires, 1941

WHITE: *Najdorf*   BLACK: *Stahlberg*

Caro-Kann Defense

1. P - K4, P - QB3; *2.* P - Q4, P - Q4; *3.* Kt - QB3, P x P; *4.* Kt x P, Kt - B3; *5.* Kt x Kt ch, KP x Kt; *6.* B - QB4, B - Q3 (the alternative *6.* . . . B - K2 saves a tempo); *7.* Q - K2 ch, B - K2 (after *7.* . . . Q - K2 the ending is inferior, but, as we have seen, not definitely lost. However, Black prefers to try his luck in the middle game).

8. Q - R5

An innovation that almost refutes Black's entire strategy. On the older *8.* Kt - B3, O - O; *9.* O - O, B - KKt5 White's game does not have enough oomph, and the Black players were generally able to draw.

8. . . .   P - KKt3 ?

Here is the further weakness we were talking about. Necessary is the bold *8.* . . . O - O !; *9.* Kt - B3, B - K3; *10.* B - Q3,

P - KKt3; *11.* Q - R6, R - K1, and Black's game is tenable because *12.* P - KR4? is refuted by *12.* . . . . B - B1; *13.* Q - B4, B x P dis ch.

9. Q - Q1	O - O
10. Kt - B3	Kt - Q2
11. O - O	Kt - Kt3
12. B - Kt3	R - K1
13. P - KR3	

To restrict Black's QB.

13. . . .	B - B1

On *13.* . . . . B - K3; *14.* B x B, P x B exchanges the doubled Pawn for a backward Pawn. *13.* . . . . B - K3 is threatened.

14. R - K1	B - B4

Since the Bishop is out of play anyhow, he might as well have played *14.* . . . . B - K3. After *15.* B x B, R x B; *16.* R x R, P x R, there is so much material exchanged that White can hardly win.

15. R x R	Q x R
16. P - B4	R - Q1
17. B - K3	B - K5
18. Q - K2	B - Kt2

Regrouping of pieces by both sides.

19. R - Q1	B x Kt

Because of the doubled Pawns this Bishop is always awk. wardly placed, so Black decides to exchange it.

20. Q x B	P - KB4

DIAGRAM 239

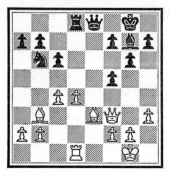

Let us pause to analyze this position. White now has two advantages—the Pawn majority and the two Bishops. Neither of these alone would be sufficient to win, but the two together are almost irresistible. Black on the other hand has no compensation; he must sit back and wait.

White thus really has two strategic goals—to weaken the Black Q-side Pawns, and to build up an attack against the King.

21. P - QR4

Threatening P - R5 - R6.

21. . . .   Q - K5

He decides to try his luck in the end game. On 21. . . . Kt - Q2; 22. P - R5, P - QR3, there could follow 23. P - Q5, Kt - K4; 24. Q - K2, P x P; 25. B - Kt6, R - B1; 26. R x P with continued pressure.

22. Q x Q   P x Q

Black has now undoubled his Pawns but at a great cost; his K-side majority is hard to mobilize.

23. P - R5   Kt - Q2
24. P - Q5 !

At last.

24. . . .   P - QB4

Forced, for if 24. . . . B x P; 25. P x P is crushing.

25. B - R4   Kt - K4

The Pawn mass cannot be neutralized. If 25. . . . B x P; 26. R - Kt1 wins.

26. B x P   Kt x P
27. B - K7   R - R1

DIAGRAM 240

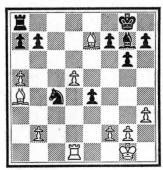

28. P - Q6 !

The decisive extra Pawn. Note that although Black has un-doubled his Pawns he does not have the time to make use of them.

28. . . .   B - B1
29. P - QKt3

The finish abounds in pretty combinations.

29. . . .   Kt - Kt7
30. R - QB1

Threatening P - Q7 and R - B8, to which there is no good defense, for if *30. . . .* B x B; *31.* P x B, Kt x B; *32.* R - Q1 decides.

$$30. . . . \qquad \text{Kt x B}$$
$$31. \text{P - Q7 !}$$

Anyhow.

$$31. . . . \qquad \text{B x B}$$
$$32. \text{R - B8 ch} \qquad \text{Resigns}$$

When the doubled Pawns do not in effect nullify a Pawn majority they may get the player into a blocked position where the enemy has all the play, i.e., it may lead to a backward Pawn as well, or to a blockaded position.

A

B

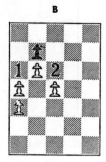

WHITE'S PAWNS ARE STILL MOBILE

WHITE'S PAWNS ARE IMMOBILIZED. BLACK STRIVES TO OCCUPY POINTS 1 AND 2

Thus in these diagrams, in A the Pawn complex still has some mobility, in B it does not. Hence the player with a Pawn complex such as that in A will strive to avoid the advance of the center Pawn.

An illustration of how disastrous the Pawn situation in B can be is *Diagram 241,* from Winter-Fine, Lodz, 1935. White

DIAGRAM 241

is unable to defend his many weaknesses. The game continued:

1. Q - K2	Q - B3
2. B - B1	K - Kt1

To gain time on the clock.

3. R - Kt2

Control of the QKt file would be assured Black in any case after . . . R - Kt3 and . . . QR - Kt1.

3. . . .	R x R
4. Q x R	Q - R5 !

Threatening . . . Kt - Kt5.

5. Q - Kt5

There is no defense: the only move to stop . . . Kt - Kt5 is 5. B - K2, and that is refuted by 5. . . . B - R3; *6.* Q - Kt3, Q x P.

5. . . .	P - QB3
6. P x P	Kt x B
7. B - Q2	

The Knight cannot be recaptured because of mate at K8.

7.	. . . .	Kt - K4
8.	P - B7	K - R2
9.	Q - K8	Q x P
10.	Q - B8	Kt - Kt5

White resigned because further drastic loss of material is unavoidable.

The Pawn complex seen in the above diagram is one that comes out of the Nimzoindian Defense. Even when an enemy piece cannot get to K4, as here, the exposed QBP is often a target that cannot be defended. We can watch the fate of this Pawn complex in a series of positions from a game Shipman-Fine, New York, 1945 (Game No. 5).

Diagram 242 arose after nine moves: *1.* P - Q4, Kt - KB3; *2.* P - QB4, P - K3; *3.* Kt - QB3, B - Kt5; *4.* P - K3, P - QKt3; *5.* B - Q3, B - Kt2; *6.* Kt - B3, Kt - K5; *7.* Q - B2, B x Kt ch; *8.* P x B, P - KB4; *9.* O - O, O - O.

DIAGRAM 242

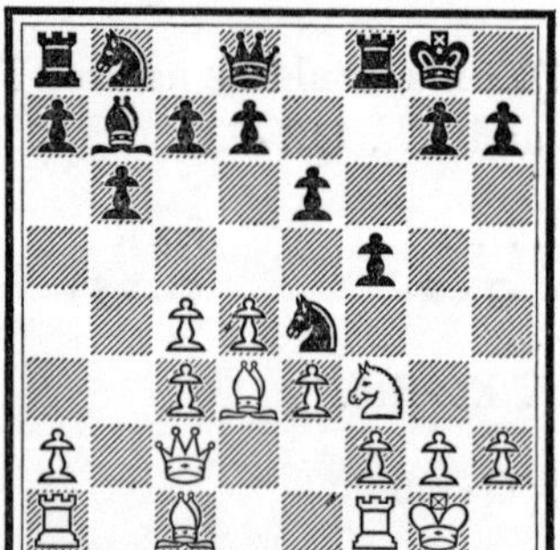

Black's ultimate aim is to force a position of type B above. White should hinder this and play for P - B5, but he does not realize the danger. The moves intervening between the diagrams are of no great moment, so we give them in abbreviated form.

From the diagram the game continued: *10.* B - R3, P - Q3; *11.* Kt - Q2, Kt x Kt; *12.* Q x Kt, Kt - Q2; *13.* P - B3, Q - K2; *14.* P - K4, P x P; *15.* P x P, P - K4 (*Diagram 243*).

DIAGRAM 243

The first goal has been reached: the Pawns have been effectively restrained. A threat of . . . P x P and . . . B x P now looms. Naturally White does not want to play P - Q5 to block this, so he tries other defensive measures.

16. Q - K3, R x R ch; *17.* R x R, R - KB1; *18.* R x R ch, Q x R; *19.* Q - B3 ? (this merely facilitates Black's plan), P - B4 (*Diagram 244*).

DIAGRAM 244

As usual, it has not been possible to force P - Q5 without this move. With it it will not be long.

20. Q x Q ch, Kt x Q; *21.* B - Kt2, Kt - K3; (*Diagram 245*) *22.* P - Q5. Finally he has no choice. Now that P - Q5 has come the next step is to attack the White QBP.

DIAGRAM 245

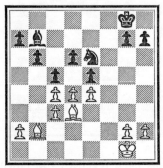

22. . . . Kt - B5 (better *22.* . . . Kt - Q1 at once); *23.* B - B2, B - R3; *24.* B - Kt3, K - B2; *25.* P - KR3 (better *25.* K - B1), Kt - Kt3 (headed for QR4); *26.* B - B1, K - B3; *27.* P - Kt3, Kt - R1; *28.* K - Kt2, Kt - B2; *29.* K - B3, Kt - Q1; *30.* B - K3, Kt - Kt2; *31.* K - K2, Kt - R4; *32.* K - Q3 (*Diagram 246*).

DIAGRAM 246

The key position in the end game. White's pieces are tied down to the defense of the QBP. The winning maneuver now involves a penetration of the K-side by the Black King.

32. . . . B - B1; 33. P - Kt4, P - KR3; 34. K - K2, K - Kt3; 35. K - Q3, P - R4; 36. B - Q1, P x P; 37. P x P (if 37. B x P, B - R3), B - R3; 38. B - Kt3, K - B3; 39. B - B1, K - Kt3; 40. B - K3, K - B3; 41. B - B1.

How is Black to break through?

41. . . . Kt x B !; 42. P x Kt, B - B1 (one of the unusual positions where Black wins because the Bishops are of opposite colors); 43. P - Kt5 ch, K - Kt3; 44. B - K3, B - Kt5; 45. B - B1, K - R4; 46. B - K3, B - Q8; 47. P - Kt4, K - Kt5; 48. B - B1, P - Kt3; 49. P x P, KtP x P; 50. B - K3, K - B6; 51. B - B1, B - K7 ch (winning three Pawns); 52. K - Q2, B x P; 53. resigns.

In the series of Diagrams 243–246 we see Black's strategy clearly delineated—restrain the Pawn complex, blockade it, exchange heavy pieces, attack the exposed Pawn, immobilize the White pieces, penetrate the enemy position with the King, gain material.

Once the doubled Pawns can be liquidated, White's game is satisfactory. E.g., in *Diagram 247*, from Reshevsky-Alekhine,

DIAGRAM 247

AVRO tournament, 1938, Black has the positionally potent threat of . . . P - K4. White saved the day with:

1. P - K5 !	P x KP
2. P x BP	KR - Q1
3. Q - K4	Q - Kt3
4. Q - K2	

He does not want to lose the BP(!), which has now suddenly become an asset (passed Pawn).

4. . . .	P - K5
5. R - B4	P x P
6. B x P	Kt - B3
7. R x P	R - Q7
8. Q x R	Q x R

White has won a Pawn, which in itself means little in such a position, but the liquidation of his doubled Pawns has left him with the freer game.

Often the doubled Pawns here are liquidated with P - B5 rather than P - K5; either way White gets a good game.

Backward Pawn

WE SPEAK of the "backward Pawn on an open file" but that is redundant, since the backward Pawn must necessarily be on an open file. This fact immediately suggests its main weakness —it is exposed to attack. At times the attack may yield a direct material gain; at other times it may simply exert a lot of pressure. It is generally not a fatal weakness; it can be serious or slight depending on the remainder of the position.

Diagram 248, from Evans-Sandrin, Dallas, 1951, shows a position where a direct attack on the backward Pawn yields a decisive material advantage. The continuation was:

1. R - B1   Q - B2

DIAGRAM 248

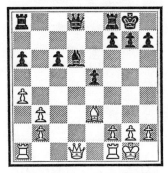

2. R - B4   KR - Q1

On 2.... KR - QB1; *3.* Q - B2, QR - Kt1; *4.* R - B1, the Pawn is again lost because of the eventual mate threat.

3. Q - B2	R(R1) - QB1
4. R - B1	Q - Kt2
5. R x P	R x R
6. Q x R	Q x P
7. Q x B	

Black resigned because of the heavy material loss.

An instance where direct attack yields a Pawn or an over-whelming position is *Diagram 249,* from Fine-Bisguier, New York, 1951. Here Black had to play *1....* P - KR3, when the threats on K6 are momentarily lifted. Instead he played:

1. . . .	B - Q2
2. B - R3 !	Q - K1

The only way to hold the Pawn was 2.... R - K1; *3.* R - K1, Q - B1; *4.* Q - K2, B - R4; *5.* B - Q2, B x B; *6.* Q x B, P - KR3; *7.* Kt - B3. But the consequent weakening of the Black squares makes Black's game positionally hopeless.

DIAGRAM 249

3. Q - K2	Q - Kt3
4. Kt x KP	B x Kt
5. Q x B ch	K - R1
6. Q - B5	Q - R3
7. B - Kt2	

and White won quickly.

As a rule even when the backward Pawn can be held temporarily, the consequent cramping of the defender's position is a serious weakness which often is tantamount to a loss. Thus in *Diagram 250*, from Tartakower-Marshall, New York,

DIAGRAM 250

1924, the Black QBP is the target. Normal build-up of pressure resulted in constriction of Black's position and eventually material gain:

1. Kt - K5	B - Q2
2. Kt x B	Kt x Kt ?

This exchange makes life too easy for White; better was 2. . . . Q x Kt and . . . Kt - K5, to block the White Bishop.

3. B x B	K x B
4. R - B1	Q - B3
5. P - K3	

To deprive Black's Rook of his threat and mobilize the White Queen.

5. . . .	QR - Q1
6. R - B2	R - K3
7. Q - Q2	R - Q3

Black is really just marking time.

8. R - Q1

There was a pseudothreat of . . . P - Q5. White's excess of caution does not matter.

8. . . .	Kt - K4
9. Q - Q4	R(Q1) - Q2
10. R(Q1) - QB1	K - Kt1

This loses the Pawn immediately. In the Tournament Book Alekhine recommends *10.* . . . R - B2, but then *11.* P - QKt4 leads to a Pawn win.

11. P - B4	Kt - Kt5
12. Q x Q	R x Q
13. B - R3	P - KR4

14. R x P	R x R
15. R x R	P - Q5
16. B x Kt	P x B
17. K - B2	

and White won the ending.

Frequently the disadvantage incurred as a result of a backward Pawn is not decisive, but the defender has to hold an inferior position all the way, and mistakes are only too likely to occur. This is the case in *Diagram 250A,* from Lasker-Rubinstein, St. Petersburg, 1914. The game continued:

DIAGRAM 250A

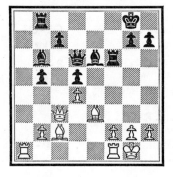

1. . . .	B - KB4
2. KR - B1	B x B
3. R x B	R - K1
4. R(R1) - B1	

The frontal attack on the Pawn here naturally does not succeed because it is held up by the Bishop, but threats can still be built up. Now it is Q - Q3, and if . . . Q - Q2; R - B6, hitting at the KtP.

4. . . .	R(B3) - K3
5. P - R3	R - K5
6. Q - Q2	R(K1) - K3

Planning . . . Q - Q2 and . . . P - B3, after which the defense cannot be broken through.

7. R - B6

A valiant try. . . .

| 7. . . . | Q - Q2 ? |

Which succeeds. With 7. . . . Q x R; 8. R x Q, R x R; 9.
Q - Kt4, R - Q3; 10. Q x P, P - R3 White wins a Pawn, but not
the game. After the text White's pressure continues indefi-
nitely.

| 8. R x R | Q x R |

A long period of seesawing followed now, in which White
was trying to provoke a weakness in the Black camp. We give
these moves in abbreviated form:

9. Q - Q3, Q - K1; 10. Q - B3, K - B2; 11. Q - Q3, K - Kt1; 12.
Q - B3, Q - K3; 13. R - R1, Q - K1; 14. K - B1, P - R3; 15. Q - Q3,
K - B2; 16. R - B1, K - Kt1; 17. Q - Kt3, Q - B2 ? (another error—
why he did not prefer . . . Q - Q2 is not clear); 18. R - Q1,
P - B3 (now 18. . . . Q - Q2 allows 19. P - B3, R - K3; 20. B - B4
and 21. B - K5); 19. P - B3, Q - B3; 20. Q - Q3, R - K2; 21. B - B2,
Q - Q3; 22. Q - B2, K - B2; 23. R - B1, R - K3; 24. Q - B5 ch, R -
B3; 25. Q - K5 !, R - K3 (Black would prefer not to exchange
Queens, but he has no choice, for if 25. . . . Q - Q2; 26. B - R4,
B - B2; 27. Q - R5 ch, R - Kt3; 28. R - K1 with a strong attack);
26. Q x Q, R x R (*Diagram 251*).

White has attained his first goal: the exchange of Queens.
By blockading the QBP he is in effect a Pawn ahead; the next

DIAGRAM 251

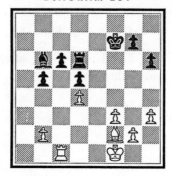

step of course will be to mobilize his K-side Pawns. There followed:

27. K - K2, K - K2; *28.* K - Q3, R - Kt3; *29.* P - KKt3, R - B3; *30.* P - B4, K - Q2; *31.* R - K1, R - B1; *32.* R - QR1, P - R4; *33.* B - K3, P - Kt3; *34.* R - KB1, K - Q3; *35.* P - KKt4, P x P; *36.* P x P (*Diagram 252*).

DIAGRAM 252

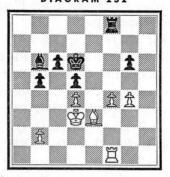

White's plan is clear: he will either advance the passed Pawn or enter via the Rook file. In desperation Black tried *36. . . .* P - B4, which was refuted by *37.* P x P ch, B x P; *38.* B x B ch, K x B; *39.* P - B5, P x P; *40.* P x P, R - B3; *41.* R - B4!,

P - Kt5; *42.* P - Kt3, R - B2; *43.* P - B6, K - Q3; *44.* K - Q4, K - K3; *45.* R - B2, K - Q3; *46.* R - QR2, R - B2; *47.* R - R6 ch, K - Q2; *48.* R - Kt6, and Black resigned.

Examination of Diagrams 250A–252 again reveals the guiding ideas behind White's play: restrain the backward Pawn, tie down the Black pieces, exchange Queens, mobilize the Pawn majority, force an entry, and gain material. This game also shows that often even when the backward Pawn can be liquidated it comes too late.

Sometimes a dogged defense of the backward Pawn suffices to hold everything. Usually this occurs when there is little material left. An example is *Diagram 253*, from Stahlberg-Fine, Warsaw, 1935. The continuation was:

DIAGRAM 253

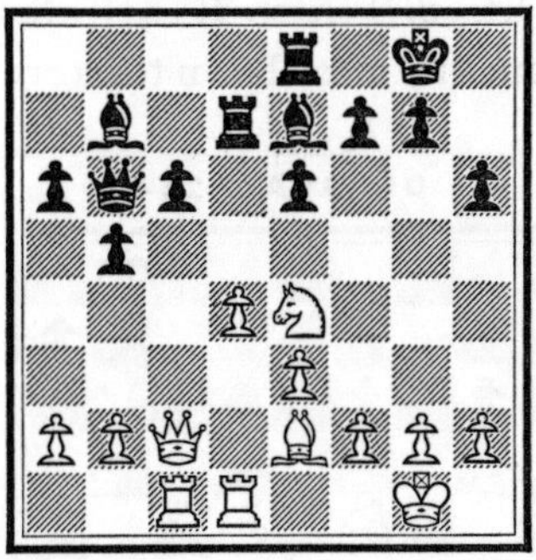

1. Kt - B5	B x Kt
2. Q x B	Q x Q
3. R x Q	K - B1
4. P - B4	K - K2
5. R(Q1) - B1	R - Q3
6. K - B2	K - Q2

And White could not win the ending.

The Isolated Pawn

NORMALLY Pawns support one another. When they are isolated, they are a prey to attack, and material loss is generally unavoidable, since the defending pieces soon become unbearably overloaded.

The cases where there are several isolated Pawns are as a rule lost for the defender, though of course there are numerous exceptions, when the defense turns out to be just adequate.

Diagram 254 is from Euwe-Alekhine, first match game, 1937. Here White advanced his RP to R6 and Black made the mistake of capturing . . . KtP x RP. After a few moves a Pawn was lost:

1. Kt x Kt   Kt x Kt

On *1.* . . . P x Kt; *2.* B - Kt5, R - Kt1; *3.* R x P, B - Q4; *4.* B - K3, Black has another loose Pawn to worry about.

DIAGRAM 254

2. Kt - B5   B x Kt
3. Q x B   P - Kt4

Desperation. On the alternative *3.* . . . Q - Kt3; *4.* Q - B3 decides. The position was untenable.

4. B - K3

Also strong was *4.* B x Kt.

4. . . .	B - Q4
5. R x P	B x B
6. K x B	R - B2
7. R(B1) - R1	Q - Q3

The RP can no longer be held; he is looking for counter-play.

8. Q x Q	R x Q
9. R x P	R x R
10. R x R	Kt - B5
11. B - B5	R - K3

Quite often when a Pawn is captured, the attack comes to a standstill, and a counterattack springs up out of nowhere. That is the case here. White just manages to hold on to his extra Pawn.

12. B - Q4	R x P
13. B x P	P - Kt5
14. K - B1	

And White won the ending with little trouble.

Frequently the Pawns are weakened as a result of a premature attack. That is a danger that the attacker must weigh in the balance when he starts out on his offensive. *Diagram 255,* from Winter-Fine, Hastings, 1935–36, came out of a counterattack by White. While Black's position is solid, White has weak Pawns at QR2, QB3, and even K4. The game continued:

1. . . .	P - K4

To force the removal of White's only well-placed piece.

2. Q - Q5 ?

DIAGRAM 255

With such weak Pawns it would have been much better to avoid the exchange of Queens, and speculate on the possibilities of a K-side attack with Q - Q3, Kt - R4, K - R1, P - KB4, etc.

2. . . .	Q x Q
3. B x Q	Kt - B4
4. Kt - Q2	B - K3
5. P - KB4	K - K2
6. Kt - B4	P x P

Surprising, but strong. 6. . . . Kt - Q2 is too cramping.

7. R x P	QR - QB1
8. Kt - K3	

Black was threatening . . . Kt - R5.

8. . . .	Kt - Q6
9. Kt - B5 ch	K - Q2
10. R - B3	Kt - K4
11. R - Kt3	B x Kt
12. P x B	P - Kt3

13. P - B4	K - K2
14. R - QR3	

Still hoping to save the Pawn.

14. . . .	R - B2
15. R - R6	R - Q1
16. P - QR4	

Loses a Pawn, but on other moves a Pawn goes another way. E.g., on *16.* R - R3, P - Kt4 is decisive.

16. . . .	Kt - Q6
17. P - R5	P - Kt4
18. R - B6	

The threat was . . . Kt - Kt5 as well as . . . P x P.

18. . . .	R x R
19. B x R	P x P
20. R - Kt1	P - B6
21. B - R4	R - Q5

And White resigned.

An examination of the play from the diagram shows that after the exchange of Queens there was no way to avoid the loss of a Pawn. Scattered Pawns, unless otherwise compensated for, are an almost certain loss against best play.

To attack an enemy King Pawns must be advanced to break a blockade. And advanced Pawns may become artifically isolated and exposed. The analogy with the military situation is quite clear—an army may advance too quickly into enemy territory, be cut off from its sources of supply and reserve support, and as a result the scattered troop units may be picked off one by one. The following game is an excellent illustration of how a poorly conducted attack may lead to the loss of prematurely advanced Pawns.

GAME NO. 6
New York, 1927
WHITE: *Alekhine*   BLACK: *Capablanca*

Queen's Pawn Game

1. P - Q4, Kt - KB3; *2.* P - QB4, P - K3; *3.* Kt - KB3, P - QKt3;
4. P - KKt3, B - Kt2; *5.* B - Kt2, P - B4 (a move still new at the
time this game was played; today it is considered inferior);
6. P - Q5, P x P; *7.* Kt - R4, P - Kt3; *8.* Kt - QB3, B - Kt2; *9.* O - O,
O - O; *10.* B - B4 ?

What the best move is is not certain, but this cannot be it.
To play for an attack the most logical way is *10.* P x P, P - Q3;
11. P - K4, QKt - Q2; *12.* P - B4, and tournament experience
favors White. He can also play to capture at Q5 with a piece,
and keep the QP backward: *10.* B - Kt5, P - KR3; *11.* B x Kt,
B x B; *12.* B x P; this too is slightly in White's favor.

10. . . .	P - Q3
11. P x P	Kt - R4

To develop his QKt.

12. B - Q2	Kt - Q2
13. P - B4	

Going in for the attack mentioned before, but now Black
has adequate counterplay.

13. . . .	P - QR3
14. B - B3	

White's play is inconsistent; he cannot form a well-con-
ceived plan.

14. . . .	Kt(R4) - B3
15. P - R4	P - B5

Artifically isolates the White Q-side Pawns.

16. B - K3	

Now on *16*. P - K4 there would follow *16*. . . . Kt - B4 - Q6. However, that was still better than the text.

16. . . .	Q - B2
17. P - KKt4	

DIAGRAM 256

An examination of this position reveals particularly clearly the weakness of the White Pawns—they are disorganized and artificially isolated. White's only chance lies in the attack; if that fails he will be lost.

17. . . .	Kt - B4
18. P - Kt5	Kt(B3) - Q2
19. P - B5	KR - K1
20. B - B4	B - K4 !

Seizing a vital center square. Black now has the initiative and does not let go.

21. B - Kt4	Kt - Kt6
22. P x P	RP x P
23. R - Kt1	B x Kt

First blood—it is surprising how quickly White's game falls apart—surprising, that is, before you have read this book.

24. P x B	Q - B4 ch
25. P - K3	

On a King move the QP goes with check.

25. . . .	Kt - K4
26. B - B3	Kt - Q6

A comparison of this diagram with the previous one reveals what has happened: Black has developed his pieces, beaten off the attack, and now the exposed White Pawns must fall.

DIAGRAM 257

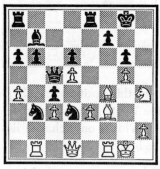

27. K - R1

There is no defense: if 27. R x Kt, Kt x B

27. . . .	B x P
28. R x Kt	Kt x B
29. QR - Kt1	R x P
30. Kt - Kt2	R x B !
31. R x R	Kt x Kt
32. K x Kt	R - K1
33. K - B1	B x R
34. Q x B	Q x P

Black is three Pawns ahead; the rest is elementary. The remaining moves were: 35. R - K1, R x R ch; 36. K x R, Q - Kt8 ch; 37. K - Q2, Q x P ch; 38. K - B1, Q - K4; 39. K - Kt2, K - Kt2; 40. Q - B2, P - QKt4; 41. Q - Kt6, P x P; 42. Q x RP, Q - K7 ch 43. resigns.

The Isolated Queen's Pawn (Isolani)

A SPECIAL case of the isolated Pawn that is of the greatest importance for theory is that of the QP. As a rule this Pawn is the only one that is isolated. If we look at the diagram,

THE ISOLATED QP

which is the usual position where the isolated QP (also known as the isolani) occurs, we see that White has two advantages: (1) he can attack the QP directly; and (2) he can occupy the square Q4 without being attacked by a Pawn. As possible compensation, Black can (1) occupy the squares K5 or QB5 (outposts); (2) play on the open QB file, (3) build up threats on the semiopen K file. The counterbalancing of these advantages and disadvantages will determine who has the upper hand. Usually White has the better of it, particularly if several pieces have been exchanged, so that he is closer to the end game; however, there are cases where Black (or White, if he has the isolani) stands better.

Diagram 258, from Euwe-Kramer, New York, 1951, is typi-

DIAGRAM 258

cal of the positions in which White has an advantage. It will take Black some time to be able to occupy either K5 or QB5, while an attack along the K file is obviously a project for the distant future. White on the other hand is already in occupation of Q4 and has a number of immediate attacking developments available. The principle behind his play will be to increase his command of space until he can gain material. The game continued:

1. Kt - R4   Q - Kt5

As Euwe shows, the weakness of Black's White squares is too serious a handicap to overcome. E.g., if *1.* . . . Q - R2; 2. Kt - Kt5, Q - Kt1; *3.* B - KB4, or *1.* . . . Q - B2; 2. Kt - Kt5, Q - Q2; *3.* Kt - Kt6, winning the exchange in either case.

2. P - QR3   Kt x Kt

3. R x Kt   Q - Q3

4. B - KB4   Q - B3

On the alternative *4.* . . . Q - K3; 5. B - B7, R - K1; *6.* Kt - Kt6, R - R2; *7.* B - B3 leaves Black hopelessly cramped.

5. R - B1	B - Q2
6. Q x Q !	

A surprising liquidation, which wins a Pawn.

6. . . .	B x Q

On 6. . . . P x Q; 7. Kt - Kt6 and 8. Kt x B wins the BP.

7. Kt - Kt6	R - R2
8. B - B7	R - K1
9. P - QR4	

Here White could have won a Pawn with 9. B - B3 as well, for after 9. . . . B - Q1; 10. B x B, R x B; 11. P - K4 is decisive. However Black could try 9. . . . P - R3; 10. Kt x P, Kt x Kt; 11. B x Kt, B x B; 12. R x B, B - B3 with counterplay.

9. . . .	B - Q1
10. B x B	R x B
11. B - Kt5	P - R3

Hoping for 12. B x B, P x B; 13. R x P, R - R3 with counter-chances. White does not oblige.

12. P - QKt3	Kt - K5
13. P - B3	Kt - B3

On 13. . . . Kt - Q3 White can take at QB6, for the QP goes immediately after that as well.

14. P - K4	B x B
15. P x B	P - R5
16. KtP x P	Kt - K1
17. R - B5	Resigns

An opening from which the isolated QP frequently arises is the Tarrasch Defense to the Queen's Gambit Declined: 1. P - Q4, P - Q4; 2. P - QB4, P - K3; 3. Kt - QB3, P - QB4. This was in fact one of the most popular defenses to the Queen's

Gambit until Rubinstein developed his attack, leading to the isolation of the QP, which virtually demolished the line. Here is a model game with this variation.

GAME NO. 7

Paris, 1938

WHITE: *Capablanca*   BLACK: *Znosko-Borovsky*

Queen's Gambit Declined

1. P - Q4, P - Q4; *2.* P - QB4, P - K3; *3.* Kt - QB3, P - QB4; *4.* BP x P, KP x P; *5.* Kt - B3, Kt - QB3; *6.* P - KKt3, Kt - B3; *7.* B - Kt2, B - K2; *8.* O - O, O - O; *9.* P x P !, B x P.

Because of the strength of this line for White, the gambit variation *9. . . .* P - Q5; *10.* Kt - QR4 has been tried, but it does not suffice against exact play.

DIAGRAM 259

Again the principle for exploitation of White's advantage remains the same: increased command of space until it can be converted into material gain.

> *10.* Kt - QR4   B - K2
> *11.* B - K3

Note how, as in the previous game, White concentrates on command of Q4 and QB5.

11. . . .	Kt - K5
12. Kt - Q4	Kt - K4

Aiming for . . . QB5 (outpost compensation).

13. R - B1	Q - R4

13. . . . Kt - B5 ? is out of the question because of R x Kt !

14. B - B4	Kt - Kt3

A better chance was the sacrifice 14. . . . Kt - B3.

15. B - B7	Q - R3

Not appetizing, but the alternative 15. . . . P - Kt3 ?; 16. Kt - B6 loses a piece at once.

16. P - QR3	B - Q2
17. Kt - QB3	Kt x Kt
18. R x Kt	B - K3
19. P - QKt4	

With no less a threat than winning the Queen with P - Kt5.

19. . . .	P - Kt3

DIAGRAM 260

20. P - K4 !

A pause for a theoretical refresher. White is in command of more space; he can utilize such an advantage in one of two ways: (1) by winning material; or (2) by building up an attack. Here is one of those unusual positions where White has his choice. With 20. P - B4 he can already win a Pawn. Instead he chooses to play for an attack; either way is good.

20. . . .	P x P
21. B x KP	QR - K1
22. Kt x B	P x Kt
23. B - B6	B - B3
24. P - Kt5	Q - B1

On 24. . . . Q - R4; 25. R - Q3, R - B1; 26. B - Q6 is also hopeless for Black.

25. R - B2	R - K2
26. B - Q6	R - Q1
27. P - B4 !	

The manner in which he coolly permits the pin is most admirable.

27. . . .	K - R1
28. R(B1) - B2	R - KB2
29. R(KB2) - Q2	

Finally threatening B - K8, which if played at once could be answered by . . . R - B2.

29. . . .	R - Kt1
30. Q - R5	Q - Q1
31. B - K4 !	

Black must lose at least a piece to stop mate temporarily. He therefore resigned.

Another method of exploiting the isolani in the Tarrasch Defense Variation described above is to exchange at QB6, and saddle Black with a backward Pawn. Thus in *Diagram 261*, from Rubinstein-Salwe, Lodz, 1908, the continuation

DIAGRAM 261

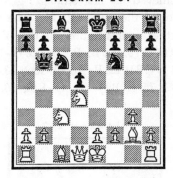

was:

1. Kt x Kt	P x Kt
2. O - O	B - K2
3. Kt - R4	Q - Kt4
4. B - K3	

Again—control of Q4 and QB5.

4. . . .	O - O
5. R - B1	B - KKt5
6. P - B3	B - K3
7. B - B5	KR - K1

DIAGRAM 262

White has achieved his first strategic goal: occupation of QB5 and control of the open QB file. The next step is exchange and further concentration on the Black weaknesses.

8. R - KB2, Kt - Q2; 9. B x B, R x B; 10. Q - Q4, R(K2) - K1; 11. B - B1, R(K1) - QB1; 12. P - K3, Q - Kt2; 13. Kt - B5, Kt x Kt; 14. R x Kt, R - B2; 15. R(B2) - B2, Q - Kt3; 16. P - QKt4.

DIAGRAM 263

The goal has been reached: occupation of the QB file. The next step is to storm the weak Pawns and capture one.

16. . . . P - QR3 (he has to meet the threat of P - Kt5); 17. R - R5 !, R - Kt1 (if 17. . . . Q - Kt2; 18. Q - B5 followed by P - R4 and P - Kt5); 18. P - QR3, R - R2 (the loss of a Pawn was unavoidable); 19. R x BP, Q x R; 20. Q x R, and the remainder was easy: 20. . . . R - R1; 21. Q - B5, Q - Kt2; 22. K - B2, P - KR4; 23. B - K2, P - Kt3; 24. Q - Q6, Q - B1; 25. R - B5, Q - Kt2; 26. P - KR4, P - R4; 27. R - B7, Q - Kt1; 28. P - Kt5, P - R5; 29. P - Kt6, R - R4; 30. P - Kt7, and Black resigned.

At times in positions such as Diagram 261 the Kt at Q4 can capture a piece at K6 and win by pressure against the center; such a case is seen in Diagram 195.

Another opening in which the isolani comes up is one varia-

tion of the Orthodox Defense to the Queen's Gambit: *1.* P - Q4,
P - Q4; *2.* P - QB4, P - K3; *3.* Kt - QB3, Kt - KB3; *4.* B - Kt5,
B - K2; *5.* Kt - B3, QKt - Q2; *6.* P - K3, O - O; *7.* Q - B2, P - B4; *8.*
P x QP, Kt x P; *9.* B x B, Q x B; *10.* Kt x Kt, P x Kt; *11.* P x P.

DIAGRAM 264

This type of position is generally drawn with best play because White cannot bring enough pressure to bear on the QB
file. However, Black remains on the defensive all the way
through and is subject to many problems.

A typical continuation is Flohr-Vidmar, Nottingham, 1936:
11. . . . Kt x P; *12.* B - Q3 (in the game this actually occurred
one move earlier), P - KKt3; *13.* O - O, B - Kt5; *14.* Kt - Q4,
QR - B1; *15.* Q - Q2, P - QR3; *16.* B - B2, Q - Kt4; *17.* P - B3,
B - Q2; *18.* KR - K1, KR - Q1; *19.* QR - Q1, Q - B3; *20.* B - Kt3,
B - R5 (note how Black does not allow the pressure against
his QP to build up); *21.* B x B, Kt x B; *22.* R - QB1, Kt - B4; *23.*
R(K1) - Q1, Q - Kt3; *24.* Kt - K2 (aiming at Q5), Kt - Q2 (a
spirited defense: if *25.* Q x P, Q x P ch, or *25.* Kt - B4, Kt - B3);
25. Q - Q4, Q x Q; *26.* Kt x Q, Kt - K4; *27.* P - QKt3, K - B1; *28.*
K - B1.

DIAGRAM 265

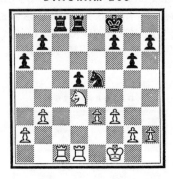

Up to this point Black had defended himself perfectly, but here he goes astray. 28. . . . K - K2 was necessary, and if then 29. Kt - K2, R x R; 30. R x R, Kt - B3 with a tenable, though still cramped, position. Instead Black played: 28. . . . R x R ?; 29. R x R, Kt - B3 ??; 30. Kt x Kt, R - B1; 31. R - B5 !, P x Kt. After this further weakening had been forced White won the ending in a masterly manner: 32. K - K2, K - K2; 33. K - Q3, K - Q3; 34. R - R5, R - QR1; 35. K - Q4, P - KB4; 36. P - QKt4, R - QKt1; 37. P - QR3, R - QR1; 38. P - K4, BP x P; 39. P x P, P x P; 40. K x P, R - R2; 41. K - B4, P - R3; 42. P - KR4, K - K3; 43. K - Kt4, R - R1; 44. P - R5, P - Kt4; 45. P - Kt3, R - R2; 46. K - B3, R - R1; 47. K - K4, R - R2; 48. K - Q4, K - Q3; 49. K - K4, K - K3; 50. R - K5 ch, K - Q3; 51. R - K8, P - B4; 52. R - Q8 ch, K - B3; 53. R - B8 ch, K - Kt3; 54. R x P, R - R2; 55. R - K5, K - B3; 56. R - K6 ch, K - Kt4; 57. K - B5, R - B2 ch; 58. R - B6, and Black resigned.

As we have pointed out, it should by no means be assumed that the isolated QP is always a handicap. There are positions in which it can be an advantage. These occur when it can be used to support outposts at K5 or QB5; when the outpost is at K5 it forms the basis for a K-side attack, when it is at QB5 for a Q-side foray.

The manner in which the isolani can be used to support an attack is beautifully illustrated in the following model game.

GAME NO. 8

Nottingham, 1936

WHITE: *Botvinnik*   BLACK: *Vidmar*

Queen's Gambit Declined

1. P - QB4, P - K3; *2.* Kt - KB3, P - Q4; *3.* P - Q4, Kt - KB3; *4.* Kt - B3, B - K2; *5.* B - Kt5, O - O; *6.* P - K3, QKt - Q2; *7.* B - Q3, P - B4; *8.* O - O, BP x P; *9.* KP x P, P x P; *10.* B x P, Kt - Kt3 (better *10. . . .* P - QR3); *11.* B - Kt3, B - Q2.

DIAGRAM 266

Let us see what the essentials of this position are. Black will attempt to consolidate by playing . . . B - B3, . . . Kt - Q4, . . . R - B1, etc. As we have seen from a number of previous instances, if White is passive this plan will yield Black a definite advantage, possibly a win.

White's aggressive strength lies in the well-placed Bishops at QKt3 and KKt5. If he can force a P to KB5, the Black Pawns at KB2 and K3 will be under attack, and the consequent pressure will yield him a strong pull. This is the plan adopted.

12. Q - Q3

On the immediate *12.* Kt - K5 Botvinnik feared the reply *12. . . .* KKt - Q4. The text prepares B - B2 under certain circumstances.

12. . . .   QKt - Q4 ?

Instead Botvinnik rightly recommends *12. . . .* KKt - Q4 !, and if then *13.* B - B2, P - Kt3. Black plays too passively and drifts into an inferior position.

13. Kt - K5   B - B3

14. QR - Q1

Defends the QP in order to be able to shift the Queen.

14. . . .   Kt - QKt5 ?

More waste of time. Better was *14. . . .* R - B1.

15. Q - R3   B - Q4

It is clear what Black's purpose was—to neutralize the White KB. But he has lost too much time.

16. Kt x B   QKt x Kt

17. P - B4   R - B1

Now *17. . . .* P - KKt3 ? is refuted by *18.* B - R6, R - K1; *19.* B - R4, winning the exchange.

Already command of the diagonal gives rise to pretty combinations: if *17. . . .* Kt - K5; *18.* Kt x P, R x Kt; *19.* Q x P regaining the material with a winning game.

18. P - B5   P x P

After *18. . . .* Q - Q3; *19.* P x P, P x P, Black is saddled with a weak KP.

19. R x P

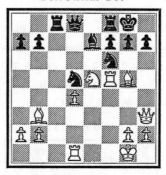

White's attack is in full swing—he has command of the open KB file, and the diagonal on which his KB is placed. Something is bound to happen.

19. . . .	Q - Q3

This allows a brilliant finish, but after 19. . . . R - B2; 20. QR - KB1, Black's game is also critical.

20. Kt x P !	R x Kt

Or 20. . . . K x Kt; 21. B x Kt, and 22. R x Kt.

21. QB x Kt	B x B
22. R x Kt	Q - B3
23. R - Q6	

Not 23. R - B5, B x P ch.

23. . . .	Q - K1
24. R - Q7	

Much more material now goes, so Black resigned.

In many cases the attack here could succeed just as well for Black. We give a model game for the Black side.

GAME NO. 9
Hastings, 1934–35

WHITE: *Botvinnik*   BLACK: *Euwe*

Queen's Gambit Accepted (by transposition)

1. P - QB4, P - QB3; *2.* P - K4, P - Q4; *3.* KP x P, P x P; *4.* P -
Q4, Kt - KB3; *5.* Kt - QB3, Kt - B3; *6.* B - Kt5, P - K3; *7.* Kt - B3,
P x P; *8.* B x P, B - K2; *9.* O - O, O - O.

DIAGRAM 268

This is a position often reached in the Queen's Gambit
Accepted. In the previous game we saw model play by White;
here an ideal defense by Black is seen.

10. R - B1	P - QR3
11. B - Q3	

A preferable alternative is *11.* P - QR4.

11. . . .	P - R3
12. B - K3	

This relieves the pressure on Black's game. After *12.* B - R4
White's attacking possibilities remain.

12. . . .	Kt - QKt5
13. B - Kt1	P - QKt4
14. Kt - K5	

Preparing the advance of the KBP, as in the previous game.

14. . . .   B - Kt2
15. Q - Q2

Threatening B x P.

15. . . .   R - K1

A "mysterious Rook move" Nimzovitch would have said. It meets the threat for if now 16. B x P?, P x B; 17. Q x P, B - B1 is an adequate defense.

16. P - B4   QKt - Q4
17. Kt x Kt   Q x Kt
18. P - B5   B - Q3
19. P x P   R x P

DIAGRAM 269

The position is ideal for Black. As a result of the White Pawn advance he has a strong aggressive stand in the center and is bound to win a Pawn sooner or later.

20. B - B5

White is faced by a choice of poor alternatives. On 20. Kt - Q3?, R x B wins a piece. If 20. Kt - B3, Kt - Kt5; 21. B - B4,

B x B; 22. Q x B, Kt - K6; 23. R - KB2, QR - K1 with a winning attack.

20....	R - K2
21. B - R3	

The Pawn cannot be held: on 21. B - B4, B x Kt it goes. However White then has good end-game chances. The correct reply to 21. B - B4 is 21.... Kt - R4.

21....	B x Kt
22. P x B	Q x KP
23. B - B4	

Or 23. B - Q4, R - Q1.

23....	Q - Q4
24. Q x Q	Kt x Q

and Black won the ending.

Another advantage that can be coupled with the isolani is possession of the QB file. This is seen in *Diagram 270*, from Nimzovitch-Taubenhaus, St. Petersburg, 1913. In order to ease the pressure against his QRP Black played:

DIAGRAM 270

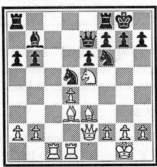

1. . . .	Kt x B ?
2. P x Kt	P - QKt4 ?

A second mistake, after which he is lost. With 2. . . . P - QR4 he can still preserve equality.

3. R - B5 !	KR - B1
4. R(Q1) - B1	P - Kt3
5. P - QR3	Kt - K1
6. P - QKt4	Kt - Q3
7. Q - KB2	P - B4

In order to play . . . Q - Kt4.

8. Q - B4	Kt - K1
9. B - K2	Kt - Q3

Black is completely constricted.

10. B - B3

Now Black is forced to do something because of the threat of B x B, Q x B; Kt x P.

10. . . .	R x R
11. QP x R	Kt - K1
12. R - Q1	Kt - B3
13. P - B6	B - B1
14. P - B7	R - R2
15. R - Q8 ch	K - Kt2
16. R x B	R x P
17. Kt x P	

and Black resigned.

Summing up our discussion of the isolated QP, we can say:

Other things being equal, the isolani is a weakness. However, it is not a fatal weakness. It can be exploited by (a) occupation of the Q4 square, (b) direct attack on it. This is best done in an end-game-like situation. On the positive side, it can be used to support an attack on the KB file or K-side, and under certain circumstances play on the QB file.

"Hanging" Pawns

THE term "hanging" refers to the two Pawns in the center at QB4 and Q4. These Pawns, since they are exposed, are apt to be a source of weakness. They are subject to a direct

DIAGRAM 271

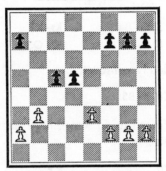

HANGING PAWNS

attack that can frequently be disastrous. But as a rule they can be defended with a cramped though on the whole satisfactory game. *Diagram 272*, Bernstein-Teichmann, Carlsbad, 1923, is an illustration.

1. Q - R3	Kt - K5
2. R - Q3	KR - Q1
3. KR - Q1	Q - K3

We see here the typical course of events: White can bring pressure to bear on the hanging Pawns, but Black can just manage to defend.

DIAGRAM 272

4. Kt - Q2	Q - QKt3
5. Kt - B1	Kt - B3
6. Kt - Kt3	QR - B1
7. P - KR3	P - KR3
8. Kt - K2	R - Q2
9. Kt - B3	Q - K3
10. Q - R5	

White still has no direct threats, but Black decides to take advantage of the tactical situation to force a favorable liquidation.

| 10. . . . | P - Q5 |
| 11. P x P | P x P |

With the following drawing variation in mind: 12. R x P, R x R; 13. R x R, Q - K8 ch; 14. K - R2, Q x P; 15. Q x P, Kt - Kt5 ch!; 16. P x Kt, Q - R5 ch; 17. K - Kt1, Q - K8 ch with perpetual check.

12. Kt - Kt5

Seems to win a Pawn.

| 12. . . . | Q - B4 ! |

But Black has rightly seen that he has sufficient counter-play.

13.	Q - R4	R - B8 !
14.	R x R	

Not 14. Kt x P, Q x R !

14.	. . .	Q x R
15.	R - B8 ch	K - R2
16.	Q - B2	Q x Q
17.	R x Q	P - Q6

The QP has now become a useful passed Pawn.

18.	R - Q2	Kt - K5
19.	R - Q1	R - Kt2

The final liquidation which assures the draw.

20.	Kt - B3	Kt x Kt
21.	P x Kt	R - Kt7
22.	R x P	R x RP

The remaining Pawns on the Q-side will soon be exchanged, so a draw was agreed to here.

At times the hanging Pawns may prove to be an advantage for their possessor because they are in the center after all and can therefore support a flank attack, e.g., one on the QKt file. An example is *Diagram 273*, from Rubinstein-Nimzovitch, Carlsbad, 1907. This continued:

1.	. . .	Q - Kt3

Hitting the target (QKt2) immediately.

2.	Q - R3	P - B5

DIAGRAM 273

A combination of aggression and defense. On the one hand
he weakens his hold on White's Q4, on the other he strengthens
his attack on the QKt file.

3. B - K2	P - QR4
4. KR - Q1	Q - Kt5
5. R - Q4	KR - Q1
6. R(B1) - Q1	R - Q2

We see how the opposing forces are drawn up: White concentrates on the Q-file, Black on the QKt.

7. B - B3	R(R1) - Q1
8. Kt - Kt1 ?	

Rubinstein becomes impatient and errs. Better was 8.
R(Q1) - Q2 immediately.

8. . . .	R - Kt1
9. R(Q1) - Q2	Q x Q
10. Kt x Q	K - B1

Not 10. . . . R(Q2) - Kt2 at once because of 11. Kt x P. Now
the move is threatened.

11. P - K4

Desperation. On *11.* R - B2, R(Q2) - Kt2; *12.* R(Q4) - Q2, B - B4 wins the Pawn.

11. . . .	P x P
12. R x R	Kt x R
13. B x P	Kt - B4
14. R - Q4	

Or *14.* B - B6, R - Kt5; *15.* B - Q5, Kt - R5 and should win.

14. . . .	Kt x B
15. R x Kt	R x P
16. Kt x P	R - Kt5

With the outside passed Pawn it is better to have minor pieces.

17. Kt - Q6	R x R
18. Kt x R	B x P

And Black won.

To sum up: the hanging Pawns are usually a minimal weakness. Direct attack on them may force a permanent weakness or material gain. As a rule they can be adequately defended, at the cost of a slight constriction of the position. As compensation they can be used as the basis for a counterattack on the flank, e.g., the open QKt file.

Blockaded Pawns

WE USE the term "blockaded" to refer to those Pawns that are held back by pieces other than Pawns. The Pawn that is held back must either be a backward Pawn or a passed Pawn, for otherwise the blockader could be driven away by one of the supporting Pawns. In general, theory tells us that the blockade of a Pawn by a Knight is advantageous, since the mobility of a Knight is not reduced by its position as a blockader. In contrast, the other pieces make poor blockaders because their mobility is reduced.

Diagram 274, from Pilnik-Euwe, Amsterdam, 1950, is an

DIAGRAM 274

excellent illustration of the effectiveness of a blockade. White's QP is held by a Knight, the KP by the Queen; the Queen as blockader is undesirable, so Black will eventually try to replace her. White's efforts are directed toward lifting the blockade, Black's toward maintaining it. The game continued:

> *1.* Kt - Kt3 ?

Euwe rightly calls this a positional blunder because it is totally unrelated to the blockade problem. Better was *1.* K - R1 followed by Kt - Kt1 - B3.

1. . . .	R - K2
2. B - B1	B - B1
3. B - K2	B - Q2

Black has a Q-side majority, which he can advantageously mobilize.

4. R(K1) - B1	R - KB1
5. Q - B1	Kt(B2) - K1

Heading for K4, as we shall see.

6. K - R1	P - B3
7. R - Kt1	Kt - Kt2

Loss of time, but it makes no difference, White is condemned to passivity.

8. B - B3	Q - Kt4

Getting into an end game is more important than maintaining the Pawn equilibrium. Black sees that the two passed White Pawns will be harmless because of the blockade.

9. Q x Q	P x Q
10. R(Kt1) - KB1	Kt(Kt2) - K1
11. B - K2	R x R
12. R x R	K - Kt2
13. P - KR3	Kt - B3
14. B - Q3	B - K1
15. R - K2	Kt - Q2

DIAGRAM 275

16. R - Q2

Here White misses a golden opportunity that comes right out of the principles of blockade: he should have played 16.

Kt - Kt5, to hit at the blockader. If then *16. . . . Kt x Kt; 17.
B x Kt* at least one blockader is gone. Best for Black is *16. . . .
Kt - QB1; 17. P - Q6, R - K4; 18. K - Kt2, P - QR3; 19. Kt - B7.*

16. . . .	Kt - K4
17. B - K2	

Black has reached one strategic goal. The next step is to
mobilize his Q-side majority.

17. . . .	P - QKt4
18. R - B2	R - QB2
19. Kt - Q1	P - B5
20. P x P	P x P
21. Kt - B3 ?	

Again he misses an opportunity to attack a blockader: he
should have played *21.* Kt - Kt2 and if then *21. . . . P - B6; 22.
Kt - Q3.*

21. . . .	K - B3
22. Kt - Kt1	R - Kt2
23. Kt - Q2	B - R5
24. R - B1	R - Kt7

DIAGRAM 276

| 25. Kt x P | Kt(K4) x Kt |
| 26. B x Kt | B - B7 |

All in line with Nimzovitch's principle: *restrain—blockade—destroy*. The blockade has served its purpose; now it is time for destruction.

| 27. B - Kt3 | R - Kt8 |

The simplest way to win.

| 28. R x R | B x R |

Now both the once blockaded Pawns will go.

29. Kt - K2	B x P ch
30. K - R2	K - K4
31. Kt - B3	B - Q6
32. K - Kt3	Kt - K5 ch
33. Kt x Kt	B x Kt

The remainder is relatively easy. The conclusion was:

34. P - Q6, K x P; *35.* B - Kt8, P - KR3; *36.* B - B7, B - Q4; *37.* B x P, B x P; *38.* P - R4, P - QR4; *39.* P x P, P x P; *40.* K - B3, P - R5; *41.* K - K3, B - K3; *42.* K - Q4, B x P; *43.* K - B3, B - Q8; *44.* B - B5 (so that if *44.*. . . . P - Kt5 ??; *45.* B x P ! draws since the Bishop is of the wrong color), K - K4; *45.* B - Q7, K - B5; *46.* K - Kt4, B - B7; *47.* K - B3, B - Kt6; *48.* K - Kt4, B - B2; *49.* K x P, B - Kt3; *50.* K - Kt4, B - B4; *51.* B - B6, P - Kt5; *52.* K - B5, B - K5; *53.* B - Q7, P - Kt6; *54.* B - R3, K - K6; *55.* K - Q6, B - B4; *56.* B - Kt2, K - B7, and Black must queen so White resigned.

To sum up: the blockaded Pawn is immobilized and therefore weak. For the blockader the rule is: restrain—blockade—destroy. For the blockaded the rule is: remove the blockader. Tactical considerations will determine which of these plans is more effective.

The Minority Attack

WE SPEAK of a minority attack when two Pawns can force a weakness among an opposing three, as in the adjoining diagram. By advancing his QKtP to Kt5, White will force Black

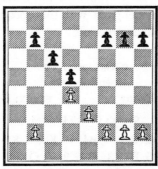

WHITE BUILDS UP A MINORITY ATTACK BY ADVANCING HIS QKtP TO Kt5

BLACK BUILDS UP A MINORITY ATTACK BY ADVANCING HIS KBP TO B5

into a dilemma: (1) . . . P x P leaves the QP isolated and the KtP exposed; (2) if he does nothing P x P, P x P leaves the BP backward; (3) an earlier . . . P - QKt4, to stop P - Kt5, leaves the BP backward and exposed. The whole situation is so bad for Black that he must necessarily seek compensation elsewhere; if he cannot find it he generally loses. One exception to this is that exchanges can free Black's game to a considerable extent. For if, say, the only pieces left are a Rook for each side, the advance can easily be contained, since the backward Pawn can be defended by the King.

It should be noted that in the diagramed position above Black also has a minority attack on the K-side, with . . . P - KB4 - B5. Again White is faced with the same dilemmas. Since these Pawns are near the King, the opening of this situation leads to an attack, whereas the opening of the other wing leads to an end-game advantage. However, since White usually has the initiative his minority attack will generally get there first.

The opening which this Pawn position comes out of most often is the Exchange Variation of the Queen's Gambit Declined. We give a model game with this opening, which shows how the minority attack proceeds.

GAME NO. 10
Dubrovnik, 1950

WHITE: *Evans*   BLACK: *Opsahl*

Queen's Gambit Declined

1. P - Q4, Kt - KB3; *2.* P - QB4, P - K3; *3.* Kt - QB3, P - Q4; *4.* B - Kt5, QKt - Q2; *5.* P - K3, B - K2; *6.* Q - B2, O - O; *7.* P x P, P x P; *8.* Kt - B3, P - B3; *9.* B - Q3, R - K1; *10.* O - O, Kt - B1.

DIAGRAM 277

White has the desired position, and now proceeds to the minority attack. *11.* QR - Kt1, Kt - K5; *12.* B x B, Q x B; *13.* P - QKt4, P - QR3 (this move is played not so much to prevent P - Kt5, which it does not do, as to exchange an extra Pawn when that inevitable advance does come); *14.* P - QR4, Kt x Kt;

15. Q x Kt, B - Kt5; *16.* Kt - Q2, Q - Kt4 (threatening . . . B -
R6); *17.* KR - B1, R - K3 (Black rightly plays for a K-side
attack, but it is not enough); *18.* P - Kt5, RP x P; *19.* P x P,
B - R6; *20.* P - Kt3, QR - K1; *21.* P x P, P x P; *22.* B - B1, B x B;
23. Kt x B.

DIAGRAM 278

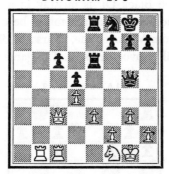

An almost ideal position for White. As a result of the
minority attack Black has a backward Pawn on an open file,
and the logical pressure brought to bear on this Pawn leads to
the gain of material. Note that Black has not had the time to
build up his own minority attack. There followed:

23. . . . Kt - Kt3; *24.* R - Kt6, Kt - K2; *25.* Q - Kt4, P - R4; *26.*
R - Kt8 (exchanges of course favor White, since he is playing
for the end game, while Black relies on the middle game),
R x R; *27.* Q x R ch, K - R2; *28.* Q - B4 !, Q x Q; *29.* KtP x Q,
P - Kt3 (better . . . P - B3); *30.* Kt - Q2, R - Q3; *31.* K - B1,
K - Kt2; *32.* R - R1, R - Q2; *33.* Kt - Kt3, R - Kt2; *34.* Kt - B5,
R - Kt7 (giving up the second rank to White loses, but it is
doubtful whether any defense would have held the ending);
35. R - R7, K - B3; *36.* R - R6 (correct is *36.* Kt - Q7 ch as later,
but the loss of time does not matter), R - Kt8 ch; *37.* K - Kt2,
R - Kt7; *38.* R - R7, R - Kt8; *39.* R - B7, R - QR8; *40.* Kt - Q3,
K - K3; *41.* Kt - B5 ch, K - B3; *42.* Kt - Q7 ch, K - K3; *43.*

Kt - B8 ch !, K - B3; *44.* Kt - R7 ch, K - K3; *45.* Kt - Kt5 ch, K - Q3
(if instead *45.* . . . K - B3; *46.* P - B3 followed by P - K4 decides); *46.* R - Kt7, P - B3; *47.* Kt - R7, K - K3; *48.* Kt - B8 ch
(finally wins a Pawn because *48.* . . . K - Q3 ?; *49.* R - Q7 ch
is mate), K - B2; *49.* Kt x P, K x Kt; *50.* R x Kt, and White won
with his extra Pawn.

Even when the Black QP is missing in a position such as
Diagram 277, the minority attack might be effective. Thus in
Diagram 279, from Vidmar-Fine, Warsaw, 1935, the advance
on the Q-side still proved decisive. The game continued:

DIAGRAM 279

| *1.* . . . . | QR - Q1 |
| *2.* P - QR4 | R - Q3 |

Hoping for eventual counterplay on the K-side.

| *3.* P - Kt5 | RP x P |

The reply *3.* . . . BP x P; *4.* P x P, P - QR4 is tempting. But
White then continues with *5.* B - Kt3, and the control of the B
file will eventually lead to the win of a Pawn.

4. P x P	B - Q2
5. P x P	B x P
6. B - Kt5	B - Q4

7. B - K2   P - R3
8. Q - Kt4

DIAGRAM 280

This is the position White was aiming for. After the exchange of Queens Black will be unable to avoid the loss of a Pawn.

8. . . . R - K3; 9. Q - R5, Q - Q1; 10. Q x Q, R x Q; 11. B - B4 (removes the support for the QKtP), B x B; 12. R x B, R - Kt3; 13. R - B8, R x R; 14. R x R ch, K - R2; 15. K - B1, R - Kt7; 16. K - K1, R - R7; 17. R - B5, R - R8 ch; 18. K - K2, R - R7; 19. P - R3, P - QKt3; 20. R - QKt5, Kt - Q2; 21. K - Q1 (finally winning a Pawn, for if 21. . . . R - R8 ch; 22. K - B2, R - R7 ch; 23. K - B1), P - Kt3; 22. Kt x P. The remaining moves are of purely technical interest: There followed: 22. . . . K - Kt2; 23. P - Kt4, R - R8 ch; 24. K - K2, R - R8; 25. K - B3 (saves the Pawn ingeniously: if 25. . . . R x P ch; 26. K - Kt2, R - R5; 27. P - B3 and the Rook is stuck), K - B1; 26. K - Kt2, R - QB8; 27. P - R4, K - K2; 28. P - Kt5, P x P; 29. P x P, K - Q1; 30. K - B3, K - B2; 31. R - Kt3, K - B3; 32. K - K2, K - Q4; 33. K - Q3, R - Q8 ch; 34. Kt - Q2, K - B3; 35. R - B3 ch, K - Kt2; 36. K - B2, R - QR8; 37. Kt - K4 (wins another Pawn—the principle holds: one Pawn deserves another), P - Kt4; 38. Kt - Q6 ch, K - Kt3; 39. P - B4, P - Kt5; 40. R - B4, R - R7 ch; 41. K - Kt3, R - R6 ch; 42. K x P,

R x P; *43.* Kt x P, R - K5; *44.* Kt - K5, and Black faced with the loss of more material resigned.

To sum up: against passive defense the minority attack, which attacks the semiexposed Pawn, sets up a completely exposed Pawn, and eventually leads to the gain of material. The defender can either try for a counterattack, or attempt to exchange so much material that there is not enough left to exploit the advantage.

The Pawn Chain

THE Pawn chain consists of a series of Pawns in a diagonal, directly confronted by an enemy series. Thus in the diagram

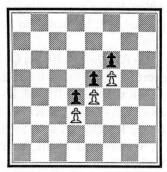

**PAWN CHAIN; WHITE'S BASE IS AT Q3;
BLACK'S BASE IS AT KB3**

we have a Pawn chain with the White Pawns at Q3, K4, KB5, the Black at Q5, K4, KB3. The *base* of the Pawn chain is Q3 for White, KB3 for Black. Nimzovitch pointed out the important principle that one should *attack the base of the Pawn chain.* For if White hits the Pawns at Q5 or K4, they are defended, and nothing happens, but if he can reach out to KB6, the base may fall, and the other Pawns will be undefended. Conversely, Black should attack White's base, the Pawn at Q3.

The Pawn chain cannot be adequately evaluated without considering the general mobility of the pieces, so we shall defer the fuller discussion of it until the next chapter.

Unequal Distribution of Pawns

WHEN there is an unequal distribution of Pawns, without any doubled Pawns both sides either have passed Pawns or potential passed Pawns. In such cases *the potential passed Pawn away from the King position confers an advantage.* Since most players generally castle on the K-side, this means that *the majority of Pawns on the Q-side is an advantage.* It is of course an end-game advantage, i.e., one that is best exploited in the end game. The following game is a model for the use of the Pawn majority.

GAME NO. 11
Stockholm, 1937

WHITE: *Collet*   BLACK: *Fine*

Queen's Gambit Declined

1. P - Q4, Kt - KB3; *2.* P - QB4, P - K3; *3.* Kt - KB3, P - Q4; *4.* B - Kt5, QKt - Q2; *5.* P - K3, P - B3; *6.* QKt - Q2, B - K2; *7.* B - Q3, O - O; *8.* O - O, P - B4; *9.* P x QP, KP x P; *10.* R - B1 ?, P - B5 !

DIAGRAM 281

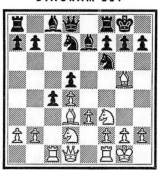

With this move Black sets up the Q-side majority. Since he has an end-game advantage, the next step is to exchange pieces. White unwisely conforms to Black's plan.

11. B - B5, P - QKt4; *12.* P - QR3, R - K1; *13.* Q - B2, P - Kt3; *14.* B - R3, Kt - Kt3; *15.* B x B, R x B; *16.* Kt - K5, KKt - Q2; *17.* B x B, Q x B; *18.* Kt x Kt, Q x Kt; *19.* Kt - B3, Q - Q3; *20.* P - KR4 (White's only chance is an attack), P - QR4; *21.* P - R5, Kt - Q2 (Black must take some steps to safeguard the King); *22.* P - KKt3, Q - K3; *23.* K - Kt2 (intending to double on the KR file), Q - K5; *24.* Q x Q (the exchange is not favorable, but alternatives are worse: on *24.* Q - B3, P - Kt4 wins a piece), P x Q; *25.* Kt - Q2, Kt - Kt3.

DIAGRAM 282

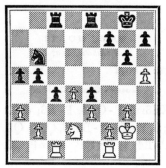

Black has reached the favorable ending he was looking for. The next step is to get a passed Pawn on the Q-side, or to force entry that leads to a passed Pawn.

26. P x P, RP x P; *27.* R - B2, P - B4; *28.* P - B3 (hoping to get some air), Kt - Q4; *29.* R - K1, K - Kt2; *30.* P x P, P x P; *31.* P - R4 (desperation: on other moves the slow methodical advance decides), P x P; *32.* R x P, R x R; *33.* Kt x R, R - QB1; *34.* Kt - R3 (if *34.* Kt x P, R - B7 ch forces the passed Pawn), K - B3; *35.* R - K2, K - K3; *36.* K - R3, R - R1 ch; *37.* K - Kt2 (not *37.*

K - Kt4, R - R4 and mates), R - QKt1; *38.* K - R3, R - Kt6; *39.*
Kt - B4, P - R6; *40.* P x P, P - R5 (threatening . . . R - B6); *41.*
R - QB2, Kt x P; *42.* Kt x Kt, R x Kt; *43.* R - B6 ch, K - Q4; *44.*
R x P, R x P.

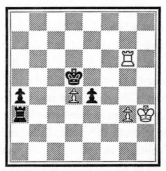

DIAGRAM 283

Black has achieved his goal; a passed QRP. Now the two
passed Pawns decide. *45.* K - Kt2, R - R7 ch; *46.* K - B1, P - R6;
47. P - Kt4, R - QKt7. White resigns because he must give up
his Rook for the passed Pawn.

IX. *Command of Space—Superior Mobility*

I N T H I S C H A P T E R we shall discuss the various types of positional advantage that do not involve a weakness in the Pawn structure directly. These are the positions that manuals on the opening refer to as ± or "a slight pull" or "White has a minimal superiority." They are the most difficult positions to handle, even though the principles involved are fairly simple.

In line with our general theoretical discussion, we note first of all that *an advantage in space is temporary in character*. If it is not exploited in short order, it will as a rule disappear. This is true even when there are definite weaknesses, such as a bad Bishop; it is all the more true when there is nothing tangible to put one's finger on. Hence the first concern of the superior player is to *restrain the* opponent.

Restraint alone, however, is merely the prelude; the advantage conferred by it is still temporary. In many cases it will be possible to *weaken* the enemy further, by forcing a Pawn advance, or getting the two Bishops, or some other method. Such weakening cannot always take place, but when it can it is most helpful. It is a kind of softening-up process.

Weakening soon reaches its limits. Still there is no permanent advantage. The next step is *combinative—a break-through* of some kind must be achieved. What this break-through consists of depends entirely on the position—usually but not always it involves some sacrifice.

Finally, the break-through leads to *destruction,* which may be either a mating combination or the decisive capture of material or both.

Thus the ideal procedure against a position with inferior mobility consists of four steps:

1. Restrain
2. Weaken
3. Break-through combination
4. Destruction

It is only the third and fourth steps that lead to a permanent advantage.

In a great many cases, the majority in actual practice, the defender does not submit passively to the attrition process. He attempts to break out of the encirclement, he weakens his Pawn structure, he counterattacks, he does something that is a gamble. Many times the result is good for him; many times it only leads to a permanent disadvantage all the sooner. In practice it is rare to find the ideal procedure, but it is still present in the back of both people's minds.

The Cramped Position

OFTEN there is no clear-cut weakness as such, but the opponent is merely cramped. It is against such positions that we are apt to find the ideal procedure worked out most precisely. Some model games will help to make the principles clearer.

GAME NO. 12
AVRO Tournament, 1938

WHITE: *Alekhine*　　　BLACK: *Capablanca*

French Defense

1. P - K4, P - K3; *2.* P - Q4, P - Q4; *3.* Kt - Q2, Kt - KB3 (better is *3.*. . . . P - QB4); *4.* P - K5, KKt - Q2; *5.* B - Q3, P - QB4; *6.*

P - QB3, Kt - QB3; 7. Kt - K2, Q - Kt3 (and here 7. . . . P - B3 is preferable); 8. Kt - B3, P x P; 9. P x P, B - Kt5 ch.

DIAGRAM 284

First Stage: Restraint

In this position White has superior mobility—his pieces are more aggressively placed, and they have more room to maneuver. Hence his main concern now is restraint. In this phase, exchanges are to be avoided as much as possible, since *a cramped position is always freed by exchanging.* So White played:

10. K - B1 !	B - K2
11. P - QR3	Kt - B1 ?

In his urge to avoid any weaknesses at all Black plays too passively. Two alternatives were better than the text: A. *11.* . . . P - B3, to loosen the White center; B. *11.* . . . P - QR4, to avoid at any rate the weakening that follows.

12. P - QKt4	B - Q2
13. B - K3	Kt - Q1

Planning to free himself by . . . P - QR4.

14. Kt - B3

Restraint! The purpose becomes clearer as we go on.

14. . . .   P - QR4

Second Stage: Weakening

Sooner or later in a cramped position a weakening move of some kind is bound to come. Here Capablanca weakens his Pawns in the hope of getting some kind of counterplay. Note that although we have separated restraint and weakening for theoretical purposes, in practice they go on together. This of course also applies to the other stages: at any point a decisive combination may be possible.

15. Kt - QR4   Q - R2

But this only leads to further constriction. In general exchanges are a good idea in cramped positions, so *15. . . .* B x Kt should have been tried. After *15. . . .* B x Kt; *16.* Q x B ch, Kt - B3; *17.* B - Kt5, Kt - Q2; *18.* R - B1, Kt(Q2) - Kt1, followed by . . . R - R2, Black gets some relief.

16. P - Kt5

Restraint!

16. . . .   P - QKt3

A real weakness has been formed—the Pawn at QKt3, which is under constant attack.

17. P - Kt3   P - B4

Another weakness, but after *17. . . .* Kt - Kt3; *18.* P - KR4, O - O ?; *19.* Kt - Kt5 White has a decisive attack.

DIAGRAM 285

In this position there are several targets for attack: the Pawn at QKt3, the Pawn at KB4, the open QB file. White strengthens his position before the break-through.

18.	K - Kt2	Kt - B2
19.	Q - Q2	P - R3

Creating a "hole" at KKt6. Again it is easy to criticize Black's moves, but in such cramped positions nothing is really feasible.

20.	P - R4

Preventing . . . P - KKt4, and preparing to occupy the hole.

20.	. . . .	Kt - R2
21.	P - R5	Kt(B2) - Kt4 ?

This leads to a decisive break-through sooner than anticipated. Here Black would have done best to rely on passive defense with . . . O - O.

22.	Kt - R4	Kt - K5
23.	Q - Kt2	

Restraint again. For now the freeing move 23. . . . B x Kt ? is impossible because of 24. P x B, and P - B3 then wins a piece.

| 23. . . . | K - B2 |
| 24. P - B3 | Kt(K5) - Kt4 |

DIAGRAM 286

Third Stage: Break-Through (Opening of Lines)

The time has come for the decisive break-through, which is, as we have mentioned, purely combinative in character. Here it involves the gain of *material;* in other positions it could lead to a *decisive attack.* In either case it begins by *opening lines.*

25. P - Kt4

Wins at least a Pawn.

25. . . . P x P

The only chance.

26. B - Kt6 ch

A subtle in-between move. On 26. P - B4 ? right away Black escapes too easily, since after 26. . . . Kt - K5; 27. B x Kt.

P x B; 28. Kt - B3, Q - Kt2; 29. QR - K1, while White still wins a Pawn, the game has opened up and Black has counterplay.

26. . . .	K - Kt1

On 26. . . . K - B1 there follows simply 27. P x P with a decisive attack along the open KB file.

27. P - B4	Kt - B6

Desperation. On 27. . . . Kt - B2 there would follow 28. Q - K2, later Q x P, and a winning attack on the open KKt file.

28. B x Kt ch	R x B
29. Kt - Kt6	B - Q1
30. QR - QB1	

A note of caution: if at once 30. K - Kt3, R - QB1 gives Black some counterplay.

30. . . .	B - K1
31. K - Kt3	Q - KB2
32. K x P	

Fourth Stage: Destruction

After the opening of lines we have reached a position where Black must lose a piece. The remainder is easy.

32. . . .	Kt - R5
33. Kt x Kt	Q x P ch

Spite check!

34. K - Kt3	Q - B2
35. Kt - KB3	

And Black resigned the hopeless struggle.

GAME NO. 13

Moscow, 1935

WHITE: *Botvinnik*   BLACK: *Tchechover*

Nimzovitch's Attack

1. Kt - KB3, P - Q4; *2.* P - B4, P - K3; *3.* P - QKt3, Kt - KB3; *4.* B - Kt2, B - K2; *5.* P - K3, O - O; *6.* B - K2, P - B3 (better is *6.* . . . P - B4; Black gets into a cramped position now); *7.* O - O, QKt - Q2; *8.* Kt - B3, P - QR3 (to free himself).

DIAGRAM 287

In this position White has a minimal advantage because of the cramped development of the Black pieces.

First Stage: Restraint

Black is threatening to free himself with . . . P - QKt4. Hence:

> *9.* Kt - Q4   P x P ?

Unnecessarily weakening. . . . P - QB4 was better.

> *10.* P x P   Kt - B4

Threatening . . . P - K4 and . . . Kt - Q6.

> *11.* P - B4   Q - B2

Again threatening . . . P - K4.

12. Kt - B3

Again restraint!

| 12. . . . | R - Q1 |
| 13. Q - B2 | |

Not 13. P - Q4 at once because of 13. . . . Kt(B4) - K5, forcing an exchange and thereby some freeing.

13. . . .	Kt(B4) - Q2
14. P - Q4	P - B4
15. Kt - K5	

Occupation of the center—the prelude to an attack and further weakening.

15. . . .	P - QKt3
16. B - Q3	P x P
17. P x P	B - Kt2
18. Q - K2	Kt - B1

Black is still cramped, but there are no obvious weaknesses. The next step is to induce one.

| 19. Kt - Q1 | R - R2 |
| 20. Kt - B2 | Q - Kt1 |

Second Stage: Weakening

21. Kt - R3 !

With the threat of Kt - Kt5, White induces a weakening of the Black Pawns defending the King.

| 21. . . . | P - R3 |

Third Stage: Break-Through

DIAGRAM 288

22. Kt - Kt5

As the sequel shows, this move can be played anyhow. The opening of the KB file justifies the piece sacrifice.

22. . . .	P x Kt
23. P x P	Kt(B1) - Q2

On the alternative 23. . . . Kt(B3) - R2; 24. Kt x P wins another Pawn for the piece, and continues the attack. Black hopes for 24. P x Kt, Kt x P with some amelioration.

24. Kt x P

Anyhow! The sacrifice now leads to a winning attack.

24. . . .   K x Kt

Fourth Stage: Destruction

25. P - Kt6 ch   K - Kt1

There is no defense. On both 25. . . . K - B1 and 25. . . . K - K1; 26. Q x P wins, e.g., 25. . . . K - K1; 26. Q x P, Kt - B1; 27. Q - B7 ch, K - Q2; 28. B - B5 ch, K - Q3; 29. B - R3 ch.

26. Q x P ch	K - R1
27. Q - R3 ch	K - Kt1
28. B - B5	

Threatening mate in two.

28. . . .	Kt - B1
29. B - K6 ch	Kt x B
30. Q x Kt ch	K - R1
31. Q - R3 ch	K - Kt1

DIAGRAM 289

32. R x Kt

Obvious but pretty.

32. . . .	B x R
33. Q - R7 ch	K - B1
34. R - K1	

Botvinnik proceeds with mating threats.

| 34. . . . | B - K4 |

With a forlorn hope in 35. R x B, Q x R; 36. P x Q, R - Q8 ch; 37. K - B2, R - Q7 ch; though even then White wins. But Botvinnik goes straight for mate.

35. Q - R8 ch	K - K2
36. Q x P ch	K - Q3
37. Q x B ch	K - Q2
38. Q - B5 ch	K - B3
39. P - Q5 ch	K - B4
40. B - R3 ch	K x P
41. Q - K4 ch	K - B6
42. B - Kt4 ch	K - Kt7
43. Q - Kt1 mate	

GAME NO. 14
Margate, 1937

WHITE: *Fine*   BLACK: *Alekhine*

Dutch Defense

1. P - Q4, P - K3; *2.* P - QB4, P - KB4; *3.* P - KKt3, Kt - KB3; *4.* B - Kt2, B - Kt5 ch; *5.* B - Q2, B - K2 (one of Alekhine's favorite variations); *6.* Kt - B3, Kt - B3; *7.* P - Q5, Kt - K4; *8.* Q - Kt3, O - O; *9.* Kt - R3, Kt - Kt3.

DIAGRAM 290

Black's pieces are crowded and cramped, but he threatens to free himself with . . . P - K4.

First Stage: Restraint

10. P x P

An exception to the usual rule: in this case the opening of lines leads to further positional advantages for White.

10. . . .	P x P
11. R - Q1	

Holding the Bishop in its strong position.

11. . . .	P - B3
12. O - O	P - K4

Better was *12.* . . . Q - B2, though Black remains cramped.

Second Stage: Weakening

13. P - B5 dis ch	K - R1
14. Kt - KKt5	Q - K1

Forced.

15. Kt - K6	B x Kt
16. Q x B	B x P
17. Q x BP	R - Q1
18. Q - B2	

DIAGRAM 291

A comparison of the two diagrams, 290 and 291, shows that Black has managed to free himself somewhat, but at the cost of conceding White the two Bishops and weakening his Pawn structure. In what follows he is unable to maintain his position because of these weaknesses.

18. . . .	Q - K3
19. Kt - R4	B - K2
20. P - QR3	

Preparing a minority attack against the Q-side, and defending the QRP. The immediate threat is Kt - B5, which cannot be played right away because the QRP is loose after 20. Kt - B5, B x Kt; 21. Q x B, Q x P.

20. . . .	R - Q5
21. P - KR3	

A restraining move: White wishes to play B - K3, and to do that he prevents . . . Kt - Kt5.

21. . . .	P - QKt4

Taking the bull by the horns—he attempts a counterattack on the Q-side. This removes the need for a break-through combination on White's part—all that he has to do is exploit the weakened Black Pawns.

22. Kt - B3	P - QR4
23. B - K3	R x R
24. R x R	P - Kt5
25. P x P	P x P
26. Kt - R4	

The pressure against Black's Q-side Pawns now leads to the loss of a Pawn.

26. . . .	Kt - Q4
27. B - B5	Q - B2

Black's only hope lies in the counterattack against KB2, but it is insufficient.

28. P - K3   R - B1
29. Q - B4

After this a Pawn must go. The immediate threats include
P - K4.

29. . . .   Q - B1

Other defenses are no better, e.g., 29. . . . B x B; 30. Kt x B,
R - B1; 31. R - Q2.

Fourth Stage: Destruction

As we have seen, the need for a third stage did not come up
here because Black initiated a weakening counterattack.

30. B x B   Kt(Kt3) x B

Forced, for if 30. . . . Q x B; 31. B x Kt.

31. P - K4   Kt - B3
32. Q x KtP

After the win of the Pawn the technical difficulties were
minimal. The conclusion was:

32. . . . R - Q1; 33. R x R, Q x R; 34. Kt - B5, Q - Q3; 35. Q -
B3, P - R3; 36. Kt - Q3, Kt - Q2; 37. P - R4, Kt - Kt3; 38. B - R3,
Kt(Kt3) - B1; 39. P - QKt4, P - R4; 40. Kt - B5, Kt - B3; 41.
Q - B4, Q - K2; 42. Kt - Kt3 (wins another Pawn), Q - Q3; 43.
Kt - R5, Q - Q7; 44. Kt x P, Q - K8 ch; 45. B - B1, Kt x P; 46.
Q - K2, Q x Q; 47. B x Q, P - Kt3; 48. Kt x P, Kt - B6; 49. B - Q3,
K - Kt2; 50. P - B4, Kt - Q4; 51. P - Kt5, K - B3; 52. K - B2, Kt -
Kt3; 53. K - K3, Kt - R5; 54. K - Q4, Kt - K3 ch; 55. K - Q5, Kt -
B2 ch; 56. K - B6, Kt - K3; 57. P - Kt6, Kt - Q1 ch; 58. K - Q7,
Kt - K3; 59. P - Kt7, Kt(R3) - B4 ch; 60. K - B8, and Black re-
signed.

GAME NO. 15
Budapest, 1928

WHITE: *Capablanca*   BLACK: *H. Steiner*

Queen's Gambit Declined

1. P - Q4, Kt - KB3; *2.* P - QB4, P - K3; *3.* Kt - QB3, P - Q4; *4.* B - Kt5, QKt - Q2; *5.* P - K3, B - K2; *6.* Kt - B3, O - O; *7.* R - B1, P - B3; *8.* B - Q3, P x P; *9.* B x P, Kt - Q4; *10.* B x B, Q x B; *11.* O - O, Kt x Kt; *12.* R x Kt.

DIAGRAM 292

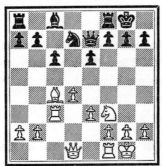

This whole opening is an excellent illustration of the principles of restraint and liberation in a cramped position. White's seventh move, *7.* R - B1, e.g., is strongest because it prevents the freeing . . . P - QB4. Black can now equalize theoretically with *12.* . . . P - K4. Instead he played:

12. . . .   P - QKt3 ?

which met with a model refutation.

First Stage: Restraint

13. Q - B2

Threatening to win a Pawn with B - Q3 and B - K4, and thereby forcing Black into a more cramped position.

13. . . .	P - QB4
14. P x P	Kt x P
15. P - QKt4	Kt - R3

The fact that this move is forced is the ingenious point to Capablanca's brilliant restraining combination, for the task of getting the Black Knight back into the game will be a permanent headache. On the alternative *15.* . . . Kt - Q2; *16.* B - Q3, P - R3; *17.* R - B7 is too hard for Black to meet.

16. P - QR3	B - Kt2

Second Stage: Weakening

The only real weaknesses in Black's position are the poorly placed Knight at QR3 and White's possession of the open QB file; both of these are purely temporary. White must force further weaknesses.

17. B - Q3

Prevents . . . QR - B1 and weakens the K-side.

17. . . .	P - Kt3
18. R - B1	

Again . . . QR - B1 is stopped because White gets R, Kt, and B for the Q: *18.* . . . QR - B1; *19.* R x R, R x R; *20.* Q x R ch, B x Q; *21.* R x B ch, K - Kt2; *22.* B x Kt and should win.

18. . . .	QR - Q1

Intending . . . Kt - Kt1 and if then R - B7, R - Q2. This calls for restraining action.

19. Kt - K5

Meanwhile also threatening to win the exchange with B x Kt and Kt - B6.

19. . . .	Q - Q3

The tempting *19. . . .* Q - Kt4 is also met by P - B4.

20. P - B4

DIAGRAM 293

White now threatens to win a Pawn with *21.* Q - R4, and Black is helpless against this threat.

Third Stage: Break-Through

20. . . .   **Kt - Kt1**

Also inadequate was Black's only other try *20. . . .* P - B3; *21.* Kt x P !, P x Kt; *22.* B x Kt, B x B; *23.* Q x P ch, K - R1; *24.* P - Kt5 (not *24.* P - K4, Q - Q5 ch, and Black mates), B x P (if *24. . . .* B - Kt2; *25.* P - K4, Q - Q5 ch; *26.* K - B1, and R - R3 ch is decisive); *25.* Q - R5 ch, and Q x B.

21. R - B7   **B - R1**

On the tempting *21. . . .* R - B1 White also wins a Pawn with *22.* Kt x BP, Q x R; *23.* Q x Q, R x Q; *24.* Kt - R6 ch, K - Kt2; *25.* R x Q ch, and *26.* R x B.

Fourth Stage: Destruction

22. R x RP

After the win of this Pawn the remainder is not difficult. The conclusion was:

22. ... Kt - B3; 23. R x B, Kt x Kt; 24. R x R, R x R; 25. B - K2, Q - Q7; 26. Q x Q (the simplest: if instead 26. P x Kt, Q x P ch and . . . R - Q7 can make life difficult), R x Q; 27. R - B8 ch, K - Kt2; 28. K - B1, Kt - Q2; 29. R - Q8 (forcing the exchange of the remaining pieces), K - B3; 30. B - Kt5, R - Q4; 31. P - QR4, R x B (desperation: if 31. . . . K - K2; 32. R x Kt ch, R x R; 33. B x R, K x B; 34. P - QR4 with an elementary win); 32. P x R, K - K2; 33. R - QB8, P - K4; 34. R - B6, P - K5; 35. K - K2, P - B4; 36. K - Q2, K - B2; 37. K - B3, and Black resigned the hopeless fight.

If we re-examine these examples to see what they show about the ideal procedure involved, several comments become apparent about each step:

1. *Restraint.* In this stage the task is twofold—to avoid exchanges and to prevent liberating Pawn moves.

2. *Weakening.* Generally a weakness is forced by some tactical threat. In a great many cases a desperate defender voluntarily submits to weaknesses to ease his position somewhat.

3. *Break-through.* The method here involves *opening lines.* However, this must not be done indiscriminately, because in some cases the open lines may be to the defender's advantage. The line opening may lead to either the gain of material or an attack against the King.

4. *Destruction.* This stage goes hand in hand with the preceding one. Often at the crucial stage there are several possibilities that must be carefully weighed.

Other Positional Advantages

WE HAVE described positional advantages consisting of a superior Pawn structure and of a generally more mobile position.

The specific character of the weaknesses that this latter leads to can now be broken down further. The advantage can fall into any one of the following categories; naturally there may be two or more of these advantages combined.

1. Superior Pawn structure
2. A decisive attack against the King
3. The open file
4. The semiopen file
5. Superiority on the long diagonal
6. The two Bishops
7. Command of the center
8. Occupation of an advanced post
9. Weak squares in the enemy camp
10. Superiority in the Pawn chain
11. The "bad" Bishop

Category 1 has been treated in the last chapter; category 2 has the next chapter devoted to it. Each of the others will be discussed in more detail here.

The Open File

The open file is one that is occupied by a Rook, or can be occupied by one. Such occupation in itself does not mean anything. But it can lead to penetration by the Rook to the seventh or eighth rank, where it is almost certain to gain material if unopposed, or to support a decisive attack. Once the Rook reaches the seventh or eighth ranks the air is ripe with combinations.

A simple example of how the open file can lead to a decisive combination is the position in *Diagram 294*, from Fine-Becker, Zandvoort, 1936. If White's Rook can reach Q7 he wins a Pawn. Hence:

DIAGRAM 294

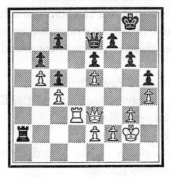

1. Q - B3

Threatening Q - B6, and preventing . . . R - R1.

1. . . . Q - K1

The only defense, but it leaves exposed the "hole" at KB6.

2. Q - KB6 R - R1

Black has been forced on the defensive. However, he threatens to free himself with . . . P - B3, so White must make the most of his temporary advantage. He does this by going over to the attack.

3. P - Kt4 P x P

Or *3. . . .* P - B3; *4.* P x RP, P x KtP; *5.* BP x P with an easy win.

4. P - R5 Q - B1

The alternative *4. . . .* P x P; *5.* Q - Kt5 ch is no better.

5. P x P Q - Kt2
6. R - Q8 ch

The quickest road to victory.

6. . . .	R x R
7. Q x R ch	Q - B1
8. P x P ch	K x P
9. Q - B6 ch	K - Kt1
10. Q x P ch	K - R2
11. Q - Q7 ch	K - R3
12. P - K6	

The passed Pawn decides.

12. . . .	Q - R1 ch

One spite check is permitted.

13. Q - Q5	Q - K1
14. Q - K5	Q - K2
15. K - Kt3	Resigns

Diagram 295, from Nimzovitch-Capablanca, New York, 1927, is another instance where quick penetration via the open file leads to a surprisingly speedy victory.

DIAGRAM 295

1. . . .	R - B7
2. Q - R6	

Although this has been severely criticized, there is really nothing better. If *2.* Q - B3 ?, R x B and if *2.* Q - Q1, P - K4;

3. R - QB1, R x R; 4. Q x Q, R x R ch and 5. . . . P x B. The
best chance was 2. Q - B1.

2. . . .	P - K4

Clearing the road for the other Rook.

3. B x KP	R(Q1) - Q7
4. Q - Kt7	

Despair. On 4. R - KB1 there follows the pretty 4. . . .
Q x KP; 5. B - B4 (or 5. P x Q, R - Kt7 ch; 6. K - R1, R x P ch;
7. K - Kt1, R(B7) - Kt7 mate), R x P ! (anyhow); 6. B x Q,
R - Kt7 ch and mates as in the note.

4. . . .	R x P
5. P - Kt4	

White is in a mating net.

5. . . .	Q - K3
6. B - Kt3	R x P

The last straw. If now 7. B x R, Q x KtP ch; 8. K - R1, Q - R6,
and mates.

7. Q - B3	R(R7) - Kt7 ch
8. Q x R	R x Q ch
9. K x R	Q x KtP

Now the march of the Pawns decides. The conclusion was:
10. QR - Q1, P - KR4; 11. R - Q4, Q - Kt4; 12. K - R2, P - R4;
13. R - K2, P x P; 14. P x P, B - K2; 15. R - K4, B - B3; 16. R - KB2,
Q - Q4; 17. R - K8 ch) the Rook cannot maintain itself in a
good spot: if 17. R(K4) - KB4, P - R5; 18. B x P, B - K4), K - R2,
and White resigned.

Diagram 296, from Lasker-Teichmann, Cambridge Springs,
1904, is typical of positions where penetration to the seventh
rank leads to a winning end game. Black can hold material

even for a while, but the steady pressure of the White Rook decides. The game continued:

DIAGRAM 296

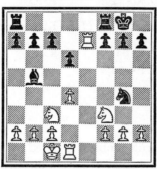

1.. . .   **B - R3**

On *1.. . .* B - B3; *2.* P - Q5 is ruinous.

2. R x QBP   **Kt x BP**

The only way to preserve material equality for a while.

3. R - K1   **KR - K1**
4. R(K1) - K7   **R x R**
5. R x R   **R - Q1**

White was threatening to win a Pawn with R - Q7.

6. Kt - KKt5   **Kt - Kt5**

Already material loss is unavoidable. If *6.. . .* P - B3; *7.* Kt - K6, and if *6.. . .* R - KB1; *7.* Kt - K4 (even stronger than R - Q7), Kt x Kt; *8.* Kt x Kt, P - Q4 (if *8.. . .* R - Q1; *9.* Kt x P); *9.* Kt - Q6.

7. Kt x BP

In the actual game Lasker played *7.* P - KR3, which gave Black more counterplay.

7. . . .	R - KB1
8. Kt x P	R - B8 ch
9. K - Q2	R - B7 ch
10. Kt - K2	P - R3

On 10. . . . R x P at once, 11. R - K8 is mate.

11. P - B4	R x P
12. P - Kt4	

And White wins a piece.

The Semiopen File

A much more difficult problem is posed by the semiopen file, in which the Rook cannot penetrate directly but is held back by an enemy Pawn. In that event the technique consists of forcing an entry either by exchanging the Pawn, or by tying down the enemy pieces to the defense of the Pawn, which allows a decisive attack elsewhere.

A model game demonstrating the utilization of the semiopen file is Bogoljubow-Capablanca, New York, 1924, which led to the position in *Diagram 297*. Here White's QBP is exposed and weak, so the first step is to increase the pressure against it.

1. R(R1) - B1	R(B1) - B1
2. R - QB2	Kt - K1

Aiming for QKt4.

3. R(B1) - B1	Kt - Q3
4. Kt - K5 ?	

While Black plays consistently, White is "swimming." As Alekhine shows in the Tournament Book, White's best chance was 4. Kt - B5 and if then 4. . . . P - QKt3; 5. Kt - R4.

4. . . .	Q - R4

DIAGRAM 297

Already threatening to win a Pawn with . . . Kt - Kt4.

5. P - QR4

Another weakening, but this time scarcely avoidable. On 5. Kt - Q3, Kt - Kt4; 6. Kt - B5, Q - Kt3; the threat of . . . P - K4 is hard to meet.

5. . . .   Q - Kt3

Suddenly White finds that he must lose a Pawn. The main variations are:

A. *6.* P - QKt4, P - QR4; *7.* P - Kt5, Kt - B5; *8.* Kt x Kt, R x Kt; *9.* R - R1, P - K4, and the QP goes.

In this last variation White can also win two Pawns with *9.* . . . R x QP; *10.* P x R, R x R; *11.* Q x R, Q x P ch; *12.* K - B1, Q x R ch; *13.* K - K2. However, the resulting Queen ending is less easily won than the Rook and Pawn ending.

B. *6.* R - Kt2, Kt - B4; *7.* R(Kt2) - Kt1, P - B3; *8.* Kt - Kt4, P - K4, and again the QP goes.

6. Kt - Q3	Q x KtP
7. Kt - B5	Q - Kt3
8. R - Kt2	Q - R2
9. Q - K1	P - QKt3

After this the pressure against the White QBP remains, and Black wins fairly easily with his extra Pawn. The remaining moves were:

10. Kt - Q3, R - B5; *11.* P - R5, P x P; *12.* Kt - B5, Kt - Kt4; *13.* R - K2 (. . . P - K4 was threatened), Kt x QP; *14.* P x Kt, R(B1) x Kt; and White resigned. For if *15.* P x R, Q x P ch, and *16.* . . . R x R.

Another case where the semiopen file leads to the win of a Pawn in a surprising manner is *Diagram 298,* from Lasker-Tarrasch, Nuremberg, 1896. At first sight it does not look as if White has any real advantage. Yet after

DIAGRAM 298

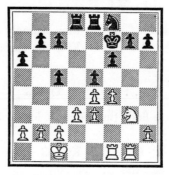

1. Kt - R5

Black suddenly finds that he must lose a Pawn. If *1.* . . . Kt - K3; *2.* P - B5, Kt - Kt4; *3.* P - R4. So the reply was:

1. . . .	P - KKt3
2. P x P	R x KP

For capture of the Knight leads to mate in two: *2.* . . . P x Kt; *3.* R x P ch, K - K2; *4.* R - Kt7 mate.

3. Kt x P K - Kt2
4. R - B2

and White won easily with his extra Pawn.

We have already seen one example of the use of the semi-open file in the minority attack in the Queen's Gambit Declined (p. 256). There the Pawn advance is used to force a weakness on the QB file. Another way in which such a Pawn structure can be used is to force an entry via an advanced square (an "outpost" Nimzovitch called it). A model example is *Diagram 299* from Nimzovitch-Capablanca, New York, 1927.

DIAGRAM 299

Here Black's plan is to penetrate to QB5 and K5 and attack the weakened White Pawns. The game continued:

1. Kt - Q4, Q - Kt3; *2.* R - B2, KR - B1; *3.* P - QR3, R - B2; *4.* R - Q3, Kt - R4 (this excursion leads to nothing. After some inconsequential loss of time Capablanca finds the right way); *5.* R - K2, R - K1; *6.* K - Kt2, Kt - B3; *7.* R(K2) - Q2, R(K1) - QB1; *8.* R - K2, Kt - K2; *9.* R(K2) - Q2 (White can do nothing), R - B5; *10.* Q - R3, K - Kt2; *11.* R - KB2, P - R4; *12.* R - K2, Kt - B4; *13.* Kt x Kt ch (avoiding this exchange was slightly better), KtP x Kt; *14.* Q - B3, (if *14.* Q x RP, R - KR1; *15.* Q - B3, R - KR5 regaining the Pawn with the better game), K - Kt3.

DIAGRAM 300

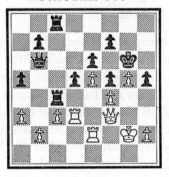

Black has reached the position he was aiming for. By playing along the fifth rank he now forces further weaknesses.

15. R(K2) - Q2	R - K5
16. R - Q4	R - B5
17. Q - B2	

Better was *17.* R x R(B4), but Black's pressure still remains.

17. . . .	Q - Kt4
18. K - Kt3	R(B5) x R

Surprising, since it shuts in the Black Rook.

19. P x R

Forced, for if *19.* R x R, R - K7.

19. . . .	Q - B5
20. K - Kt2	

White is still able to do nothing but mark time, yet it is
not clear how Black will win.

20. . . .   P - Kt4

Creating further pressure along the QB file.

21. K - Kt1	P - Kt5
22. P x P	P x P
23. K - Kt2	Q - B8

Pinning down both the White Queen and Rook.

| 24. K - Kt3 | Q - KR8 |

The ending has a problemlike character. If now 25. R - K2, R x R; 26. Q x R, Q - Kt8 ch wins the QP. And if 25. P - R4, R - K8 wins.

25. R - Q3	R - K8
26. R - KB3	R - Q8
27. P - Kt3	

White is almost in *zugzwang*. If 27. K - R3, R - Q7 decides, while if 27. R - Kt3, Q - K5; 28. R x P, R - Q6 ch; 29. K - R4, R - KB6.

| 27. . . . | R - QB8 |
| 28. R - K3 | |

There just are no moves: if, e.g., 28. P - R3, R - Kt8 ch; 29. K - R4, R - Kt5 mate, or 28. K - R4, R - B7.

| 28. . . . | R - B8 |

Now everything goes: on 29. Q - K2 there follows 29. . . . Q - Kt8 ch; 30. K - R3, R - K8. White resigned.

In the previous example we saw that the semiopen file could be used to shift the pieces to another part of the board. There the win came in end-game style. In *Diagram 301* from Reshevsky-Capablanca, Margate, 1935, White uses his advantage to force a winning attack. The game continued:

DIAGRAM 301

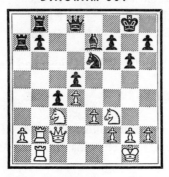

1. P - QR4 (holds the QKtP back), Kt - B2; *2.* Kt - K5, Q - K1;
3. P - B4 (threatening P - B5 under the proper circumstances),
P - B3; *4.* Kt - Kt4, Q - Q2; *5.* P - R3, K - Kt2; *6.* Kt - B2, B - R6; *7.*
R - R2, B - Q3; *8.* Kt(B2) - Q1, P - B4; *9.* Kt - Kt5 (strengthen-
ing the pressure against the QP), R - R4; *10.* Kt x Kt, B x Kt;
11. Kt - B3, Q - K3; *12.* Q - B2, P - Kt3; *13.* Q - B3 (ties Black's
pieces to the defense of the QP), R - Q1; *14.* R(R2) - Kt2
(threatening R - Kt5, which apparently wins a Pawn).

Black seems to be lost, but he finds an inspired defense.

DIAGRAM 302

14. . . .   Q - K2

For if now *15.* R - Kt5, R x R; *16.* R x R, Q - R6; *17.* Kt x P, P - B6 with too much counterplay.

> *15.* R - Kt4   R - Q2
> *16.* K - R1

White has another idea now: while all the Black pieces are placed so clumsily to defend the weak Pawns, he will open lines on the K-side and start an attack.

> *16.* . . .   B - Q1
> *17.* P - Kt4   P x P

To allow another weakness at KB4 would be ruinous.

> *18.* P x P   Q - Q3
> *19.* K - Kt1   B - B2
> *20.* K - B2

Preparing to march to QB2, when he can afford to go after the QP.

> *20.* . . .   R - B2

Another ingenious defense: he threatens . . . P - Kt4.

> *21.* P - Kt5   B - Q1
> *22.* K - K2   B x P

But this yields White an open file instead of a semiopen one, and leads to a quick loss. The best chance was *22.* . . . Q - K3; *23.* K - Q2, Q - B4; *24.* Q - K2, though White should still win in this line.

> *23.* R x P   Q - R6
> *24.* K - Q2   B - K2
> *25.* R - Kt7

With this penetration the game is virtually decided. The immediate threat is R(Kt1) - Kt6, Q - Kt4 - K6, etc. Black resorts to a desperate gamble.

25. . . .   R x RP
26. Q x P

Naturally not 26. Kt x R ??, Q - Q6 ch; 27. K - B1, B - R6 ch, and Black wins.

26. . . .   R - R4
27. Q x P

After this the game is virtually over. The remaining moves were: 27. . . . R - R4; 28. K - Q3, Q - R1; 29. Q - K6, Q - R6; 30. R - Q7, R(R4) - KB4; 31. R - Kt3, Q - R8; 32. R x B, Q - B8 ch; 33. K - Q2, and Black resigned.

The Long Diagonal

The possession of the long diagonal by the Bishop is analogous to the occupation of an open file by a Rook. There is however this important difference: that while the Rook can penetrate to the seventh or eighth rank the Bishop is not so strong and must create a permanent weakness in some other manner. Sometimes it can be done by an exchange, leaving a weak Pawn; at other times the consistent pressure will force the win of a Pawn.

We must distinguish two main cases here. When the long diagonal is bearing down on the enemy King position (for White: QR1 to KR8) its occupation is directed toward an attack against the enemy King. We have already seen some examples (Diagrams 78, 79, and 101–109) of combinations inherent in such a situation. In this section we wish to confine ourselves to the other alternative, where the long diagonal does not hit at the King.

Illustrative of the possibilities is the position in *Diagram 303*, from Fine-Kashdan, New York, 1938. Here White's only real advantage lies in his KB, which can potentially control

the long diagonal. The game continued:

1.	B - B5	Q x Q
2.	QR x Q	R - Q1
3.	R x R ch	B x R
4.	P - QKt3	B - Kt3

Naturally hoping to free himself by exchanges.

5.	Kt - R4	B x B
6.	Kt x B	Kt(B5) - K4

He must be prepared to drive the Kt away: on *6. . . .*
Kt - Kt3 there would follow *7.* R - Q1 and if *7. . . .* P - QR3;
8. Kt - B7, R - Kt1; *9.* P - K5 with a winning position.

7.	P - B4	Kt - Q2
8.	Kt x Kt	B x Kt
9.	R - Q1	B - K1
10.	Kt - Q6	R - Kt1

Black cannot hold on to everything. If *10. . . .* P - QKt3; *11.*
P - K5, and the Knight is lost.

11. P - K5 !

At last. The power of the Bishop now makes itself felt.

11. . . .	K - B1
12. P - QR3	K - K2
13. P - QKt4	P - QR3
14. R - B1	P - B3

The only way to free himself: on *14. . . . K - Q2; 15.* Kt x P is immediately decisive.

| 15. R - B5 | P x P |
| 16. P x P | |

The Pawn is indirectly defended: if *16. . . .* Kt x P; *17.* Kt x B wins a piece.

| 16. . . . | B - Q2 |

Now he threatens to win a Pawn, so White goes over to the decisive liquidation.

DIAGRAM 304

| 17. Kt x P | |

Wins a Pawn.

| 17. . . . | R x Kt |
| 18. B x Kt | R - B2 |

The Rook and Pawn ending is also hopeless.

19. B - K4   R x R
20. P x R

With a Pawn ahead, and Black still so cramped, the win is easy. The conclusion was:

20. . . . P - R3; *21.* K - B2, K - Q1; *22.* K - K3, K - B2; *23.* K - Q4, P - QR4; *24.* B - Q3, B - K1; *25.* B - B4, B - Q2; *26.* B - Kt3, B - B1; *27.* B - R4, B - Kt2; *28.* K - B4, B - R3 ch; *29.* B - Kt5, B - Kt2; *30.* K - Kt3, and Black faced by the loss of his QRP as well resigned.

Command of the long diagonal can also give rise to brilliant combinative possibilities. In *Diagram 305*, from Keres-Flohr, Semmering-Baden, 1937, Black has just played . . . BP x QP,

DIAGRAM 305

expecting P x P. Instead Keres replied

1. Kt x P

And suddenly the tremendous power of White's fianchettoed Bishop makes itself felt. How is Black to develop now? He cannot play . . . Kt - B3. So he tries to get his Kt to QB4.

1. . . .   Q - B2
2. Q - Kt3

Again hitting the weak spot.

2. . . .   B - B3 ?

But this is too optimistic. He had to take the first opportunity to neutralize White's Bishop with . . . Kt - B3, in spite of all its dangers.

3. KR - Q1   Kt - Q2
4. P - QB4   Kt - B4
5. Q - Kt4   Kt - K3

A natural try, which fails. 5. . . . Kt - R3 was better, though still not wholly satisfactory.

6. Kt - Kt5   Q - K4
7. QR - B1   R - Q1

It is much too dangerous to take the KP: there would follow after 7. . . . Q x KP; 8. Kt - B3, B x Kt; 9. Q x B, threatening B - Kt2, and Black is in a bad way.

8. R - Q5

Note how the control of the long diagonal makes all kinds of combinations possible.

8. . . .   R x R

The alternative 8. . . . Q x KP is refuted convincingly by 9. Kt - B7, R - Kt1; 10. R - K1, Q x RP; 11. R x R ch, Kt x R; 12. R x P, B x R; 13. Q x B with a decisive attack.

9. P x R   P - QR3
10. Kt - R7

An elegant winning combination.

10. . . .   Kt - Q5

There is no defense: if 10. . . . R x Kt; 11. R x B ch, Kt - B1; 12. Q - Kt6.

11. R x B ch	R x R
12. Kt x R	Q x KP
13. P - R4	Kt - B4
14. Q - K4	

And Black resigned.

The Two Bishops

Other things being equal, a Bishop is slightly stronger than a Knight. When there are two Bishops against Bishop and Knight, or two Knights, the advantage is even greater. Naturally such an advantage is again temporary. In the end game the two Bishops are a very potent force, and consequently one way to utilize them is to head for the finale. However, they are also strong in the middle game and can lead to many entrancing attacking possibilities.

In *Diagram 306*, from Alekhine-Fine, Kemeri, 1937, we see the purely positional use of the two Bishops. Black has a hard time developing.

1.... Kt - K5 ?

After this Black is definitely lost. The only good try was *1....* P - QR3, so that if then *2.* P - Kt6, Kt - Q4; *3.* R - Kt1, Kt - Q2 with sufficient counterplay.

DIAGRAM 306

2. B - B7

Now 2. . . . P - QR3 is bad because of 3. P - Kt6.

2. . . .	Kt - Q2
3. Kt - Q4	Kt - Kt3
4. P - B3	Kt - Q4

Hoping to exchange one of the Bishops, but White does not oblige.

5. B - R5	Kt(K5) - B3
6. Kt - B2	

Again avoiding exchanges: if 6. P - K4 ? at once, Kt - K6 gets the KB.

6. . . .	B - Q2
7. P - K4	R - QB1
8. K - Q2	Kt - Kt3

Threatening an exchange with . . . Kt - B5 ch.

9. Kt - K3

Which is promptly prevented.

9. . . .	O - O
10. P - QR4	

Preparing to drive the Knight away.

10. . . .	KR - Q1
11. B - Q3	P - K4
12. KR - QB1	

Better than 12. B - B3, Kt x P, for if 13. R x Kt, B x P.

12. . . .	B - K3
13. R x R	R x R
14. B - Kt4	Kt - K1

Even exchanges do not help any more. If here *14. . . .*
Kt - B5 ch; *15.* Kt x Kt, B x Kt; *16.* R - QB1, B - K3; *17.* R x R ch,
B x R; *18.* B - Q6, Kt - Q2; *19.* B - B4, and Black is completely
bottled up.

15. P - R5	Kt - Q2
16. Kt - Q5	B x Kt
17. P x B	Kt - B4
18. B - B5	R - Q1

On *18. . . .* Kt - Kt6 ch; *19.* K - Q3, R - Q1; *20.* R - K1 wins.

19. K - B3	P - QKt3

The alternative *19. . . .* R x P loses a piece after *20.* K - B4.

20. P x P	P x P
21. B x Kt	

Part of the power of the two Bishops is that they can be
exchanged at an appropriate point to force a winning end
game; that is what happens here.

21. . . .	P x B
22. P - Kt6	Kt - Q3
23. B - Q7	R x B
24. R - R8 ch	

Black resigned because he is mated in a few moves.

Another convincing demonstration of the strength of the
two Bishops is seen in *Diagram 307*, from Fine-Najdorf, New
York, 1948. White has sacrificed a Pawn to get to this position.
He played:

1. R - QB1

And Black soon found himself hopelessly lost.

1. . . .	Kt - Q2

DIAGRAM 307

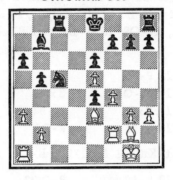

If the Knight ventures too far, the Bishops cut off its line of retreat, and it may not get back. E.g., *1.* . . . Kt - R5; *2.* R x R ch, B x R; *3.* R - B2, B - Q2; *4.* P - Kt3.

2. R x R ch	B x R
3. R - B2	O - O

If *3.* . . . B - Kt2; *4.* B x P wins at once, as does *4.* R - B7.

4. B x P	P - B3
5. B - Q4	P x P
6. P x P	

Black is hopelessly cramped. The remaining moves were:
6. . . . R - Q1; *7.* R - B7, Kt - B1; *8.* B - QB5, B - Q2; *9.* R - R7, B - K1; *10.* B - Q6, B - Kt3; *11.* B - B6, B - Q6; *12.* P - QKt4, P - KR4; *13.* R x RP, R - B1; *14.* K - B2, P - R5; *15.* P x P, Kt - Kt3; *16.* K - Kt3, K - R2; *17.* P - R5, Kt - R1; *18.* K - B4, Kt - B2; *19.* B - B5, R - B2; *20.* B - B3, B - B5; *21.* B - K4 ch, K - R3; *22.* B - B5, Kt - Kt4; *23.* B - KKt6, Kt x P ch; *24.* K - Kt3, Kt - Kt4; *25.* R - R8, and Black about to be mated resigned.

An example of the attacking power of the two Bishops is seen in *Diagram 308*, from Alekhine-Em. Lasker, New York,

1924. Note how Black uses one Bishop to force weaknesses, and the other to attack.

DIAGRAM 308

1. . . .	B - KR4
2. P - KKt4	B - KB2
3. P x P	R - B1
4. Q - Kt2	P x P
5. P - B5	

Sooner or later this move would be forced, against a threat such as . . . Q - Q3, so White plays it immediately.

5. . . .	Q - Q3

Preparing to bring the other Bishop into the attack.

6. Kt - Kt2	B - B2

Now the Knight is tied to the defense of the KRP. Black need only attack this Knight and it will be all over.

7. KR - K1	P - KR4
8. P - KR3	Kt - R2
9. R x R ch	R x R
10. R - K1	R - Kt1

After this the threat of . . . Kt - Kt4 is decisive.

11.	Q - Q2	Kt - Kt4
12.	Kt - K5	

Desperation.

12.	. . .	P x Kt
13.	Q x Kt	P - K5
14.	P - B6	P - Kt3

With 14. . . . Q x P he would also have won, but he prefers to crash through in the attack.

15.	P - B4	RP x P
16.	B - K2	

Or 16. P x P, P x B.

16.	. . .	P x P
17.	B - R5	R - Kt7
18.	Kt - R4	Q x P
19.	Q x Q	B x Q

and White resigned.

Command of the Center

Since control of the center is implicit in much of the previous discussion, especially that of the cramped position, we need not add much here. Clearly such command is temporary and must be converted either into material gain or a decisive attack. One example will suffice to illustrate the principles. *Diagram 309* is taken from Reshevsky-Shainswit, New York, 1938. Here White's Queen is in a dominating position, and it looks as if Black's game will soon collapse. However, the second player has hidden resources, and the win is by no means as easy as it looks. There followed:

DIAGRAM 309

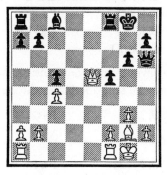

1. . . .	Q - Kt2
2. Q - Q6	

A good alternative was 2. KR - K1. But White must be careful, for 2. Q x BP, B - K3 gives Black counterplay. Such positions can be awfully tricky because the defender has no permanent weaknesses, and if he once manages to develop, all the advantage is gone.

2. . . .	P - B5

After 2. . . . Q x P ?; 3. B - Q5 ch wins at once, for if 3. . . . K - Kt2; 4. Q - K7 ch.

3. B - Q5 ch	K - R1
4. QR - K1	

To keep the KBP defended.

4. . . .	B - B4
5. R - K7	Q - Q5
6. Q - K5 ch	

White can win almost as he pleases, but this is the simplest. On 6. Q - B7, P - KKt4 Black has counterchances.

6. . . .	Q x Q
7. R x Q	P x P
8. RP x P	QR - Kt1
9. KR - K1	

Control of the seventh rank now ensures White the gain of material. Note how he still dominates the center.

9. . . .	P - QKt4

A desperate try.

10. P - Kt3	P x P
11. B x P	KR - B1
12. R - K7	P - QR4
13. R - R7	R - R1
14. R(K1) - K7	R x R

He has no defense: if 14. . . . P - Kt4; 15. R x R, R x R; 16. R - K5, and many Black Pawns go.

15. R x R	B - K5
16. R x P	R - Q1
17. K - B1	R - Q8 ch

Or 17. . . . B - B6; 18. B - K2.

18. K - K2	R - QR8
19. P - QR4	

and Black resigned because he must lose a second Pawn.

Occupation of an Advanced Post

The secure occupation of an advanced post by a piece is one of the strongest positional advantages that a player can have. By "advanced" we generally mean on the fifth rank or beyond, but usually it is the occupation of the sixth rank that is most effective. The most useful piece for occupation is the Knight, which thereby commands a large number of important squares.

Next in order of usefulness is the Rook, which uses the advanced post as a point of entry on an open file. Bishop and Queen are as a rule less effective in advanced positions, because they can frequently work just as well at a distance.

The square that is available for occupation is popularly called a "hole." A hole at K6 or Q6 is a very serious handicap, one more to the sides can be bad, but is not necessarily so.

A

B

**WHITE SEEKS TO OC-
CUPY THE HOLE AT Q6**

**WHITE SEEKS TO MAKE
USE OF THE HOLES AT
KB6 AND KR6**

In Diagram A the hole is at Q6, in B there are two, one at KB6, the other at KR6.

Once a hole is occupied, the enemy position becomes terribly constricted. In effect the first two stages have been completed: restraint and weakening. All that is needed now is to look around for the break-through combination. Several examples will make the principles clearer.

Diagram 310 is from the famous game Lasker-Capablanca, St. Petersburg, 1914. White's Knight has occupied the hole at K6, and Black is terribly constricted. White's plan must involve the opening of more lines; the most obvious way in which that can be done is via the KKt file—P - KKt4 - Kt5. But he need not be in a hurry. The game continued:

DIAGRAM 310

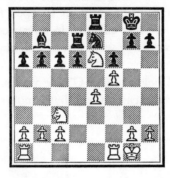

1. QR - Q1

One of White's major concerns must be to avoid the exchange of the powerfully placed Knight. Black might wish to try . . . P - B4 followed by . . . P - Q4; after the exchange White's Knight is attacked. To stop that White first occupies the Q file.

1. . . .	Kt - B1
2. R - B2	P - QKt4

Hoping to get some freedom by play with the Knight, which is headed for QB5 and K4. This plan is however easily parried. In such positions the best bet is to give up the exchange with . . . K - B2 and . . . R x Kt. While the resulting position with two R's, Kt, and 6 P's *vs.* R, B, Kt, and 7 P's is theoretically won for White the technical difficulties are enormous, and Capablanca might well have drawn.

3. R(B2) - Q2

Tying down the Knight.

3. . . .	R(Q2) - K2
4. P - QKt4	K - B2

5. P - QR3	B - R1
6. K - B2	R - R2

With the thought that the opening of the Rook file may give him some more air.

7. P - Kt4	P - R3
8. R - Q3	P - QR4
9. P - KR4	P x P
10. P x P	R(R2) - K2

While White steadily strengthens his position, Black, choked by the enemy Knight in his innards, is reduced to marking time.

11. K - B3	R - Kt1
12. K - B4	

Threatening P - Kt5.

12. . . .	P - Kt3
13. R - Kt3	P - Kt4 ch
14. K - B3	Kt - Kt3

Desperately he tries to get counterplay.

15. P x P	RP x P

DIAGRAM 311

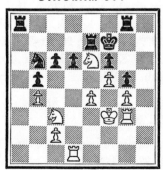

Lines have been opened for the White Rooks, and now they can enter for the kill.

16. R - R3

The capture of the Pawn is deceptive here: on *16.* R x P there follows *16. . . .* Kt - B5; *17.* R - Q1, Kt - K4 ch; *18.* K - B2, R - R1 with counterplay.

16. . . .   R - Q2
17. K - Kt3

In order to be able to play P - K5 under certain circumstances without fearing a discovered check.

17. . . .   K - K1
18. R(Q1) - KR1

Forcing a decisive penetration. The threat is R - R7, or R - R8, after due preparation. Because of White's Kt at K6, Black is unable to co-ordinate his Rooks and is helpless.

18. . . .   B - Kt2
19. P - K5 !

The entrance of White's second Knight is decisive.

19. . . .   QP x P

There are many pretty ways to lose. If *19. . . .* P - B4; *20.* R - R8, R x R; *21.* R x R ch, K - B2; *22.* R - B8 ch, K - K2; *23.* P x BP mate. Or *19. . . .* BP x P; *20.* Kt - K4, Kt - Q4; *21.* R - R8, R x R; *22.* R x R ch, K - K2; *23.* Kt(K6) x P, Kt - B3; *24.* Kt x Kt, K x Kt; *25.* R - R6 ch, K - K2; *26.* P - B6 ch with an easy win.

20. Kt - K4   Kt - Q4
21. Kt(K6) - B5

Winning the exchange to begin with, for if *21. . . .* R - QB2; *22.* Kt x B, R x Kt; *23.* Kt - Q6 ch.

21.	B - B1
22. Kt x R	B x Kt
23. R - R7	R - B1
24. R - R1	

In addition to all his other woes Black is in a mating net.

24.	K - Q1
25. R - R8 ch	B - B1
26. Kt - B5	Resigns

Even when the advanced occupier can be exchanged, the resulting position is often unfavorable for the defender because a strong protected passed Pawn results. An example is *Diagram 312*, from Botvinnik-Flohr, Moscow, 1936. Here the hole is at Q6, which White heads for posthaste.

1. Kt - Kt1	Q - B1
2. Kt - R3	B - Q1
3. Kt - B4	B - B2
4. Kt - Q6	R - Kt1

DIAGRAM 312

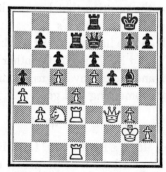

5. R - QKt1

Once the hole is occupied, the next step is to open lines. Now P - QKt4 is threatened.

5. . . .	Q - Q1
6. P - QKt4	P x P
7. R x P	B x Kt

Forced, since otherwise the QKtP will go.

| 8. KP x B | Q - R4 |
| 9. R(Q3) - Kt3 | |

DIAGRAM 313

Let us examine the position that has resulted from the exchange of White's Knight. White's pieces are still more aggressively placed, and he has two direct weaknesses to aim at: the Pawns at QKt7 and K6. Black on the other hand is hemmed in behind his own and the enemy Pawns. It can only be a question of time before something will go.

9. . . .   R - K1

Speculating on *10.* R x P, R x R; *11.* R x R, Q - Q7 ch; *12.* Q - B2, Q - Q6 with possibilities of perpetual check.

10. Q - K2

White decides to play solidly.

10. . . .	Q - R1
11. R - K3	K - B2
12. Q - B4	P - QKt4

A trap.

13. Q - B2 !	

Which White sees through. If 13. P x P e.p.?, P - B4 dis ch; and if 13. RP x P, P x P dis ch.

13. . . .	R x P

This leads to a quick loss. But after the more peaceful 13. . . . P x P; 14. R x RP, R - R2; 15. R(K3) - R3 Black is also lost in the long run.

14. P x R	P - B4 dis ch
15. K - R3	P x R
16. Q - B7 ch	K - Kt1
17. P - Q7	R - KB1
18. Q - Q6	

There were already many ways to win. The immediate threat now is Q x P ch and Q - K8.

18. . . .	P - R3
19. Q x P ch	K - R2
20. Q - K8	P - Kt6

A last try—if 21. Q x Q ?, R x Q; 22. R - K8, P - Kt7, and Black queens.

21. Q x Q	R x Q
22. P x P	R - Q1
23. R x P	R x P
24. P - Kt6	Resigns

A hole at K5 or Q5 can be the prelude to a very strong attack; examples of this will be seen in the next chapter, on the attack against the King.

Occupation of an advanced square by a heavy piece frequently gives rise to a decisive combination. Thus in *Diagram 314,* from Fine-Reshevsky, Hollywood, 1945, with

1. R - Q6

White wins a Pawn. There followed:

1. . . .   QR - Q1

DIAGRAM 314

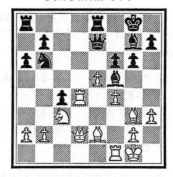

2. Kt - Q5

The simplest. In the game White played 2. R - Q1, R x R; 3. Q x R, Q x Q; 4. R x Q ?? (4. P x Q still wins), Kt - B1; 5. B x P ch, K - B1 and Black drew.

2. . . .   Kt x Kt
3. Q x Kt ch   K - R1
4. B x P

and should win easily.

A surprising combination comes out of *Diagram 315,* from Reshevsky-Simonson, New York, 1938, where White has occupied the hole at KB6 with his Queen.

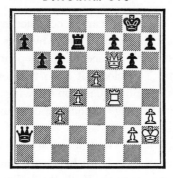

Reshevsky played:

1. P - Q5 !

The Pawn can be captured in three ways, and each way loses:

A. *1. . . .* Q x P; 2. R - Q4, winning the Rook.
B. *1. . . .* P x P; 2. P - K6, P x P; 3. Q - B8 mate.
C. *1. . . .* R x P; 2. Q x BP ch and 3. Q - B8 mate.
Black tried

1. . . .   R - Kt2

to reply to 2. P - K6 with *2. . . .* Q x P. But

2. P - K6

anyhow. In the game White played 2. P x P and also won. The text is quicker.

2. . . .   Q x P
3. R - Q4

and Black must give up his Queen or be mated.

Weak Squares

A weak square is one which can be occupied by a piece without any danger of being chased away by enemy Pawns. Naturally the value of such an occupation depends on the location of the square. The closer it is to the center, the more important it becomes. But equally on the wings, if the squares are too weak, the advantage is considerable, and material loss is often unavoidable.

In our discussion of Pawn structure a number of examples of weak squares came out. With backward Pawns the square in front of the Pawn is weak. With the isolated Pawn, again the square in front of it is weak; most often the adjacent squares as well, such as QB5 and K5 against the isolated QP.

WHITE MUST PLAY FIRST 1 P - Q Kt3, TO DRIVE BLACK'S KNIGHT AWAY; IF 1 P - Q R3, P - R5 THE KNIGHT IS UNTOUCHABLE

As soon as a weak square is set up, it should be occupied, preferably by a Knight, but often other pieces will do as well.

Where weak squares may become involved, Pawn play becomes very important. Thus in the diagram Black has a Knight at QB4, which White threatens to chase away with P - QKt4. Black safeguards his Kt with . . . P - QR4. In order to drive it away White should now continue with P - QKt3, P - QR3,*

---

* It is assumed that the KtP is protected.

and then P - QKt4, but not P - QR3 first, because Black then replies . . . P - R5, disrupting the communications of the Pawns. Now P - QKt4 would be met by . . . P x P e.p., so that Black's Knight at QB4 has become soldily anchored.

Indiscriminate Pawn advances frequently set up weak squares. Thus a Pawn storm in coffee-house style has two disadvantages—it weakens the Pawns and sets up weak squares which, when occupied by the enemy, form the basis for a decisive counterattack.

Let us take a look at *Diagram 316*, a position that arises out of the Q-Indian Defense. Here the chances are about even: Black has the semiopen QKt file to maneuver on, White the Queen file. Often however White makes the mistake here of playing P - K4; this makes his own Q4 a weak square which, if occupied, will give Black a clear advantage. E.g., a game Soultanbeieff-Sultan Khan, Liege, 1930, continued:

DIAGRAM 316

1. P - K4 ?	Q - B2
2. KR - K1	

Hoping to play P - K5 at any rate.

2. . . .	P - Q3
3. QR - B1	

The point to White's moves hereabouts becomes obscure to the annotator, and probably was obscure to Soultanbeieff as well.

3. . . .   P - KR3

Preparatory to the main event.

4. P - QR3   Kt - Q2

Weakening the defenses of Q5.

5. Q - B3

To play P - QKt4 . . .

5. . . .   P - QR4

. . . which is promptly stopped.

6. Kt - R4   P - Kt4

He accepts the invitation.

7. Q - K3

Speculating on 7. . . . P x Kt; 8. Q x RP. But Black need not allow the counterattack.

7. . . .   Q - Q1
8. Kt(R4) - B3   Q - K2
9. P - R3   QR - Kt1
10. P - Kt3   B - R1

This maneuver serves to increase the value of an eventual occupation of Q5, for then the QKtP will be under attack.

11. Kt - Kt1 ?

Another foolish move which weakens him even more. But then one is always grateful for such games where the bad moves help to bring out ideal play by the opponent.

11. . . .	Kt(Q2) - K4
12. P - QR4 ?	Kt x Kt ch
13. B x Kt	Kt - Q5

DIAGRAM 317

Black has reached his first goal. The rest is surprisingly easy.

14. B - Q1

This forced defense weakens the long diagonal, which Black promptly takes advantage of.

14. . . .	P - B4
15. P x P	R x BP
16. R - B3	R(Kt1) - KB1
17. R - KB1	R - B6

A decisive break-through combination.

| 18. B x R | R x B |

Wherever the Queen moves, Black can win in several ways. Thus if 19. Q - Q2, R x R, and either way the Rook is recaptured, a Knight check will win the Queen. Or on 19. Q - Q2, Q - Kt2 also wins with mating threats. So White resigned.

Weak squares on the wings can often be exploited by direct

occupation, which as usual sooner or later leads to material gain. *Diagram 318*, from Nimzovitch-Pritzel, Copenhagen, 1922, is an excellent example of how careless Pawn play sets up weak squares that prove the defender's downfall.

DIAGRAM 318

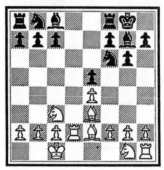

Here White's only advantage lies in the possession of the open Q file. But in such a position with a full board this advantage is of minimal value. Thus quick development would be indicated with . . . Kt - B3, . . . B - K3, eventually, if possible, . . . Kt - Q5. Instead Black played:

> 1. . . .   P - B3 ?
> 2. P - QR4

An excellent move, typical in such positions. White wishes to continue with P - R5, Kt - R4 and eventually Kt - B5.

Thus we begin to see what the move *1. . . .* P - QB3 has done. It has weakened Black's Q3, but that does not play a role until much later. More immediately it has weakened all the squares on the Q-side, which White now aims at.

> 2. . . .   Kt - Kt5
> 3. B x Kt   B x B
> 4. KKt - K2   Kt - Q2 ?

This "normal" developing move is bad because the Knight can go nowhere. A better idea was 4. . . . Kt - R3, followed by . . . KR - K1, . . . B - KB1, and . . . B - B4, which would have held the Q-side weaknesses most dynamically.

5. KR - Q1	Kt - Kt3

With a momentary threat (. . . Kt - B5) that is easily parried.

6. P - QKt3	B - B3

Hoping to challenge possession of the Q-file.

7. P - B3	B - K3
8. P - R5	Kt - B1

Black's weaknesses have compelled him to disrupt communications again.

9. Kt - R4	

Threatening to force an entry with Kt - B5, Kt x B, and R - Q7.

9. . . .	P - Kt3

An excellent rejoinder. The Pawn cannot be taken because of 10. P x P ?, P x P; 11. Kt x P, Kt x Kt; 12. B x Kt, B - Kt4, winning the exchange.

10. R - Q3	

Now the Pawn is threatened.

10. . . .	P x P ??

In spite of his previous mistakes, Black still had a defense. But after this gross positional blunder it becomes hopeless. 10. . . . R - Kt1 was necessary, with a tactical point: 11. R - B3, P - QB4; 12. R(B3) - Q3, P - B5; 13. R - B3, P x KtP; 14. BP x P,

P x P, and Black suddenly has counterthreats. After *10. . . .*
R - Kt1; *11.* Kt - Kt2 is best for White, but then Black has much
more counterplay than in the game.

11. R - B3	Kt - K2
12. R - B5	

Note how the weak squares on the Q-side are occupied one
by one.

12. . . .	KR - Kt1
13. Kt(K2) - B3	

Stops . . . R - Kt1. As Nimzovitch says, the QRP won't run
away.

13. . . .	P - QR3
14. R x RP	K - Kt2
15. Kt - Kt6	R - R2
16. Kt(B3) - R4	

DIAGRAM 319

Now we see the fruits of Black's weakening moves. Several
vital weak squares have been occupied by White, and a Pawn
must fall. The immediate threat is *17.* Kt - B5, against which
there is no adequate defense.

| 16. . . . | R(R2) - Kt2 |
| 17. R x RP | Kt - B1 |

Even after the loss of a Pawn Black's game has not been eased.

18. Kt x Kt	R x Kt
19. Kt - B5	R(Kt2) - B2
20. R - Q6	

Seizing the point made weak by Black's first move (. . . P - QB3). Now another Pawn goes.

| 20. . . . | R - Q1 |

Or 20. . . . B - K2; 21. Kt x B ch, P x Kt; 22. R x KP

| 20. R x B | Resigns |

The Pawn Chain

A Pawn chain, as the reader will recall, is one in which two sets of Pawns confront one another. Thus in the diagram the

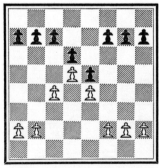

PAWN CHAIN; WHITE'S
BASE IS AT K4;
BLACK'S BASE
IS AT Q3.

Pawn chain consists of the White Pawns at Q5 and K4, Black Pawns at Q3 and K4. The *base of the Pawn chain* is the last Pawn in the chain; White's base here is the Pawn at K4, Black's the Pawn at Q3.

Generally speaking, *the advantage in Pawn chain positions accrues to the side whose Pawns extend farthest forward.* This is easily understandable. As we shall see, the strategy involved is to attack the base of the Pawn chain. In order to defend the base, pieces will have to be shifted, and if the base is, say, on the third or second rank their maneuverability thereby becomes more limited. Furthermore, if the base is removed, a protected passed Pawn is set up, which becomes increasingly stronger as it gets closer to the eighth rank. However, Pawn chains cannot really be evaluated without considering the rest of the position—much depends, e.g., on the location of the Pawn chain, whether in the center or on the wings, the forces available to defend the base, and the results of forcing open a file by the attack on the base.

A model example of Pawn-chain play is seen in *Diagram 320*, from Capablanca-Treybal, Carlsbad, 1929. There is a

DIAGRAM 320

Pawn chain with White Pawns at Q4 and QB5, Black Pawns at QB3, Q4. Naturally White's long-range strategic goal is to attack Black's base at QB3; for him this is a possibility, while for Black the attack against Q4, White's base, is out of the question. On the other hand it must not be supposed that the attack against QB3 will automatically give White the better of it; the timing must be correct, and the consequences carefully calculated. The game continued:

1.	P - QR4	Kt - Kt5
2.	Q - K1	Kt - R3
3.	P - R3	

White reasons that P - Kt5 would give Black the open QR file and possible counterplay, so he undertakes a diversion on the K-side first.

3.	. . .	Kt - B2
4.	P - Kt4	B - Q2
5.	R - B2	K - R1
6.	R - KKt2	R - KKt1
7.	P - KKt5	

Setting up another Pawn chain (White P's at KB4, KKt5, Black P's at KB4, KKt3). Again White's base at KB4 is unassailable, while Black's at KKt3 is easily hit. With Pawn chain advances possible on both wings Black's task is not easy.

7.	. . .	Q - Q1
8.	P - R4	K - Kt2
9.	P - R5	

The sacrifice of a Pawn in such positions is purely temporary; hence Black does not accept.

9.	. . .	R - R1
10.	R - KR2	Q - B2
11.	Q - B3	Q - Q1
12.	K - B2	Q - B2

Typical of such Pawn-chain defenses: Black can do no more than mark time.

13.	R(Kt1) - KR1	QR - KKt1
14.	Q - R1	R - Kt1
15.	Q - R3	QR - Kt1
16.	P - Kt5	

Now White feels that the time is ripe: the reason will soon be clear.

16.	. . .	RP x P
17.	P - R6 ch	

Blocking off Black's Rooks temporarily.

17.	. . .	K - B1
18.	P x P	K - K2

Taking the Pawn is no better: after *18.* . . . P x P White replies *19.* R - QKt1 with pressure on the QKt file.

19.	P - Kt6	Q - Kt1

DIAGRAM 321

Let us re-examine the position. There are now two sets of Pawn chains, one, on the Q-side, with White P's at QKt6,

QB5, Q4, the other, on the K-side with White P's at KB4, KKt5, KR6. In both cases Black's base is on the second rank, which leaves him quite constricted. White must now proceed to the attack against these bases with pieces.

There followed: 20. R - R1, R - QB1; 21. Q - Kt4, KR - Q1; 22. R - R7, K - B1; 23. R - KR1, B - K1; 24. R(R1) - R1, K - Kt1; 25. R(R1) - R4, K - B1; 26. Q - R3, K - Kt1; 27. K - Kt3, B - Q2; 28. K - R4 (to gain time on the clock), K - R1; 29. Q - R1, K - Kt1; 30. K - Kt3, K - B1; 31. K - Kt2, B - K1.

32. Kt - Q2 !

White now begins the deciding maneuver: a break-through combination against QKt7.

32. . . .	B - Q2
33. Kt - Kt3	R - K1

Black is so cramped that he finds it impossible to defend. On 33. . . . B - K1 the conclusion would come with 34. Kt - R5, R - Q2; 35. Kt x KtP, R x Kt; 36. R - R8.

| 34. Kt - R5 | Kt - Q1 |

DIAGRAM 322

35. B - R6

An elegant break-through, but expected by the attentive readers of this book.

35. . . .	P x B
36. R x B	R - K2
37. R x Kt ch	R x R
38. Kt x P	

and Black resigned.

Note that once Black's base at QKt2 fell his position went to pieces.

In *Diagram 323*, from Landau-Fine, Amsterdam, 1936, we see a Pawn-chain battle. White has the advantageous Pawn chain on the Q-side, Black on the K-side. The game continued:

DIAGRAM 323

1. P - KR4 ?

But this is illogical. He should have consolidated his position with O - O, R - Kt1, KR - B1, and then proceeded to P - Kt5.

1. . . .	Kt - B3
2. Q - B3	

Still speculating on a K-side attack.

2. . . .	Kt - K3
3. P - R5	P - B5

Black on the other hand follows through consistently with his Pawn-chain.

4. P x BP	Kt x BP
5. P x P	P x P
6. QKt - B1	

An unavoidable Pawn sacrifice. For if instead 6. K - B1, P - K6 wins a Pawn anyhow. Again with the base of the Pawn chain gone the position becomes untenable.

6. . . .	Kt x P ch
7. K - Q2	Kt - Kt5

The remaining moves are of little interest for our purpose. Black won as follows:

8. R - KKt1, P - K6 ch; 9. K - B2, Kt - B5; 10. P - B3, Kt - B7; 11. R - K1, Kt(B7) - R6; 12. R - R1, Kt - Kt7; 13. R - B1, Kt (R6) - B5; 14. K - Kt2, B - Q2; 15. R - B2, K - Kt2; 16. R - Kt1, R - KB1; 17. B - Q1, B - R6; 18. Kt - K2, B - B4; 19. Kt x Kt, Kt x Kt; 20. Kt x P, B x R; 21. B x B, QR - K1; 22. Kt - B5 ch, R x Kt; 23. B x R, Q - K7 ch; 24. Q - B2, Q - K6, and White resigned.

The Bad Bishop

We speak of a "bad" Bishop when it is blocked by its own Pawns, i.e., a number of Pawns are on squares of the same color with it. This is a pronounced end-game disadvantage, and the opponent should strive to simplify in order to reach the finale as quickly as possible.

Diagram 324, from Capablanca-Reshevsky, Nottingham, 1936, illustrates the principles involved. Here Black's Bishop is blocked and the KP weak. White aims first to exchange:

DIAGRAM 324

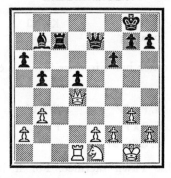

1. P - K3, Q - K5 (hoping to straighten out his Pawns if White exchanges); *2.* P - KR4, P - QR4; *3.* P - B3, Q x Q; *4.* R x Q, R - B8; *5.* K - B2, R - R8; *6.* R - Q2, P - R5; *7.* Kt - Q3, R - QKt8 ? (allows the exchange of Rooks; *7.* . . . K - B2 was better); *8.* R - Kt2, R x R; *9.* Kt x R, B - B3; *10.* Kt - Q3, P - Kt4 (a counterattack because he rightly feels that passive defense is hopeless); *11.* P x KtP, BP x P; *12.* Kt - Kt4, P x P; *13.* P x P, B - Kt2; *14.* P - Kt4, K - Kt2; *15.* K - K2, K - Kt3; *16.* K - Q3, P - R4; *17.* P x P ch, K x P; *18.* K - Q4, K - R5; *19.* Kt x P (decisive), K - Kt6; *20.* P - B4, P - Kt5; *21.* P - B5, B - B1; *22.* K - K5, B - Q2; *23.* P - K4, B - K1; *24.* K - Q4, K - B6; *25.* P - K5, P - Kt6; *26.* Kt - K3, K - B5; *27.* P - K6, P - Kt7; *28.* Kt x P ch, K x P; *29.* K - Q5, K - Kt5; *30.* Kt - K3 ch, K - B5; *31.* K - Q4 resigns.

X. *The Attack against the King*

O F A L L T H E S P E C I A L W E A P O N S available to the chess player, the attack against the King is at once the most spectacular and the most important. When the positional advantage consists of superior mobility, to convert it to an attack is often the most promising continuation. When a player is material down, the most rewarding compensation that he can look for is the attack. In a dull lifeless position an attack can create fireworks as nothing else can.

How does the attack proceed? What principles does it adhere to? What defenses is it likely to run up against, and how can these be demolished? This chapter is concerned with the answers to these and related questions.

In general, *the attack against the King does not depend on the total amount of material on the board but on the immediately available material.* That is why sacrifices are possible, and why a loss of material is less important than usual. It does the defense no good to have a Queen and Rook stuck in one corner while his King is being mated in another. The situation is directly analogous to the military one again: reserve man power and equipment are useful for future battles but are useless when there is a danger that has to be parried immediately.

Because the attack depends on what material is available now, its main guiding principle is: *Open the lines leading to the enemy King.* This can be done in either of two ways. One, the more usual, is to strip the King of his defenses—remove Pawns, divert pieces. The other, actually even more effective when it can be done, is to drive the King out into the open, especially the center of the board. Once the King is stripped of his defenses, or driven out into the open, an opportunity for a decisive combination presents itself.

Sacrifices naturally abound in the attack on the King. These occur for two reasons. First, the outcome of the attack often depends on the amount of material present in the area of the King. E.g., if White has Q, R, and B attacking the K, while Black has only R and B defending, even if Black has an extra piece on the other side of the board, the attack is likely to crash through. The second reason why sacrifices abound is that mate can be administered by a lowly Pawn. Frequently the King is blocked by his own pieces and mate comes because the King is too blocked.

A second general principle that guides the attacker is to *avoid exchanges*. This too follows quite naturally from theory. As we know, in a cramped position exchanges free the defender. Furthermore, the attacker depends on his temporary material superiority in the crucial area, hence any exchanges will reduce that superiority.

Defense against the attack on the King will be treated in more detail in the next chapter. Suffice it to say that the defender tries to avoid those situations that favor the attack; in particular he tries to keep the lines closed and to induce exchanges.

In the further discussion we must distinguish the attack on the uncastled King from that on the castled, since the techniques differ somewhat, although they adhere to the same general principles.

The Uncastled King

IN ORDER to attack the uncastled King we follow the general principles of the attack, namely open the lines to the enemy King, avoid exchanges, look for a decisive combination, especially when the King is stripped of his defenses. But there is one additional weapon that can be tremendously effective: *prevent castling.* For if the defender cannot castle, his pieces remain disunited, and thereby create the material inferiority in the crucial area that the attacker is looking for.

Diagram 325, a position from the Giuoco Piano, is an illustration of how effective the prevention of castling can be. The opening moves are:

DIAGRAM 325

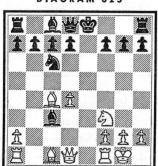

1. P - K4, P - K4; *2.* Kt - KB3, Kt - QB3; *3.* B - B4, B - B4; *4.* P - B3, Kt - B3; *5.* P - Q4, P x P; *6.* P x P, B - Kt5 ch; *7.* Kt - B3, Kt x P; *8.* O - O, Kt x Kt; *9.* P x Kt, B x P? (correct is *9.* . . . . P - Q4). Now analysis has established that

10. **B - R3 !**

gives White a won game. If now *10.* . . . . B x R; *11.* R - K1 ch is immediately decisive. Other alternatives are no better; the main possibilities are:

A. *10.* . . . . P - Q4; *11.* B - Kt5, B x R; *12.* R - K1 ch, B - K3; *13.* Q - R4, R - QKt1; *14.* Kt - K5, Q - B1; *15.* B x Kt ch, P x B; *16.* Q x P ch, K - Q1; *17.* Kt x P ch, B x Kt; *18.* B - K7 mate.

B. *10.* . . . . P - Q3; *11.* R - B1, B - R4; *12.* Q - R4, P - QR3; *13.* B - Q5, B - Kt3; *14.* R x Kt, B - Q2; *15.* R - K1 ch, K - B1; *16.*

R x QP, P x R; *17.* B x P ch, K - Kt1; *18.* Kt - Kt5, P - Kt3; *19.* B x P ch, K - Kt2 (*Diagram 326*); *20.* B - K5 ch, K - R3; *21.* Kt - K6, B x Q; *22.* B - Kt7 ch, K - R4; *23.* R - K5 ch, K - R5; *24.*

DIAGRAM 326

P - Kt3 ch, K - Kt5; *25.* P - R3 ch, K x P; *26.* Kt - B4 ch, K - Kt5; *27.* B - K6 ch, K - B6; *28.* R - K3 mate.

C. *10.* . . . . Kt - K2; *11.* Q - Kt3, P - Q4; *12.* Q x B, P x B; *13.* KR - K1, B - K3; *14.* B x Kt, K x B; *15.* P - Q5, Q x P; *16.* QR - Q1, Q - QB4; *17.* R - K5, Q - Kt3; *18.* R x B ch, Q x R; *19.* R - K1, and wins.

These variations illustrate some of the principal methods of attack against the uncastled King. We note especially:

1. Prevention of castling by seizing the diagonal QR3 to KB8 or the open K-file or both.

2. Exploitation of Black's weak KB2.

3. Use of the pin of the Kt at QB3.

4. Sacrifices that drive the King out into the open—this last is exemplified in the continuation from Diagram 326.

In the days before modern theory was crystallized people blithely exposed their Kings to attack and went down in a blaze of glory. E.g., the position shown in *Diagram 327* was one frequently reached in Morphy's days; it comes out of the Evans Gambit.

DIAGRAM 327

The opening moves are: *1*. P - K4, P - K4; *2*. Kt - KB3, Kt - QB3; *3*. B - B4, B - B4; *4*. P - QKt4, B x P; *5*. P - B3, B - R4; *6*. P - Q4, P x P; *7*. O - O, B - Kt3; *8*. P x P, P - Q3; *9*. Kt - B3. Here the best defense for Black is to try for exchanges with *9*. . . . B - Kt5; *10*. B - Kt5, B x Kt; *11*. P x B, K - B1 (Black must forgo castling: if *11*. . . . P - QR3; *12*. B - R4, B - R2; *13*. P - Q5, P - QKt4; *13*. Kt x P and wins); *12*. B - K3, KKt - K2; *13*. P - Q5, Kt - QKt1, and Black has a position that offers some defensive chances. Instead a game Morphy-Stanley, New York, 1857, continued from the diagram:

9. . . .	Kt - B3 ?
10. P - K5	P x P

Here too, a modern player's first thought would be *10*. . . . P - Q4, to exchange a piece, but it fails against *11*. P x Kt, P x B; *12*. P x P, R - KKt1; *13*. R - K1 ch, B - K3; *14*. P - Q5.

11. B - R3

Naturally. The numerous open lines now spell Black's downfall.

11. . . .	B x P
12. Q - Kt3	B - K3

More or less forced. If *12. . . .* Q - Q2; *13.* Kt x B, Kt x Kt (not *13. . . .* P x Kt; *14.* R - K1 ch); *14.* Q - Kt2, and Black is helpless against the routine development of White's Rooks.

13. B x B	P x B
14. Q x P ch	Kt - K2
15. Kt x B	P x Kt
16. KR - K1	Kt(B3) - Kt1

A losing defensive move, but what else is there? If *16. . . .* P x Kt; *17.* QR - Q1 is immediately decisive.

17. Kt - Q5

and White wins a piece to begin with.

Once the lines are open, as we have seen, the attack almost conducts itself. One defensive resource should however always be borne in mind: if Black (or White, if he is the defender) is unable to castle legally, he may be able to castle artifically, by playing his King to the corner, either directly or by first playing . . . P - KB3, . . . K - B2 and so on.

When, as is usually the case, the lines are not completely open, the attacker has two important resources at his disposal: *diversion of enemy pieces,* and *sacrifices to strip the enemy King of his defenses.*

DIAGRAM 328

Diagram 328, from Janowski-Schallopp, Nuremberg, 1896, is a simple example that shows how helpless a King undefended by the Queen can be. White plays:

> 1. B - Q5

and Black is lost. There followed:

> 1. . . .　　　　P x B
> 2. Q x P ch　　K - Q1

To venture out would be worse: 2. . . . K - K2; 3. Kt x P ch.

> 3. Q x R ch　　K - Q2
> 4. Q - Kt7 ch　K - K3

Hoping to escape. On 4. . . . K - K1 White wins most simply with 5. K - Q2.

> 5. Q - B6 ch　　B - Q3
> 6. B - B4

Now after 6. . . . Q x R ch; 7. K - Q2, Q x R; 8. Q x B ch leads to mate: 8. . . . K - B4; 9. Q - K5 ch, K - Kt3; 10. Q - Kt5 mate. So Black resigned.

Let us now examine the anatomy of some more complicated attacks against the uncastled King. As we know, apart from the general principles of opening lines and preventing castling, these usually sooner or later involve sacrifices.

GAME NO. 16
Moscow, 1943

WHITE: *Ravinsky*　　　　BLACK: *Panov*

Sicilian Defense

1. P - K4, P - QB4; 2. Kt - KB3, P - K3; 3. P - Q4, P x P; 4. Kt x P, Kt - KB3; 5. Kt - QB3, P - Q3; 6. P - KKt3 (an excellent continuation), Kt - B3; 7. B - Kt2, B - Q2; 8. O - O, P - QR3; 9. B - K3, R - B1; 10. Q - K2, P - QKt4; 11. P - QR3, Kt - K4; 12.

QR - Q1, Kt - B5; *13.* B - B1 (a Pawn sacrifice that should not have been accepted), Kt x RP.

DIAGRAM 329

How is White to continue his attack? As we know, he proceeds in four stages, which overlap at many points:

1. Open lines.
2. Avoid unfavorable exchanges.
3. Mass against the enemy King.
4. A decisive combination, and probably involving a piece sacrifice.

First Stage: Open Lines

14. P - K5	P x P

Forced.

15. Kt - B6	Q - B2
16. Kt x KP	Kt - B5

At this point exchanges cannot be avoided completely, so White removes a piece which is guarding the enemy King.

Second Stage: Avoid Unfavorable Exchanges

17. Kt x B	Kt x Kt

Now White has the open Q-file and the semiopen K-file. More material must be brought up.

Third Stage: Mass against the Enemy King

> 18. Kt - Q5 ! Q - R2
> 19. Kt - B4

Threatening to win with Kt x KP.

> 19. . . . Kt(B5) - K4 ?

As so often the defender does not find the best. 19. . . . Q - Kt3 was stronger, though White still preserves his attack.

Fourth Stage: The Decisive Combination

> 20. R x Kt Kt x R
> 21. Kt x P P x Kt
> 22. Q x P ch B - K2

After the more evasive 22. . . . K - Q1 White has a crushing mate with 23. B - Kt5 ch, K - B2; 24. Q - B6 ch, K - Kt1; 25. B - B4 ch, R - B2; 26. B x R ch, Q x B; 27. Q - R8 mate.

> 23. R - K1 Q - B4

With a whole Rook ahead one would think that Black had some chance, but the attack continues unabated.

> 24. P - QKt4 !

Diversion of a major enemy piece.

> 24. . . . Kt - B1 ?

Black loses himself in the maze of combinations. The best bet was to return the material with 24. . . . Q x KtP; 25.

B - Kt5, Q x R ch; 26. Q x Q, Kt - B3 and while White should win in the long run Black's drawing chances are excellent.

25. Q - Kt4 !

Avoid exchanges!

25. . . .   Q - B6

The decisive combination is followed up by an even more decisive one.

DIAGRAM 330

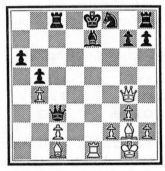

26. R x B ch !

Leads to mate or the loss of almost all the pieces.

26. . . .   K x R
27. B - Kt5 ch   K - Q3
28. Q - Q1 ch

Very pretty. The King out in the open is helpless against the Queen and Bishops. If, e.g., 28. . . . K - K3; 29. Q - Q5 mate !

28. . . .   K - B2
29. B - B4 ch   K - Kt3
30. Q - Q6 ch

In such positions it is almost essential for the attacker to continue checking.

> 30. . . .   K - R2
> 31. Q - K7 ch

Mate is nigh. If 31. . . . K - Kt3; 32. Q - Kt7 mate.

> 31. . . .   R - B2
> 32. B x R

He can afford to pause for digestive purposes.

> 32. . . .   Q - R8 ch

Necessary: if at once 32. . . . Kt - Kt3; 33. B - Kt6 dbl ch and mate next.

> 33. B - B1   Kt - Kt3
> 34. Q - B5 ch   K - Kt2
> 35. B - R5

Threatening Q - Kt6 ch and mate. On 35. . . . Q - B3; 36. B - Kt2 mates. Black is helpless.

> 35. . . .   R - KB1
> 36. Q - Kt6 ch

It is mate after 36. . . . K - R1; 37. Q - B6 ch, K - Kt1; 38. B - Kt6 ch, and so on. Black resigned.

GAME NO. 17
AVRO Tournament, 1938

WHITE: *Fine*   BLACK: *Flohr*

French Defense

1. P - K4, P - K3; 2. P - Q4, P - Q4; 3. Kt - QB3, B - Kt5; 4. P - K5, P - QB4; 5. B - Q2, Kt - K2; 6. Kt - B3, Kt - B4 ?; 7. P x P, B x P; 8. B - Q3 (threatening to split Black's Pawns), Kt - R5; 9. O - O, Kt - B3; 10. R - K1, P - KR3 (in order to castle).

DIAGRAM 331

White has an obvious advantage; how is he to proceed? He decides to undertake an attack against the King.

First Stage: Prevent Castling

11. Kt - R4　　　　　B - B1

Falls in with White's plan, but he had no choice. On **11. . . . B - K2; 12.** Kt x Kt, B x Kt; **13.** Q - Kt4 compels a weakening move because . . . O - O ? is refuted by B x P. After the text he hopes to be able to play . . . P - KKt3 and . . . B - Kt2, which would allow him to castle, but White has other intentions.

Second Stage: Open Lines

12. R - QB1

Preparing to bring this Rook into the game.

12. . . .　　　　　B - Q2

With the threat of . . . Kt x Kt ch and . . . Kt x P.

13. Kt x Kt

This exchange was unavoidable, but it also has the advantage of forcing Black's Queen to an unfavorable square.

13. . . .	Q x Kt
14. P - QB4	P x P
15. R x P	Q - Q1

Black is now threatening . . . P - QKt4. To answer this White goes over to the:

Third Stage: Mass against the Enemy King

16. Q - R5

Hitting at the weak point KB2. On 16. . . . P - QKt4 ? now 17. R - B4 is decisive, while 16. . . . P - KKt3 is refuted by 17. B x KtP.

16. . . .   Kt - K2

To reply to 17. R - B4 with . . . P - Kt3. He is also threatening . . . B x Kt.

Fourth Stage: Avoid Exchanges

17. R - Q4	P - KKt3
18. Q - B3	Q - B2
19. Kt - B3	Kt - B4
20. Kt - Kt5	Q - Kt3

The Queen remains harassed. On 20. . . . Q - B3 White wins with 21. Q x Q, P x Q; 22. Kt - B7 ch, K - Q1; 23. B x Kt, K x Kt; 24. B - R5 ch, K - B1; 25. R(K1) - Q1.

DIAGRAM 332

Fifth Stage: The Decisive Combination

White has come as far as he can with purely positional means; now the King must be driven out into the open with a sacrifice.

21. R x B !	K x R
22. P - KKt4	Kt - R5

An attempt to counterattack. After 22. . . . Kt - K2; 23. Q x BP White's pressure is irresistible.

23. Q x P ch	B - K2
24. B - Kt4	QR - K1

With the threat of . . . KR - B1.

25. B x B	R x B
26. Q - B6	P - R3

Hoping for 27. Q x R, Kt - B6 ch. But White has a speedier decision in mind.

27. R - Q1	P x Kt
28. B - K4 dis ch	Resigns

On 28. . . . K - B2 there would follow 29. Q x R (R8), R - Q2; 30. R - B1 ch.

The Castled King

THE attack against the castled King again follows the principles of opening lines and avoiding exchanges. In the process of opening lines, however, there are two special techniques that should be mastered. One is the *Pawn storm*, the other the *piece sacrifice*. The piece sacrifice does not differ essentially from that against the uncastled King, but the Pawn storm follows some other rules.

We have already seen that the attacker's prime desire is to open lines. However, it naturally makes a difference which lines are opened. The most important are the KKt and KR files, against the King castled on the K-side. When the Pawns in front of the defending K are unmoved, it is impossible to open one of these two vital files without a sacrifice. But when any one of the three Pawns (KB2, KKt2, KR2) are moved, one of the two files can be forced open.

A

WHITE CANNOT FORCE AN OPEN FILE WITH-OUT A SACRIFICE

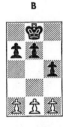

B

WHITE FORCES AN OPEN FILE WITH P-R5 FOL-LOWED BY P-Kt5

Thus in Diagram A, on *1.* P-R6, Black plays *1. . . .* P-Kt3, on *1.* P-Kt6, BP x P; *2.* BP x P, P-R3. With *1.* P-B6 White can force the Bishop file open, or sacrifice after *1. . . .* P x P; *2.* P-Kt6. Of course the success or failure of such a sacrifice depends on the rest of the position.

On the other hand in Diagram B White plays his P to R5, and then continues with P-Kt4-Kt5, which gives him the KKt file. Thus the rule is: *blockade the Pawn that has advanced, and attack it with the Pawn on the adjacent file.* In Diagram B if White plays instead P-Kt5 first, Black can keep the position closed with . . . P-R4.

C

D

WHITE FORCES AN OPEN
FILE WITH P-Kt5 FOL-
LOWED BY P-R5 OR
P-B5

WHITE FORCES AN OPEN
FILE WITH P-B5 FOL-
LOWED BY P-Kt5

In Diagram C the procedure is to advance the KtP to Kt5, then the KRP, but again not vice versa because Black can block with . . . P-Kt4. In Diagram D White plays the KBP to B5, then the KtP to Kt5.

E

F

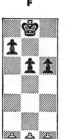

WHITE CANNOT FORCE
AN OPEN FILE WITH-
OUT A SACRIFICE

WHITE CAN ONLY FORCE
THE KB FILE OPEN WITH
P-Kt5 AND P-B5

As far as the Pawn play is concerned, the above holds true wherever the Pawns are. Thus in Diagram E they are on Black's third rank, yet White cannot force the KKt or KR files open without a sacrifice. In Diagram F likewise only the KB

G

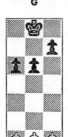

**WHITE CAN FORCE THE
KR FILE OPEN WITH
P - Kt 5 AND P - R 5**

file can be opened and in Diagram G again the KtP can advance to Kt5 and then the KR file can be opened.

H   I

   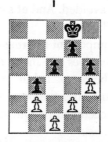

**WHITE CAN FORCE EI-
THER THE KKT OR
KR FILE OPEN**

**WHITE CANNOT FORCE A
FILE OPEN WITHOUT
A SACRIFICE**

If one Black Pawn is missing, naturally a vital file can easily be forced open. Thus in Diagram H White plays 1. P - B6: if then 1. . . . P x P; 2. P x P, if 1. . . . P - Kt3; 2. P x P and finally if Black does nothing P x P followed by P - R6 and P - Kt6.

With two Pawns against three a vital file cannot be forced open. Sometimes this happens artificially, as in Diagram I. Here the KKtP and KRP are to advance against three Pawns; White's KBP is blocked. White can do nothing.

The other method of forcing files open, by sacrifices, depends, of course, entirely on the position. We have already given a number of examples and shall give more in what follows.

Since Steinitz, it has been well known that an attack on the wings is not likely to succeed unless the center is under control. If, as is usually the case, it is not, it is best to lock it. Hence *closing the center in one way or another, either by appropriate exchanges or Pawn advances is a wise prelude to any wing attack.*

We can now draw up the general schema for the attack against the King. The central idea is to open the lines leading to the King. This can be done either by Pawn advances or a piece sacrifice or both. To assure its success it is wise to lock the center or to have it under control. Throughout exchanges will be avoided. And at some point a decisive combination can be available.

One important intermediate step must be mentioned. If the defender does not move the Pawns shielding the King, often he can be compelled to do so by threats of one kind or another.

In most cases the possession of an open KR or KKt file which can be occupied by Queen and Rook is tantamount to victory.

DIAGRAM 333

Thus in *Diagram 333* from Marshall-Marco, Paris, 1900, White to move wins at once with

1. Q - R3

If now *1. . . .* P - B4; *2.* Q - R7 ch wins a piece; if *1. . . .* Q - R4; *2.* Q - Kt3 wins the Queen. Black tried:

1. . . .	Kt - B3
2. P - B4	Q - K3
3. Q - R6 ch	K - B3
4. Q - Kt5 ch	

It is essential to keep Black's King confined.

4. . . .	K - Kt2
5 P - B5	Q - K4
6. P - B6 ch	Q x P
7. Q - R6 ch	K - Kt1
8. Q - R7 mate	

The mate conclusion is by no means unusual for such positions; the open file is simply more than the defender can take.

As we have mentioned, the most difficult position for the attacker to break through is the one where the Pawns defending the King have not been moved. In that case the attack has four stages:

1. Preparatory—here control of the center must be assured.

2. Massing material to force a weakness move (of Pawns defending the King).

3. Open lines by hitting at the weakness.

4. The decisive combination.

The following game is a model for this procedure.

GAME NO. 18

Paris, 1900

WHITE: *Pillsbury*   BLACK: *Marco*

Queen's Gambit Declined

1. P - Q4, P - Q4; *2.* P - QB4, P - K3; *3.* Kt - QB3, Kt - KB3; *4.* B - Kt5, B - K2; *5.* P - K3, O - O; *6.* Kt - B3, P - QKt3 (popular at that time, but rarely seen today); *7.* B - Q3, B - Kt2.

DIAGRAM 334

Although it is still the opening, Pillsbury here already conceives the idea of the attack.

First Stage: Preparatory—Control of the Center

8. P x P

To lock the center.

8. . . .   P x P

In modern times Tartakower has revived this variation with the move 8. . . . Kt x P, which is theoretically superior because it forces exchanges and keeps the center fluid.

9. Kt - K5

Again in the attempt to control the center.

| 9. . . . | QKt - Q2 |
| 10. P - B4 | P - B4 |

Black on the other hand ignores the center and gets in trouble. The correct defense is 10. . . . Kt x Kt; 11. BP x Kt, Kt - K5 or even 10. . . . Kt - K5 at once.

| 11. O - O | P - B5 ? |

Serenely he proceeds with the Q-side advance, which leads to his doom. 11. . . . Kt - K5 was still good enough.

| 12. B - B2 | P - QR3 |

Second Stage: Massing Material to Force a Weakness

| 13. Q - B3 |

Now the defense of . . . Kt - K5 will no longer be permitted.

| 13. . . . | P - Kt4 |
| 14. Q - R3 | P - Kt3 |

Allows the line-opening P - B5, but already he had no choice. For if now 14. . . . Kt x Kt; 15. B x Kt, Kt - Kt3; 16. B x B, Q x B; 17. P - B5, Kt - R1; 18. P - B6 and wins.

Third Stage: Open Lines

DIAGRAM 335

                    15. P - B5   P - Kt5
                    16. P x P

Black was figuring on 16. Kt - K2, Kt - K5, but White has other ideas.

                    16. . . .   RP x P

The knight cannot be taken: on 16. . . . P x Kt; 17. P x BP ch, K - R1; 18. R x Kt, Kt x R; 19. B x Kt ch mates.

                    17. Q - R4   P x Kt
                    18. Kt x Kt   Q x Kt
                    19. R x Kt

Stronger than 19. B x Kt. We are still in the line-opening stage.

                    19. . . .   P - R4

Naturally 19. . . . B x R ?; 20. B x B leads to mate.

                    20. QR - KB1   R - R3

Fourth Stage: The Decisive Combination

                    21. B x P

Black was hoping for 21. R x R, B x B; 22. Q x B, B x R; 23. B x P, P x B; 24. Q x KtP ch, Q - Kt2; 25. Q x B, R x R ch; 26. K x R, P - B7 and White loses.

                    21. . . .   P x B
                    22. R x R ch   B x R

White now announced mate in six:

                    23. R x B ch   K x R
                    24. Q - R8 ch   K - B2
                    25. Q - R7 ch   K - B1

Or 25. . . . K - K1; 26. Q - Kt8 mate.

26.	Q x Q	any
27.	B - R6 ch	K - Kt1
28	Q - Kt7 mate	

In a previous chapter we saw many examples of mating combinations involving the sacrifice of Pawns, pieces, or more. *Diagram 336*, from Pilnik-Adams, Hollywood, 1945, is another such case. White has been unable to force a Pawn weakness, but wins anyhow with:

| 1. Kt - B6 | Q - Q1 |

DIAGRAM 336

On 1. . . . P x Kt; 2. P x P followed by Q - Kt4 leads to mate.

2.	Q - R5	P x Kt
3.	P - Kt6	BP x P
4.	R x KtP	Q - K1
5.	QR - KKt1	Q - B2
6.	R(Kt6) - Kt4 !	

The Queen must give up her hold on KKt1, and then mate follows. Black resigned.

Sometimes mere pressure along a file or diagonal is enough to bring about the defender's downfall. Thus in *Diagram 337,*

DIAGRAM 337

from Lasker-Reshevsky, Nottingham, 1936, the strong hold Black has on the long diagonal is decisive. Black played:

1. . . .	Kt - Kt4
2. P x P	P x P
3. B x P	

He can only choose among different ways of losing. If 3. Kt - K1, Kt - R6 ch; 4. K - R1, Kt - B5; 5. Q - B3, Q x Q; 6. P x Q, B x P ch; 7. Kt x B, Kt x B; 8. R - B2, Kt x B; 9. R x Kt, R x P, and Black with two extra Pawns has an elementary win in the end game.

3. . . .	Kt x Kt ch
4. P x Kt	Q - Kt4 ch

After 5. K - R1, Q - Kt5 wins White's Queen.

Weakening Pawn Moves

But in a great many cases, the majority, in fact, the unweakened King position is unassailable. Pawn advances lead to nothing, piece sacrifices are unsound. It is well to remember that the successful attack is made possible by weaknesses in the enemy position; no weaknesses, no attack. We turn now to these weaknesses, i.e., moves of Pawns guarding the King, and the various typical possibilities that arise for each.

Black's Pawn at KR3

This Pawn move allows two possible combinative inroads: first along the KKt file via a Pawn storm, second along the

diagonal QKt1 - KR7, by means of a massing of the Q and B.

The following game illustrates both of these; it is instructive because of Black's mistakes.

GAME NO. 19

Folkestone, 1933

WHITE: *Fine*   BLACK: *Thorvaldsson*

Queen's Gambit Declined

1. P - Q4, Kt - KB3; 2. P - QB4, P - K3; 3. Kt - QB3, P - Q4; 4. B - Kt5, QKt - Q2; 5. P x P, P x P; 6. P - K3, B - K2; 7. B - Q3, P - B3; 8. Q - B2, P - KR3 ? It is surprising yet true that after this weakening move Black is strategically lost.

DIAGRAM 338

White's plan is now clear: to storm the K-side with P - KKt4 - Kt5.

9. B - KB4	O - O
10. O - O - O	

If he castled short the advance of the Pawns would endanger his own safety. So he removes his King to the other side to have full freedom for the attack. In so doing White exposes himself to a counterattack on the Q-side, but that is easily warded off.

10. . . .	P - QKt4
11. Kt - B3	P - QR4
12. P - KKt4	

A typical Pawn sacrifice. If now 12. . . . Kt x P; 13. QR - KKt1, P - R4; 14. P - KR3, Kt(Kt5) - B3; 15. Kt - Kt5, Kt - Kt3; 16. P - B3, P - Kt5; 17. Q - Kt2 !, Kt - K1 (if 17. . . . P x Kt; 18. Kt - K6); 18. Kt - K2, and White's attack is overwhelming; the immediate threat of Kt - R7 can be parried only by 18. . . . B x Kt when 19. B x B, Q - Q3 (if 19. . . . P - B3; 20. B - R6 and Q - B6); 20. Kt - B4 followed by Kt x P is conclusive.

12. . . .	Kt - K1

Anything to avoid opening the KKt file.

13. P - KR4	B - Q3
14. P - R5	

Threatening of course P - Kt5.

14. . . .	B x B
15. P x B	P - B3

DIAGRAM 339

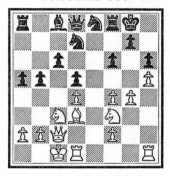

Now White can win in either of two ways: by P - Kt5, after safeguarding the Knight (for if *16.* P - Kt5 ? at once, BP x P, and the Pawn cannot recapture because the Knight is loose), or Kt - R4, as played.

16. Kt - KR4   P - KB4

Desperation. The weaknesses on the diagonal make Black's position untenable. If *16.* . . . R - B2; *17.* B - Kt6, R - K2; *18.* B - R7 ch, K - B2 (or *18.* . . . K - R1; *19.* Kt - Kt6 ch, K x B; *20.* Kt x R dis ch); *19.* Kt - Kt6, R - K3; *20.* P - B5, R - Q3; *21.* QR - K1, Kt - Kt3; *22.* R - K3, R - R2; *23.* R(R1) - K1 with decisive threats.

17. QR - Kt1

The open lines are more important than the Pawn.

17. . . .   Kt(Q2) - B3

If instead *17.* . . . P x P; *18.* B - R7 ch, K - R1; *19.* Kt - Kt6 ch, K x B; *20.* Kt x R ch, K - Kt1; *21.* Kt - Kt6 wins the exchange and preserves the attack.

18. Kt - Kt6   R - B2
19. Kt - K5   R - B2

20. B x BP	B x B
21. Q x B	Q - B1
22. Q - Kt6	

Naturally avoiding exchanges. The game is now decided by the routine advance of the Pawns.

22. . . .	Kt - R2
23. P - Kt5	Kt - B1

If 23. . . . P x P first White can even sacrifice his Queen: 24. P x P, Kt - B1; 25. P - R6, Kt x Q; 26. P - R7 ch, K - R1; 27. Kt x Kt mate.

24. Q - Q3	Q - K3
25. P - B5	Q - Q3
26. P - B6	KtP x P
27. P x RP dis ch	

Equally good is 27. P x BP dis ch, K - R1; 28. Q - Kt3, Q - K3; 29. P - B7.

27. . . .	K - R1
28. Q - Kt3	Q - K3
29. Kt - Kt6 ch	Kt x Kt
30. P x Kt	

There is now no defense against the Pawn advance, so Black resigned.

The Pawn at KR3 also gives rise to a piece sacrifice when the other pieces are aggressively placed. A typical position is that shown in *Diagram 340*, from Leonhardt-Spielmann, Nuremberg, 1906. Black plays:

DIAGRAM 340

1. ...	O - O - O

inviting P x B. White should have declined the sacrifice with
Kt - QKt5, removing Black's most dangerous attacking piece,
in which case we could not have included this example in
our book. But he took, so we can.

2. P x B	Kt x KtP

Threatening to win with . . . B - R7 ch; K - R1, Kt x QP;
Kt x Kt, B any dis ch and . . . Q - R7 mate.

3. P - KKt3

A forced weakening: if instead *3.* R - K1, B - R7 ch; *4.* K - B1,
B - K4; *5.* B - QKt5, Kt x QP; *6.* Kt x Kt, R x Kt; *7.* Q - B2, Kt -
R7 ch; *8.* K - Kt1, R - KR5; *9.* P - B3 (or *9.* P - B4, Kt - Kt5),
Kt x P ch; *10.* P x Kt, R - R8 ch and wins.

3. ...	Q - R6

The threat is now . . . P - KR4 - R5 with a decisive opening
of the KR file. And if *4.* R - K1, B x P; *5.* P x B, Q x P ch leads
to mate next move.

4. Kt - K4

Hoping to relieve himself with Kt - Kt5.

	4. . . .	B - K2

A powerful retreat: now there is a new threat of . . .
Kt x QP.

5. B - K3	P - B4
6. Kt(K4) - Q2	Kt x B
7. P x Kt	Q x P ch
8. K - R1	R - Q3
9. Kt - R2	R - R3
10. B - R5	

Desperation.

10. . . .	B - Q3
11. R - B4	B x R
12. P x B	Q - R5

White must lose another piece, and still no relief in sight,
so he resigned.

Note that in a great many of these examples the attack does
not lead to mate but to a decisive material gain—which of
course for all practical purposes is just as good.

Black's Pawn at KKt3

In this position, which is usually accompanied by a fianchetto
of Black's KB, for otherwise the Black squares become hope-

lessly weak, White again has several attacking
setups. 1. He can try to force an open KB file
with P - KB4 - B5. 2. He can try to force an open
KR file with P - KR4 - R5. 3. He can try to play
on the weakness of the Black squares by aiming
at the exchange of Black's KB.

Our next game is a model illustration of the technique of
attack involving the opening of the KR file.

GAME NO. 20

Havana, 1892

WHITE: *Steinitz*   BLACK: *Tchigorin*

Ruy Lopez

1. P - K4, P - K4; *2.* Kt - KB3, Kt - QB3; *3.* B - Kt5, Kt - B3; *4.* P - Q3 (one of Steinitz's favorite variations: he locks the center to be able to attack on the wings), P - Q3; *5.* P - B3, P - KKt3 (this fianchetto defense is weak, but Tchigorin was unfamiliar with the principles of sound play in such positions—they were still being formulated and elaborated on by Steinitz and Tarrasch); *6.* QKt - Q2, B - Kt2.

DIAGRAM 341

In this procedure, which was still pretty much of a mystery to his contemporaries, Steinitz evolves a plan of attacking on the K-side. To do this he must, however, keep the center under control and castle long to keep his KR mobile. The attacking procedure can now be divided into four stages.

First Stage: Preparatory—Control of the Center

7. Kt - B1   O - O

Naturally Tchigorin did not understand what he was letting himself in for. A modern player, wise in the ways of such positions, would at least wait until White had declared which side he was going to castle on, and then follow suit.

8. B - R4

Avoiding exchanges.

8. . . .   Kt - Q2 ?

Again ignoring the center completely.

9.	Kt - K3	Kt - B4
10.	B - B2	Kt - K3

After all this horsing around Black might almost give up.

Second Stage: Line Opening

11. P - KR4

Steinitz on the contrary knows what he is after.

11. . . .   Kt - K2 ?

The least he could have done was keep the file closed for a while with . . . P - KR3.

12. P - R5   P - Q4

One gets tired of question marks. If a break was necessary he should rather have tried . . . P - KB4.

13.	P x KtP	BP x P
14.	P x P	Kt x P
15.	Kt x Kt	Q x Kt
16.	B - Kt3	Q - B3

Although the center has been opened White still has control of it.

17. Q - K2   B - Q2

White controls two important lines: the diagonal QR2 to KKt8, and the KR file. To exploit his advantage he goes to the:

Third Stage: Massing of Material

18. B - K3	K - R1
19. O - O - O	QR - K1
20. Q - B1	

A profound trap.

20. . . .	P - QR4

Black does not see it, but there was no defense anyhow.

21. P - Q4	

More line opening.

21. . . .	P x P
22. Kt x P	B x Kt

Already the air is ripe with combinations. If 22. . . . Kt x Kt; 23. R x P ch crashes through for a mate: 23. . . . K x R; 24. Q - R1 ch, etc.

23. R x B	Kt x R

In despair. Now comes the:

Fourth Stage: The Decisive Combination

DIAGRAM 342

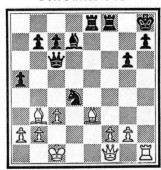

24. R x P ch	K x R
25. Q - R1 ch	K - Kt2
26. B - R6 ch	K - B3
27. Q - R4 ch	K - K4
28. Q x Kt ch	K - B4
29. Q - B4 mate	

If the defender is unable to keep the file closed, passive play is generally useless. Here is another model game.

GAME NO. 21
New York, 1934

WHITE: *Horowitz*   BLACK: *Fine*

Dutch Defense

1. P - Q4, P - KB4; *2.* Kt - KB3, Kt - KB3; *3.* P - KKt3, P - K3; *4.* B - Kt2, B - K2; *5.* O - O, O - O; *6.* P - B4, P - Q3; *7.* Kt - B3, Q - K1; *8.* Q - B2, Kt - B3; *9.* P - QR3 ? (correct is 9. P - Q5 with advantage to White), P - K4 (consolidation of the center before the flank attack is begun); *10.* P - Q5, Kt - Q1; *11.* P - QKt4, B - Q2; *12.* Kt - Q2, Q - R4; *13.* P - B3 (to set up a Pawn chain, but Black now gets the initiative), Kt - B2; *14.* P - K4, P - B5; *15.* P - Kt4.

DIAGRAM 343

Black now blockades this Pawn and opens a file in the theoretically prescribed manner.

15. . . . Q - R5; *16.* Kt - Kt3, P - KR4; *17.* P x P (unpleasant, but on *17.* P - R3, Kt - Kt4 decides), Q x P; *18.* R - B2, Kt - Kt4 (Black now wins by the simple expedient of massing material on the open files); *19.* Kt - Q2, K - B2; *20.* Kt - B1, R - R1; *21.* Kt - K2, Q - R5; *22.* Q - Q2 (White is living in cramped quarters), Kt - R4; *23.* Kt - B3, R - R3; *24.* R - K1 (hoping to get some relief with Q - K1), R - Kt3 (which is promptly stopped); *25.* K - R1, R - R1; *26.* R - B2.

DIAGRAM 344

With such an accumulation of material the decisive combination comes of itself.

26. . . .	Kt - Kt6 ch
27. K - Kt1	Kt - R6 ch
28. B x Kt	Kt - K7 dbl ch
29. K - R1	R - Kt8 mate

Against the Pawn at KKt3, the attacker can also operate by playing to open the KB file. Although this is as a rule somewhat less effective than opening the KR file, it is still often devastating. *Diagram 345,* from Evans-Santasiere, New York,

DIAGRAM 345

1951, is an excellent illustration of some of the combinative possibilities. White won with:

1. R x P !   K x R

He must accept: *1. . . .* Q x P; *2.* Q - R3 is worse.

2. Q - R3 ch   K - Kt1
3. P - B6

With all kinds of threats, particularly Kt - R6 ch, and P x B. Black in desperation tried:

3. . . .   Q x Kt

and the rest was easy:

4. Q x Q, B x P; *5.* P x B, R - K8 ch; *6.* K - B2, R(B1) - K1; *7.* P - KR4, R(K1) - K5; *8.* Q - Kt5, R(K5) - K7 ch; *9.* K - Kt3, Kt - Q3; *10.* K - R2, Kt - K5; *11.* Q x QP, Kt x BP; *12.* Q - Q8 ch, Kt - K1; *13.* B - Kt2, R x R; *14.* B x R, P - B3; *15.* P - Q5, R - K5; *16.* P - Q6, R x P ch; *17.* K - Kt3, R - K5; *18.* P - Q7, and Black resigned.

Black's Pawn at KB3

The attack here is usually less dangerous than that when the weakness is at KKt3 or KR3, because the KR file is kept closed.

However, the technique is the same: blockade the KBP, and open a file via P - KKt4 - Kt5. This differs in no essential respect from the case with the P at KR3, so we need not give further examples.

Black's Pawns Unmoved, but Other Targets Available

The unmoved Pawns, as we have mentioned, are the hardest defense of all to breach. Unlike the previous cases, the advance

of the Pawns yields no vital open file without a sacrifice, and naturally the effectiveness of a sacrifice depends on the total configuration of the position. If there is a further target, such as a P at K3, White can generally force open the KB file, with good effect, but if the position is otherwise satisfactory, no real attack can be built up.

Our next game is a model for the attack against the three unmoved Pawns, made possible by the presence of a target at K3.

GAME NO. 22

Debreczin, 1925

WHITE: *Vajda*   BLACK: *Kmoch*

Sicilian Defense

1. P - K4, P - QB4; *2.* Kt - KB3, Kt - QB3; *3.* P - Q4, P x P; *4.* Kt x P, Kt - B3; *5.* Kt - QB3, P - Q3; *6.* B - K2, P - K3; *7.* O - O, B - K2; *8.* B - K3, O - O; *9.* Q - Q2, P - QR3; *10.* P - QR4, Q - B2; *11.* Kt - Kt3, P - QKt3; *12.* P - B4, B - Kt2; *13.* B - B3, QR - Kt1.

DIAGRAM 346

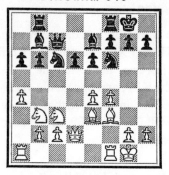

Black has a cramped but solid position. White builds up the attack now in a most ingenious manner.

> *14.* P - Kt4   KR - Q1

Hoping for counterplay in the center.

> *15.* Q - B2   B - R1
> *16.* P - Kt5   Kt - K1
> *17.* Kt - K2

The immediate advance P - B5 would merely give Black an unassailable position for his Kt at K4. White builds up his position further.

> *17.* . . . .   Kt - Kt5
> *18.* Kt(K2) - Q4   P - Q4 ?

A serious mistake, which increases the strength of White's attack. Necessary was *18.* . . . . P - K4; *19.* Kt - B5, B - B1; *20.* QR - B1, P - Q4, and Black has counterplay. Note how this variation illustrates theory: *an attack on the wing can best be met by a counterattack in the center.*

> *19.* P - K5   Kt - QB3

The blockade attempt *19. . . . P - Kt3* would of course be refuted by P - KR4 - R5.

20. B - K2

Gaining an important tempo by the attack on the QRP.

20. . . .	Kt x Kt
21. Kt x Kt	P - QR4

DIAGRAM 347

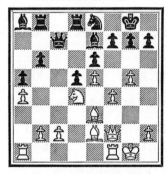

22. P - B5

The decisive break-through is made possible by a simple combination: if *22. . . .* Q x KP; *23.* B - KB4, Q - K5; *24.* B - Q3, Q x Kt; *25.* Q x Q, B - B4; *26.* Q x B, P x Q; *27.* B x R.

22. . . .	P x P
23. Q x P	B - B4
24. P - K6	

Line opening.

24. . . .	Kt - Q3
25. P x P ch	Q x P
26. Q - R3	Q - K2
27. B - Kt4	

Threatening B - K6 ch, K - R1; P - Kt6, P - R3; B x RP.

27. . . .	B x Kt
28. B - K6 ch	K - R1
29. B x B	R - K1
30. Q - R6	

Elegant defense and attack combined. The B is held indirectly and he threatens P - Kt6.

30. . . .	Kt - K5

Ingenious defense: if 31. P - Kt6, Q - Kt4 ch; and if 31. R - B7, Q x P ch; 32. Q x Q, Kt x Q; 33. B x P ch, K - Kt1, and Black wins.

31. R - B5	R - Kt2

Defending the KtP in order to be able to take the B.

32. P - Kt6	Kt - B3
33. R x Kt !	P x R

Or 33. . . . P x Q; 34. R - B8 mate.

34. B - B7	Resigns

When the Pawns are not evenly balanced, a break-through in the center can be the most vigorous prosecution of the attack. Here is a model example.

GAME NO. 23
New York, 1932

WHITE: *Fine*   BLACK: *Kevitz*

Queen's Pawn Game

1. P - Q4, Kt - KB3; *2.* P - QB4, P - K3; *3.* Kt - KB3, P - B4 ?; *4.* P - Q5, P x P; *5.* P x P, P - Q3; *6.* Kt - B3, P - QR3; *7.* P - QR4 (prevents the liberating . . . P - QKt4), B - K2; *8.* Kt - Q2, O - O; *9.* P - K4, R - K1; *10.* B - Q3, QKt - Q2; *11.* P - B4, P - QKt3;

12. O - O, Q - B2; 13. Kt - B4, B - B1; 14. Q - B3, R - Kt1; 15.
P - QKt3, P - QKt4; 16. P x P, P x P; 17. Kt - R5, B - R3; 18.
Kt - B6, R - Kt3.

DIAGRAM 348

White obviously has an overwhelming position, but how is
he to continue? The break P - K5 will probably be decisive, so
he sacrifices to make it possible.

19. R x B	R x R
20. B x P	R - Kt3
21. B - B4	Kt - Kt1

Hoping to free himself with exchanges.

| 22. Kt - Kt5 | Q - Kt2 |
| 23. P - K5 | |

Finally!

| 23. . . . | Kt(B3) - Q2 |

Countersacrifices do not help: if 23. . . . Kt x QP; 24.
Kt - R5, Q - R3; 25. Q x Kt wins.

| 24. Kt - R5 | Q - B1 |
| 25. B - Kt2 | Q - Q1 |

To take the P would open the KB file with devastating effect.

	26. Kt - B6	Q - B1
	27. P - K6 !	Kt - B3

There is nothing better: after 27. . . . P x P; 28. P x P the discovered checks are killing.

	28. B x Kt	P x B
	29. Q - Kt4 ch	B - Kt2

Or 29. . . . K - R1; 30. P x P, Q x Q; 31. P x R(Q).

	30. Kt - K7 ch	R x Kt
	31. P x P ch	K x P
	32. Q x Q	Resigns

XI. *The Art of Defense*

Although to most players the attack is more attractive, the ability to defend is just as essential a part of one's equipment. To be able to attack well actually one must foresee the best possible defenses that the opponent can put up, which means that a good attacker is almost by definition also a good defender. Of course, temperament may enter here, so that a man who is used to attacking feels uncomfortable when he is forced on the defensive; what that means is that he has the ability but not the desire. Then too, as we shall see, the best type of defense is frequently a counterattack, so that the two go hand in hand.

The general principles of defense are simply the general principles of attack in reverse. The attacker wants open lines, so the defender keeps vital lines closed. The attacker avoids exchanges, the defender encourages them. The attacker wants to keep the enemy position cramped, the defender wants freedom. The attacker wants to induce weaknesses, the defender avoids weaknesses, especially in the area of the King.

We can sum up the philosophy of the *attacker* by the statement that *he seeks to open lines and find a decisive breakthrough combination.* By contrast, the philosophy of the *defender* can be summed up in the statement *that he seeks to keep lines closed and defends only against direct threats.*

This last point, as we shall see, is the key to successful defense: defend only against direct threats. Too often we hear a player say he tried this or that move "just in case White tried an attack." The result was a weakening that really induced an attack. This kind of reasoning is prevalent even among masters. Since the attacker can prevail only against weaknesses, any voluntary weakening will merely facilitate his plans.

If we now turn to the more specific varieties of defensive play, we find that there are essentially three types: (1) counterattack, (2) philosophical defense, (3) useless defense.

The *counterattack* is an attack either in the center or on the other side of the board—here usually the enemy attack is conceded to be too strong to be held by a philosophical defense, and a counterattack is undertaken with the idea that it may succeed first. Clearly in this case timing is of the essence.

The *philosophical defense* is one adopted in an inferior or difficult position, where the defender's only line of play is to beat off the attack; he has no counterattack. This kind of defense is extremely difficult and often requires iron nerves and infinite patience. Its keynote is the elaboration of the main general principles of defense: concentrate only on the direct threats.

The *useless defense* is a passive defense in a situation where there is no real hope. Examples of this have been seen in Games 7 and 12.

Of these three forms of defense, the counterattack is preferable when there is a choice. But it should be remembered that often there is no choice, and a philosophical defense must be resorted to.

The Counterattack

As WE have pointed out, the counterattack is generally the most effective means of defense. A few examples will help to clarify in greater detail the principles involved.

Diagram 349 is from a game Lasker-Janowski, match, 1910. Here White seems to be lost: the pin on his Kt at Q4 is much

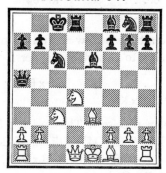

too strong. Appearances are correct here; White is lost, but he speculates on a counterattack that saves the day.

1. P - QR3	Kt - R3 ?

Now Janowski begins to falter; he becomes too fancy. The simplest way to win was *1*. . . . B - QB4; *2*. P - QKt4, B x Kt; *3*. P x Q (if *3*. B x B, Q - KKt4; *4*. Kt - Kt5, P - QR3 wins a piece), B x Kt ch; *4*. B - Q2, R x B; *5*. Q x R, B x Q ch; *6*. K x B, Kt x P, and the end game is elementary.

It is a curious psychological fact that the attacker often goes astray when there is more than one way to win; it is as if overwhelmed by his good fortune he does not know which sweet to taste first, and in the end loses them all.

The text also wins, but not as precisely as . . . B - QB4.

2. P - QKt4	Q - K4
3. Kt(B3) - Kt5	

Seizing the opportunity for a counterattack. Black already has traps to avoid: if *3*. . . . P - R3 ?; *4*. Q - B1, P x Kt; *5*. Kt x Kt, P x Kt; *6*. Q x P ch, Q - B2; *7*. Q - R6 ch, Q - Kt2; *8*. R - B1 ch, and White now has an attack, which may really turn out to be a sufficient compensation for the piece; it is already strong enough virtually to guarantee him a draw.

3. . . .	Kt - B4
4. R - B1	

White's counterattack is now in full swing. Black wins a Pawn, but is exposed to all sorts of dangers.

4. . . .	Kt x B
5. P x Kt !	

White must play precisely. The enticing 5. Kt x P ch loses after 5. . . . K - B2; 6. Kt(Q4) - Kt5 ch, K - Kt3; 7. R x Kt ch, P x R; 8. Q x R ch, K - Kt2; 9. Kt x P, B x P ch; 10. P x B, Kt x P dbl ch; 11. K - Q2, R x Q ch.

5. . . .	Q x P ch
6. B - K2	B - K2

Black has his troubles. Various alternatives have been suggested, but none is an improvement. If, e.g., 6. . . . P - QR3; 7. Kt - R7 ch, K - B2; 8. Kt(R7) x Kt, P x Kt; 9. Kt x B ch, P x Kt; 10. Q - B2 with an excellent game.

7. R - B3	

Again the best. If instead 7. Kt x P ch ?, K - Kt1; 8. Kt x Kt ch, P x Kt; 9. Kt x P ch, K - Kt2; 10. Kt x R ch, R x Kt; 11. Q - B2, R - QB1 and wins.

7. . . .	B - R5 ch ?

After this Black definitely loses. The best line was 7. . . . Q x R ch; 8. Kt x Q, Kt x Kt, when with R, B, and P for the Queen Black still has a strong attack. But this is of course a far cry from what he had before.

8. P - Kt3	Q - K5
9. O - O !	

Threatening B - B3.

9. . . .	B - B3

DIAGRAM 350

White now comes into his own.

10. R x B

Obvious and strong. He had to take the pressure off his Kt at Q4.

10. . . .	P x R
11. B - B3	Q - K4
12. Kt x P ch	K - B2
13. Kt(R7) x Kt	P x Kt
14. R x P ch	K - Kt1
15. R - Kt6 ch	K - B1

He must allow the White Q to get in, for if *15.* . . . K - R2; *16.* R - Kt7 ch followed by Q - R4 ch leads to mate.

16. Q - B1 ch	K - Q2
17. Kt x B	P x Kt
18. R - Kt7 ch	K - K1
19. B - B6 ch	

Now *19.* . . . K - B1; *20.* Q - R6 ch is mate next move, so Black resigned.

In our next illustrative example we see in action the defense that demolished the dreaded Evans' Gambit. This defense has a sprinkling of the philosophical, but is primarily a counter-attack.

Evans' Gambit

1. P - K4, P - K4; *2.* Kt - KB3, Kt - QB3; *3.* B - B4, B - B4; *4.* P - QKt4, B x P; *5.* P - B3, B - B4; *6.* O - O, P - Q3; *7.* P - Q4, B - Kt3 (Lasker's Defense—see *Diagram 351*).

DIAGRAM 351

In this position White can regain his P with *8.* P x P, but that involves the exchange of Queens which means good-by to his attack. He takes a different tack.

8. P - QR4   Kt - B3

Following common-sense principles of counterattack: the pressure on the wings is met by counterpressure in the center.

9. B - QKt5

Threatening to win a piece with P - R5.

9. . . .   P - QR3
10. B x Kt ch   P x B

11. P - R5	B - R2
12. P x P	

Hoping now for 12. . . . P x P; 13. Q x Q ch, K x Q; 14. Kt x P winning another P.

12. . . .	Kt x P
13. Q - K2	

Here he could have recovered the Pawn with 13 Q - R4, but he continues to play for an attack.

13. . . .	P - Q4
14. Kt - Q4	

To play P - B3.

14. . . .	Kt x QBP
15. Kt x Kt	B x Kt
16. Q - Q3	P - QB4

Black now goes over to the counterattack proper.

17. Q - Kt3	B - K3

The open KKt file is worth more than a Pawn.

18. B - Kt5	Q - Q2
19. QR - B1	P - KB3

Opening the KKt file anyhow.

20. P x P	P x P
21. B - B4	R - KKt1
22. Q - B3	O - O - O
23. KR - K1	

Threatening Q - K2.

23. . . .	P - B5
24. Q - K2	B - KB4
25. Q - R2	

Allows a decisive combination, but White was lost in any case.

$$25. \ldots \qquad R \times P \text{ ch}$$
$$26. \text{ K - R1}$$

Or 26. K x R, B - R6 ch; 27. K - Kt1, Q - Kt5 ch; 28. B - Kt3, Q - B6 and mates.

$$26. \ldots \qquad R \times P$$

White could not avoid heavy material loss and resigned.

In many cases the attacker weakens himself in some way in order to continue the offensive; the counterattacker of course bears this in mind, and looks for the weaknesses that have been created. The following game is a model example.

GAME NO. 25
Noordwijk, 1938

WHITE: *Spielmann*   BLACK: *Keres*

French Defense

1. P - K4, P - K3; 2. P - Q4, P - Q4; 3. Kt - QB3, Kt - KB3; 4. P - K5, KKt - Q2; 5. P - B4, P - QB4; 6. P x P, Kt - QB3; 7. P - QR3, B x P; 8. Q - Kt4, P - KKt3 ! (Black relies on the pressure exerted by his KB to give him sufficient counterplay); 9. Kt - B3, P - QR3; 10. B - Q3, P - QKt4 (he disregards the K-side, and seeks counterplay on the other wing); 11. P - Kt4, B - R2.

The lines are drawn: White's attack is on the K-side, Black's on the Q-side and in the center.

$$12. \text{ P - KR4} \qquad \text{P - KR4}$$

Up to this point Black has made moves on the K-side only in response to direct threats. The text also follows that policy: White was threatening to secure a valuable open file with P - R5.

$$13. \text{ Q - Kt3}$$

White is now threatening B x P.

13. . . .   Q - K2

which is promptly stopped, for if *14.* B x P, P x B; *15.* Q x P ch,
Q - B2.

14. P - B5 !?

A tempting move: if now *14.* . . . KtP x P; *15.* B x P, P x B;
16. Kt x P, Q - Q1; *17.* P - K6 with a decisive attack.

DIAGRAM 352

14. . . .   B - Kt1 !

Counterattack. Kmoch called this the "strongest, most surprising, and most effective move in the whole tournament."
If now *15.* B - KB4, KtP x P; *16.* B x P ?, P x B; *17.* Kt x P, Q - K3,
and White has no compensation for the piece.

15. P x KtP	Kt(Q2) x P
16. P x P ch	Q x P

Suddenly Black's attack is in full swing; the immediate
threat is . . . Kt x B ch.

17. Kt - Kt5	Q - B3
18. R - B1 ?	

Loses immediately. Necessary was 18. B - Q2, Kt - B5, but the initiative has passed to Black.

| 18. . . . | Kt - Kt5 ! |

Wins a piece, for if 19. R x Q, B x Q ch. The remainder is simple:

19. Q - B3	Q x Kt ch
20. K - Q1	Q - Kt2
21. Q - K2	R - B1

Always the most aggressive defense; if 22. Kt x P, R x R ch.

22. R x R ch	K x R
23. Kt x P ch	B x Kt
24. Q x B	Kt - B7 ch
25. K - K1	Kt x B ch

White resigns, because after 26. P x Kt, Q x R, his Bishop is pinned, so that he has no play left at all.

When the players have castled on different sides of the board, usually a wild melee ensues, in which both attack and counterattack at the same time. *Diagram 353*, from Fine-

DIAGRAM 353

Alekhine, Warsaw, 1935, serves as a model. Here Black has an advantage in that the White Pawns have been weakened

(P at KR3); however, White has some compensation in the two Bishops. The game continued:

1. P - QKt3	P - KKt4
2. P - B4	QR - Kt1
3. P - B5	B - B5
4. P - QKt4	

A routine sacrificial idea.

4. . . .	Kt x KtP

Black's decision to accept is based on the fact that he can scarcely avoid a line opening anyhow with P - QKt5 - Kt6, so he might as well be a P ahead.

5. Q - Kt3	Kt(Kt5) - B3
6. B x B	

Cedes the open Kt file because the point KKt2 is well defended.

6. . . .	P x B
7. QR - Kt1	K - R1
8. R - Kt2	Kt - B4
9. R(K1) - Kt1	R - Kt1
10. Q - R4	

White's counterattack is now in full swing.

10. . . .	P - B3

On 10. . . . Q - R4; 11. Q - Q1 preserves the pressure.

11. B - Q3	Kt(B4) - K2
12. R - Kt6	R(R1) - Kt1
13. B - Kt5	R - Kt2
14. R - Kt3	R(Kt1) - Kt1
15. K - B1	

Again in the spirit of counterattack. After 15. B - B1, Kt - Q1; 16. R - R3, Kt - B1 White must retreat.

15. . . .	R x P
16. B x Kt	Kt x B
17. R x P	Q x R
18. R x Q	K x R
19. Q - B2	

Aiming at the K-side Pawns.

19. . . .	R(Kt7) - Kt2
20. Q - Q2	P - K4
21. P x P	P x P
22. Q x P	

Thanks to his actively placed Queen White has enough counterplay to draw.

22. . . .	R - Q1
23. Q - Kt3 ch	K - B2
24. Q - K6	R - Q8 ch
25. K - K2	R(Kt2) - Kt2
26. Q x RP	

The spirit of the defense here is counterattack all the way through. The passed RP will now be a problem to Black.

26. . . .	R - QB8
27. Q - B8	

Again preventing . . . P - K5. And if 27. . . . R - B7 ch; 28. K - B1, R x RP; 29. P - R4 is very strong.

27. . . .	R - K2
28. Kt - Kt5	

So that if 28. . . . R x P; 29. Kt - K6 ch.

28. . . .	Kt - Q5 ch
29. K - Q2	R - B7 ch
30. K - Q3	R - Q2

Threatening to win the Queen with . . . Kt - K3 dis ch. It is actually hard to see a defense, for if *31*. K - K4 ?, R - K7 ch.

31. Kt - K4

Still the counterattack. If now *31*. . . . Kt - K3 ch; *32*. Q - Q6 ch, R x Q; *33*. P x R ch, K any; *34*. K x R with a won ending for White.

31. . . .	R - B7
32. K - Q2	Kt - Kt6 dbl ch
33. K - K2	Kt - Q5 ch
34. K - Q2	Kt - Kt6 dbl ch

Drawn by perpetual check

Neither side can afford to vary. If Black tries to win with . . . R - R8, Kt - Q6 is too strong, while if White tries to win with Kt - Q6 (instead of K - Q2), R x BP decides.

Our last example showed how the counterattack can be used to force a draw. This is an extremely important weapon for the tournament player, where every half point counts in the final total. We give a few more illustrations.

Diagram 354 is a variation of the Sicilian Defense; the con-

DIAGRAM 354

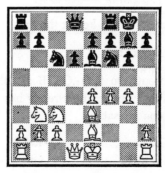

tinuation here is from the game Alekhine-Botvinnik, Nottingham, 1936. White has a threatening attack on the K-side; in accordance with theory Black counters with a break in the center.

1. . . .	P - Q4

Which turns out to be a temporary sacrifice.

2. P - B5	B - B1
3. P x QP	Kt - Kt5
4. P - Q6	

He aims for maximum mobility. The attempt to hold on to the P with 4. P x P, RP x P; 5. B - B3 fails against 5. . . . Kt x Kt !; 6. B x Kt, B x B; 7. Q x B, B x Kt ch; 8. P x B, Kt x P ch; 9. K - B2, Kt x R; 10. R x Kt, Q x P, and Black is better.

4. . . .	Q x P
5. B - B5	Q - B5

A piece sacrifice, in the spirit of the counterattack. If instead 5. . . . Q x Q ch; 6. R x Q, Kt - B3; 7. P - Kt5 followed by P - B6 wins for White.

6. R - KB1	Q x RP
7. B x Kt	Kt x P

The second sacrifice is the key to the first.

8. B x Kt	

White must accept. On 8. Q - Q3, B x P Black's attack becomes overwhelming; besides he already has three Pawns for the piece, ample compensation.

8. . . .	Q - Kt6 ch
9. R - B2	

This interposition is forced, for on 9. K - K2, Q x B ch regains both pieces.

9. . . .	Q - Kt8 ch
10. R - B1	

Again forced.

10. . . .	Q ; Kt6 ch
11. R - B2	Q - Kt8 ch

Drawn by perpetual check

Diagram 355 is from the game Botvinnik-Fine, Nottingham, 1936. Black seems to be in a bad way: White threatens to win the exchange with B - Kt6, and Black's pieces are generally disunited. He finds a way out through a counterattack.

1. . . .	P - Q6
2. B x B ch	

The only real winning try. If instead 2. B x P, Q - Kt3 ch; 3. R - B2 (not 3. K - Kt2 ?, B x B; 4. B x Kt, Q - B3 ch and wins), Q x B; 4. Q x Q, B x Q; 5. B x Kt, R - B2; 6. B - Q3, B x P with an easy draw.

2. . . .	R x B

DIAGRAM 355

3. Q x QP

Now 3. B x P or 3. P x P would fail against the reply 3. . . .
Kt x P.

3. . . .	Q x Q
4. P x Q	

An attempt to hold on to the Pawn. On 4. B x P, Kt x P
everything is even.

4. . . .	Kt - Kt3
5. B - K4	R - Q1
6. QR - B1	Kt - Q4
7. P - QR3	R(K2) - Q2

The extra Pawn does White no good; a draw was agreed to
after a few more moves.

In *Diagram 356*, from Capablanca-Fine, AVRO Tournament, 1938, Black seems to be in a hopeless position. On *1.*

DIAGRAM 356

. . . QR - Kt1; 2. R x B follows, so that the passive *1. . . .*
Kt - Q1 would appear to be forced. Then follows *2. B - K2*
with threats all over. Black finds a much more aggressive defense:

1. . . .	QR - B1
2. Q - Kt2	

Apparently White now wins a Pawn.

| 2. . . . | KR - Q1 |
| 3. R x B | Kt - K4 |

The point to the defense. If now 4. Kt - Q4, Q - Kt3, threatening . . . R x Kt and . . . R - B7, with a very powerful attack.

| 4. B - K2 | Kt x Kt ch |
| 5. B x Kt | Q - K4 |

Now Black regains the piece. He still loses a Pawn, but the aggressive placement of his pieces provides sufficient compensation.

6. Q x Q

Necessary, for on 6. Q - Kt1, Q - B6 ch wins for Black.

| 6. . . . | R - B8 ch |
| 7. B - Q1 | |

The combination is primarily a drawing device. If 7. K - K2, R - B7 ch with perpetual check unless White transposes back to the game.

7. . . .	R(B8) x B ch
8. K - K2	R(Q8) - Q7 ch
9. K - B3	P x Q
10. R x RP	P - K5 ch !

Still preserving maximum mobility.

11. K - Kt3	R - R7
12. R - R6	R(Q1) - Q7
13. R - KB1	R(Q7) - Kt7
14. R x P	R x RP

The pressure along the seventh rank now assures him of a draw since White's KR cannot get out to hold the KtP. The remaining moves were:

15. P - Kt5, K - Kt2; *16.* P - R4, R(R6) - Kt6; *17.* K - B4, R x KtP; *18.* R x R, R x R; *19.* P - Kt4, R - Kt5; *20.* R - B1, R - Kt7; *21.* K - Kt3, K - B3 ? (better *21.* . . . R - Kt5); *22.* R - B4, K - K4; *23.* R - B8 ? (correct was *23.* P - Kt5!), K - B3; *24.* R - KKt8, P - R3; *25.* P - Kt5 ch, P x P; *26.* R x P, R - Kt1; *27.* K - R3, P - K4; *28.* R - Kt1 drawn.

Summing up this section on the counterattack, we find five main principles:

1. The defender wherever feasible avoids a passive defense.

2. The counterattack is designed to post his pieces as actively as possible; material considerations are secondary.

3. The defensive area proper is held by guarding only against direct threats.

4. The most effective forms of counterattack are, by and large, (a) an attack against the King, (b) a break in the center, (c) counterplay on the other wing.

5. Often a counterattack that forces a draw is the most potent defense.

The Philosophical Defense

THERE are many positions where one side has an obvious advantage, yet the transformation of that advantage into a win is quite a problem. In such cases any voluntary weakening eases the attacker's problem immeasurably. Often the defender's only chance is to adopt a philosophical attitude—to sit back and let events take their course, *defending only against direct threats*. Even though the other side may have one or more winning lines at his disposal, they may well be overlooked in the heat of battle.

The play from *Diagram 357*, from Alekhine-Capablanca,

twenty-second match game, 1927, is a model for this type of
defense. Black can do nothing except sit back and wait for
White's threats, which will be parried as they come along. The
game continued:

DIAGRAM 357

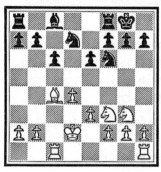

| 1. . . . | R - Q1 |
| 2. KR - Q1 | P - QKt3 |

Black must proceed cautiously. He would like to play . . .
P - K4, but the reply 3. K - K2 is too strong, so he waits.

| 3. P - K4 | B - Kt2 |
| 4. P - K5 | Kt - K1 |

It is essential to keep the White Kt out of Q6.

| 5. K - K3 | K - B1 |

Again a freeing move such as 5. . . . . P - QB4 ? is refuted by
6. P - Q5.

6. Kt - Kt5	P - KR3
7. Kt(Kt5) - K4	K - K2
8. P - B4	

White now threatens P - B5, so Black must weaken his Pawn
structure.

8....		P - KB4
9.	Kt - B3	Kt - B2
10.	Kt(Kt3) - K2	P - KKt4

Hoping to get some counterplay on the KKt file.

11.	P - KR4	P - Kt5

Forced.

12.	Kt - Kt3	P - QR4
13.	B - Kt3	QR - B1
14.	P - R3	R - B1
15.	R - Q2	B - R1

Black is waiting for the most convenient moment to play
. . . P - QB4.

16.	R(Q2) - QB2

Threatening Kt - R4, when . . . P - QB4 will be out, possibly forever.

16....		P - B4
17.	P x P	Kt x BP
18.	Kt - R4 !	Kt(B2) - R3

The only reply.

19.	B x P

An interesting sacrifice.

19....		K x B
20.	Kt x KtP	R - QKt1

The only inaccuracy in the defense. Correct was 20. . . .
R(B1) - Q1; 21. Kt x B, R - Q6 ch; 22. K - B2, R x Kt. Best for
White is 21. R x Kt, Kt x R; 22. R x Kt, R - QKt1; 23. Kt - R4
with a probable draw.

21.	Kt x B	R - Kt6 ch
22.	R - B3	R x R ch

23. P x R	R x Kt
24. R - Q1	

White already has two Pawns for the piece, and threatens to win a third; the situation is still tense.

| 24. . . . | R - KB1 |

If instead 24. . . . Kt - Kt2; 25. R - QKt1 wins.

25. R - Q6 ch	K - K2
26. R x P	Kt - B2
27. R - R7 ch	K - Q1
28. P - B4	

Prevents . . . Kt - Q4 ch.

28. . . .	Kt(B2) - K3
29. R - R7 ?	

Here White misses his golden opportunity. Alekhine later showed that 29. Kt - K2, K - B1; 30. Kt - B3, R - Q1; 31. Kt - Q5 wins for White. Capablanca now manages to slip out.

| 29. . . . | Kt - B2 ! |

As befits a philosophical defender, Black takes prompt advantage of his chance.

| 30. R x P | Kt(B4) - K3 |

For now White's Rook is out of the game, and Black can build up counterplay in the time that it takes to get the Rook back.

31. P - R5	K - Q2
32. P - R6	

Hoping for . . . R - R1; Kt x P.

32. . . .	Kt x P !
33. K x Kt	Kt - K3 ch

34. K - K3	P - B5 ch
35. K - B2	P x Kt ch
36. K x P	R - KR1
37. R - Q5 ch	K - K2
38. P - B5	R x P
39. P - B6	Kt - B1
40. R - B5	K - Q1
41. K x P	R - Kt3 ch

White's four Pawns are all disconnected and can be picked off one by one. The game was drawn after a long series of futile efforts by White to force a win.

Our next model game is also a Capablanca production; it is one of the most famous defensive masterpieces in chess history.

GAME NO. 26
New York, 1918

WHITE: *Capablanca*   BLACK: *Marshall*

Ruy Lopez

1. P - K4, P - K4; *2.* Kt - KB3, Kt - QB3; *3.* B - Kt5, P - QR3; *4.* B - R4, Kt - B3; *5.* O - O, B - K2; *6.* R - K1, P - QKt4; *7.* B - Kt3, O - O; *8.* P - B3, P - Q4.

DIAGRAM 358

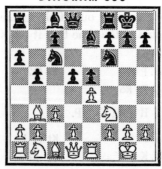

The Marshall Variation, specially prepared for the occasion.

9. P x P	Kt x P
10. Kt x P	Kt x Kt
11. R x Kt	Kt - B3

Subsequently Marshall suggested 11. . . . P - QB3, which has been analyzed a good deal in the past few years, somewhat inconclusively, though on the whole White is favored.

12. R - K1

This Rook later must move to K2, so 12. R - K2 at once has been recommended.

12. . . .   B - Q3

Threatening the familiar . . . B x P ch and . . . Kt - Kt5 ch.

13. P - KR3   Kt - Kt5

Marshall's attack is now in full swing. Capablanca could not be sure of what would happen, since he was obviously faced by a prepared variation, so he defends philosophically. There is no immediate threat; hence he develops.

14. Q - B3   Q - R5

Preventing Q x R, and hitting at the KBP.

15. P - Q4

White must have been tempted to try 15. R - K8, but in reply 15. . . . B - Kt2 wins, e.g., 16. R x R ch, R x R; 17. Q x Kt, R - K1; 18. K - B1, Q - K2; 19. Q - Q1, Q - K5; 20. P - B3, Q - K4; 21. P - Q4, Q - R7 with a decisive attack.

15. . . .   Kt x P

Now he has a threat: . . . Kt x P ch. White must find a way out. At first sight he appears lost, for if 16. Q x Kt,

B - R7 ch; *17.* K - B1, B - Kt6; *18.* Q - K2, B x P; *19.* P x B, QR -
K1; *20.* B - K3, B x R; *21.* Q x B, Q x P ch; *22.* K - B2, Q - R5 ch;
23. K - B1, Q x Q ch; *24.* K x Q, R x B ch and should win.

16. R - K2

Holds everything.

16. . . .   B - KKt5 ?

Hoping to win. The best continuation was *16.* . . . Kt - Kt5;
17. R - K8, Kt - B3; *18.* R x R ch, K x R; *19.* Kt - Q2, R - Kt1; *20.*
Kt - B1, B - Kt2; *21.* Q - B2 with about an even game.

17. P x B

Again the most precise. On *17.* Q x Kt, B - Kt6; *18.* Q - K3,
B x R; *19.* Q x B, QR - K1 wins.

17. . . .	B - R7 ch
18. K - B1	B - Kt6

Threatening mate at R8.

19. R x Kt	Q - R8 ch
20. K - K2	B x R

There is no more forceful continuation. On *20.* . . . Q x B
White wins with *21.* Q x B, Q x P ch; *22.* K - Q3, Q x R; *23.*
K - B2, P - Kt5; *24.* P - Kt5, P x P; *25.* Q x P(B3).

21. B - Q2	B - R5
22. Q - R3	QR - K1 ch
23. K - Q3	Q - B8 ch
24. K - B2	B - B7
25. Q - B3	

Now White looks safe.

25. . . .   Q - Kt8

Later Capablanca suggested a possible improvement with 25. . . . R - K7; 26. Kt - R3, R x B ch; 27. K x R, Q x R; 28. Q x B, Q x P ch; 29. Kt - B2, P - B4, and White will still find it hard to win.

26.	B - Q5	P - B4
27.	P x P	B x P
28.	P - Kt4	B - Q3
29.	P - R4	

Developing the Rook! After this it is simple.

29.	. . .	P - QR4

Hoping to create some confusion.

30.	RP x P	P x P
31.	R - R6	P x P
32.	Kt x P	B - Kt5
33.	P - Kt6	B x Kt
34.	B x B	P - R3
35.	P - Kt7	R - K6

Here Capablanca announced mate in five: 36. B x P ch, R x B; 37. P - Kt8(Q) ch, K - R2; 38. R x P ch, K x R; 39. Q - R8 ch, K any; 40. Q(8) - R5 mate.

The Useless Defense

THE useless defense is that put up in a position where there is no real hope. Many examples of it have been seen throughout the book, particularly in the section on the attack. Clearly the problem here is one of prophylaxis. The defender should manage things so that he does not get to such a position. This involves more accurate judgment of the previous possibilities. And above all it involves a mastery of preventive measures, which we turn to next.

Preventive Measures

Tarrasch had a favorite dictum: "The cramped position bears the seeds of loss." In spite of the hypermodern revolution, this dictum is still true. *By avoiding needlessly cramped positions in a great many cases the need for defense will have been avoided.*

Thus this is the first and most basic of the preventive measures. How can cramped positions be avoided is the next question. That too can be answered fairly simply in theory: *one frees a cramped position by exchanges.* This explains why *lifting a pin* is such an effective preventive measure for the defender, for removing the pin almost invariably leads to exchanges.

Very often the player is confronted with a choice of a cramped position or weak Pawns. This choice can only be resolved in terms of the individual position. E.g., in the Queen's Gambit Declined, after *1.* P - Q4, P - Q4; *2.* P - QB4, P - K3; *3.* Kt - QB3, Kt - KB3; *4.* B - Kt5, QKt - Q2; *5.* P - K3, B - K2; *6.* Kt - B3, O - O; *7.* Q - B2, Black has the choice of *7. . . .* P - QB4 and *7. . . .* P - QB3. The double advance *7. . . .* P - QB4 leaves him with weakened Pawns after *8.* P x QP, Kt x P; *9.* B x B, Q x B; *10.* Kt x Kt, P x Kt; *11.* P x P, yet it is still preferable to the cramping *7. . . .* P - QB3. On the other hand, in many variations of the Queen's Gambit Accepted White does better to avoid a weakened Pawn in the center.

We have gone through the technique of how to defend well. One important point is in order on how not to defend well. Perhaps the two most common mistakes made by both amateurs and masters are, first, unnecessary weakening Pawn moves, such as . . . P - KR3, or . . . P - KKt3, for no good reason, and, second, remaining too long in a cramped position without making an adequate effort to get out of it.

XII. *Equal Positions*

The even position has been treated only indirectly thus far. It is in order to make a few guiding principles for handling such positions explicit.

First of all, we must distinguish two types of equal positions—the balanced and the unbalanced. In the balanced neither side has any chances. In the unbalanced both sides have chances, but the two weigh about the same.

Second, we must note that the way in which a player handles an even position depends on what he wants to get out of it. *If he is playing to win,* he must strive to preserve tension. But if he is playing to draw, he should simplify. This applies equally to both types of position but the application would vary in each.

Balanced Positions

The player who is trying to win here has a rather hard time of it, but if he can keep things complicated he maintains his chances. Here is an illustration from a game between two great masters.

GAME NO. 27

Salzburg, 1942

WHITE: *Alekhine*   BLACK: *Keres*

Ruy Lopez

1. P - K4, P - K4; *2.* Kt - KB3, Kt - QB3; *3.* B - Kt5, P - QR3; *4.* B - R4, Kt - B3; *5.* O - O, B - K2; *6.* Q - K2, P - QKt4; *7.* B - Kt3,

P-Q3; 8. P-B3, O-O; 9. R-Q1, Kt-QR4; 10. B-B2, P-B4;
11. P-Q4, Q-B2; 12. B-Kt5 (a fresh idea in a rather hack-
neyed position), B-Kt5; 13. P x KP, P x P; 14. QKt-Q2.

DIAGRAM 359

This position is about even, although White has a little pull
because he may be able to occupy Q5. To avoid that, or take
the sting out of it, Black should equalize here with 14. . . .
Kt-R4, e.g., 15. P-KR3, B x Kt; 16. Kt x B, B x B; 17. Kt x B,
Kt-B5. Instead, Keres gives Alekhine too many chances to
keep the tension.

14. . . .	KR-Q1
15. Kt-B1	Kt-R4

Now essential.

16. P-KR3

His only purpose is to create complications.

16. . . .   B-K3

Which Black carelessly allows. The simplest way to preserve
equality was 16. . . . B x Kt; 17. Q x B, B x B; 18. Q x Kt,
Q-K2.

17. Kt-K3   P-B3

Hoping for *18.* B - KR4, Kt - B5.

18. Kt - R2   P - Kt3

After his failure to simplify Black is faced by real problems. On *18. . . .* B - B2 White has the speculative sacrifice *19.* Kt - Q5, R x Kt; *20.* P x R, P x B; *21.* P - Q6, B x P; *22.* Q - K4, with a rather wild game.

19. B - R6   B - KB1

To secure the square KB5.

20. B x B   K x B

21. P - KKt3

Again a move to maintain the initiative and preserve the tension. The KRP may not be taken because of the trap *21. . . .* B x KRP; *22.* Kt - Q5, Q - R2; *23.* P - KKt4, Kt - B5; *24.* Kt x Kt, P x Kt; *25.* Q - B3, and the Bishop is trapped.

21. . . .   R x R ch

Now he decides to simplify.

22. B x R

The Q file is no longer so important; White is more interested in keeping the position unbalanced.

22. . . .   R - Q1

23. P - QR4   Kt - QB5

24. P x P   P x P

The position still looks rather even, but Alekhine has a new surprise.

25. Kt - Q5   Q - QKt2

Keres is psychologically unprepared to defend against Alekhine and therefore refuses the bait. But objectively the best was *25. . . .* B x Kt; *26.* P x B, R x P; *27.* P - Kt3, Kt - Q3;

28. Q - K3, K - Kt2, and Black's position is solid though he will have to give back the Pawn sooner or later.

26.	P - Kt3	Kt - Q3
27.	P - QB4	P x P
28.	P x P	B x Kt
29.	KP x B	Kt - Kt2

Aiming for Q5.

We can pause to take stock here. From the even balanced position of Diagram 359 has come an unbalanced position with chances for both sides—thus White has gained his objective. In what followed Keres played rather inconsistently and finally lost. The remaining moves were:

30. Kt - Kt4, Q - K2; 31. B - B2, Kt(Kt2) - K1 (too passive); 32. P - R4, P - K5 ? (too weakening); 33. Kt - K3, Q - K4; 34. R - R7 (Alekhine takes prompt advantage of his opponent's errors), K - Kt1; 35. Kt - Kt4, Q - Q5 (see Diagram 203); 36. B x P, P - B4; 37. Kt - R6 ch, K - R1; 38. B - B2, Q - B3; 39. Q - K6 (transition to a favorable end game), Q x Q; 40. P x Q, R - B1; 41. Kt - B7 ch, Kt x Kt; 42. P x Kt, Kt - Q3; 43. B - Q3, K - Kt2; 44. P - B8(Q) ch, K x Q; 45. R x P, K - Kt1; 46. R - Q7, Kt - K1; 47. P - R5, P x P; 48. B x P, R - R1; 49. B - K6 ch, K - R1; 50. R - Q5 (winning another Pawn), Kt - B3; 51. R x BP, K - Kt2; 52. K - Kt2, R - R7; 53. B - B5, R - R6; 54. R - B7 ch, K - R3; 55. R - B7, R - R3; 56. P - B4, P - R5; 57. P - Kt4, resigns.

GAME NO. 28

Semmering-Baden, 1937

WHITE: *Flohr*   BLACK: *Ragosin*

Catalan System

1. P - Q4, Kt - KB3; 2. P - QB4, P - K3; 3. Kt - KB3, P - Q4; 4. P - KKt3, B - K2; 5. B - Kt2, O - O; 6. O - O, P - B3; 7. QKt - Q2, QKt - Q2; 8. Q - B2, P - QKt3; 9. P - Kt3, B - Kt2; 10. B - Kt2, R - B1; 11. QR - B1, P - B4.

DIAGRAM 360

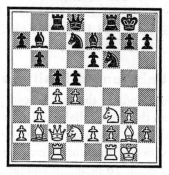

In this position the only real lack of symmetry lies in the different placement of the black-square Bishops. White, however, is content to draw and the ensuing simplifications serve his purpose.

12.	Q - Kt1	R - B2
13.	Q - R1	Q - R1
14.	KR - Q1	R - K1
15.	BP x P	B x P

This move is essential to maintain the balance.

16.	B - KR3	P - QR4

To get some counterplay with . . . P - R5.

17.	P x P	R x P

Simplification.

18.	Kt - K5	R x R
19.	R x R	Kt x Kt
20.	B x Kt	R - QB1
21.	R x R ch	Q x R
22.	Q - Kt2	Q - B3

The wholesale exchanges have left the balance essentially undisturbed. The remaining moves were:

23. Kt - Kt1, Q - B4; *24.* B - Q4, Q - Kt5; *25.* Q - B3, P - QKt4; *26.* Q x Q, B x Q; *27.* Kt - B3, B x Kt (White's two Bishops are of no importance here); *28.* B x B, P - Kt5; *29.* B x Kt, P x B; *30.* B - Kt2, B x B; *31.* K x B, drawn.

Unbalanced Positions

THE technique for handling the unbalanced position is markedly different from that for the balanced. When the Pawns are unbalanced, mechanical simplification can be almost suicidal, while the preservation of the tension may be the only way to keep the chances even. To maintain equality, we must maintain the dynamic forces in equilibrium, rather than the material situation as such. In practice this means that each side must exploit his chances as effectively as possible. Another way of looking at it is that there should be simultaneous attack and counterattack. Several model games will help to make these points clearer.

GAME NO. 29

AVRO Tournment, 1938

WHITE: *Reshevsky* BLACK: *Fine*

Catalan System

1. P - Q4, Kt - KB3; *2.* P - QB4, P - K3; *3.* Kt - KB3, P - Q4; *4.* P - KKt3, P x P; *5.* Q - R4 ch, QKt - Q2; *6.* B - Kt2, P - QR3; *7.*

DIAGRAM 361

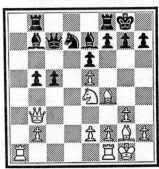

Kt - B3, B - K2; 8. Kt - K5 (a daring novelty), R - QKt1; 9.
Q x BP, P - QKt4; 10. Q - Kt3, Kt x Kt; 11. P x Kt, Kt - Q2; 12.
B - B4, P - QB4; 13. O - O, Q - B2; 14. P - QR4, O - O; 15. P x P,
P x P; 16. Kt - K4, B - Kt2.

In this position White with one Pawn to two on the Q-side
has a theoretically lost end game. His chances lie on the K-side
and in the center, in a possible attack. But he chose to simplify
mechanically, which led to his downfall:

17. R - R7 ?	Q - Kt3

Naturally not 17. . . . R - R1 ? at once because of R x B and
Kt - B6 ch.

18. KR - R1	R - R1
19. R x R	R x R
20. R x R ch	B x R
21. Q - Q3	B - B3
22. Kt - Kt5	B x Kt
23. B x B	Q - Kt2

Avoiding the trap: if 23. . . . Kt x P ??; 24. Q - Q6 and White
wins.

24. P - B3	P - R3
25. B - K7	

He cannot hold on to the Pawn, for if 25. B - B4, P - Kt4.

25. . . .	P - B5
26. Q - B3	Kt x P
27. B - B5	Kt - Q2
28. B - Q4	P - K4 !

To be able to advance the Q-side Pawns.

29. B x P	P - Kt5
30. Q - Q4	Kt x B
31. Q x Kt	P - B6

Decisive.

32. P - Kt3	Q - Kt3 ch
33. K - B1	P - B7
34. Q - Kt2	Q - B4
35. Q - B1	B - Q4
36. P - B4	B x B ch
37. K x B	Q - Q4 ch

White resigned.

Our next game is a model for the defender.

GAME NO. 30

AVRO Tournament, 1938

WHITE: *Reshevsky*   BLACK: *Euwe*

Queen's Gambit Declined

1. P - Q4, Kt - KB3; *2.* P - QB4, P - K3; *3.* Kt - QB3, P - Q4; *4.* B - Kt5, B - K2; *5.* P - K3, O - O; *6.* R - B1, P - KR3; *7.* B - R4, Kt - K5; *8.* B x B, Q x B; *9.* P x P, Kt x Kt; *10.* R x Kt, P x P; *11.* B - Q3; P - QB3; *12.* Kt - K2, Kt - Q2; *13.* O - O, Kt - B3; *14.* Kt - B4.

DIAGRAM 362

As we know from our discussion of Pawn structure, White's plan here consists in an eventual minority attack on the Q-side. Black cannot afford to play passively but must seek counter-play on the K-side. He played:

14. . . .	B - Kt5
15. Q - B2	Kt - R4

Not so much to force an exchange as to pave the way for the advance of the KBP—his own minority attack.

16. Kt x Kt	B x Kt
17. R - B5	B - Kt5
18. R - Kt1	

Still preparing P - QKt4.

18. . . .	QR - K1
19. P - QKt4	Q - Kt4

Preventing P - Kt5 for the time being by a tactical finesse. If 20. P - Kt5 ?, B - B6; 21. P - Kt3 (not 21. B - B1, B - K5), R - K5; 22. B - B1 (the threat was . . . R - R5), R - R5 (anyhow); 23. P x P, Q - R4, and wins.

20. K - R1	P - R3

To exchange another Pawn when White does play P - Kt5.

21. P - QR4	P - B4

Now Black's attack is in full swing, and White must do something about it. If, e.g., 22. P - Kt5, RP x P; 23. P x P, P - B5, and Black's chances are better.

22. P - B4	Q - K2

Again with a threat.

23. R - K1	R - B3

White is given no respite—the threat is now . . . R - K3.

24. P - R3	R - K3

For if 25. P x B, Q - R5 ch.

25. Q - B2

Forcing a drawing liquidation.

25. . . .	R x P
26. R x R	Q x R
27. Q x Q	R x Q
28. B x RP	P x B
29. P x B	P x P

Threatening . . . P - Kt6.

30. K - R2	R - Q6
31. R x BP	R x P
32. R x P	R x KtP
33. K - Kt3	

Drawn

Counterattack saved the day for both sides!

Summing up this chapter, we can say that when the position is even, further technique depends on the Pawn distribution. If the Pawns are balanced, to play for a win one must preserve the tension, if possible creating an unbalance; to play for a draw, simplify. If the Pawns are unbalanced, mechanical simplification is usually an error; instead, each side should strive to exploit his chances to the fullest. Here it is only by an equilibrium of the dynamic forces that real equality is maintained.

XIII. *Continuing the Opening*

I N   T H E S E   L A S T   T W O   C H A P T E R S we shall consider the
transition stages of the middle game, when it comes out of the
opening, and when it goes into the ending. Both openings and
endings have been treated by the writer in other works at
greater length, and the reader is referred to these * for more
detailed study.

In the continuation of the opening, our prime concern is
with the Pawn skeleton. It is the Pawn skeleton that determines the long-range plans that the game is to follow. A
thorough knowledge of Pawn structure is essential for an
adequate continuation of the most advantageous opening
variations.

Let us review briefly the theory of Pawn structure in the
openings. An advantage is obtained by having one Pawn in
the center against none. Thus in the Diagrams A and B White
has the better of it. Diagram A is the basic pattern for the QP
openings, Diagram B for the KP. Naturally these positions can
as a rule not be forced at once. To *1.* P - K4 Black can reply
1. . . . P - K4, to *1.* P - Q4, *1.* . . . P - Q4. Hence the next step
is to try to get rid of the enemy center Pawns, which leads to
Diagrams C and D. Here White's purpose will be to force an
exchange, Black's to avoid one.

In the openings where the center is not occupied by Pawns,
the difference in theory is only apparent. There two possibilities exist. The defender can either try to establish Pawns in

* For the openings see *Practical Chess Openings* and *The Ideas
behind the Chess Openings.* For the endings see *Basic Chess Endings.*

the center at a later date, or he can attack the center Pawns and force a weakness; the first possibility is the more usual one.

Let us now see how these various possibilities work out in practice.

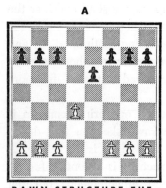

A

PAWN STRUCTURE THE-
ORETICALLY DESIRABLE
FOR WHITE IN THE
QP OPENINGS

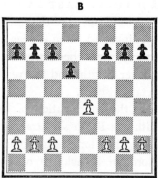

B

PAWN STRUCTURE THE-
ORETICALLY DESIRABLE
FOR WHITE IN THE
KP OPENINGS

1. Pawn at Q4 vs. Pawn at K3

THIS is a fundamental position which can come out of a variety of openings, particularly the Queen's Gambit and the French Defense. In general White has an advantage here which can be exploited in one of two ways: he can either use the square K5 as an outpost for a K-side attack, or he can tempt . . . P - QB4, exchange QP x BP, remain with three Pawns vs. two on the Q-side, and play for the end game, where he has a theoretical advantage because of the majority of Pawns on the Q-side. Two model games will serve to illustrate these two possibilities.

C

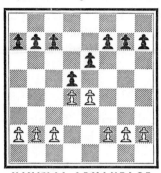

D

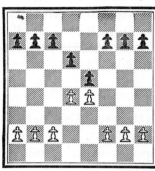

MINIMAL ADVANTAGE
FOR WHITE IN THE
QP OPENINGS

MINIMAL ADVANTAGE
FOR WHITE IN THE
KP OPENINGS

GAME NO. 31

New York State Championship, 1910

WHITE: *Capablanca*   BLACK: *Jaffe*

Queen's Gambit Declined

1. P - Q4, P - Q4; *2.* Kt - KB3, Kt - KB3; *3.* P - K3, P - B3; *4.*
P - B4, P - K3; *5.* Kt - B3, QKt - Q2; *6.* B - Q3, B - Q3; *7.* O - O,
O - O; *8.* P - K4, P x KP; *9.* Kt x P, Kt x Kt; *10.* B x Kt.

DIAGRAM 363

In this position the natural freeing move *10. . . . P - K4* is prevented by a tactical finesse: *11.* P x P, Kt x P; *12.* Kt x Kt, B x Kt; *13.* B x P ch, K x B; *14.* Q - R5 ch, and White comes out a Pawn ahead. So Black finds it necessary to submit to the attack that follows.

| *10. . . .* | Kt - B3 |

However, this does not lead to real liberation. The alternatives *10. . . . P - QB4* and *10. . . . P - KR3*, to hold . . . P - K4 open, were both better.

| *11.* B - B2 | P - KR3 |

Now he must prevent the pin.

12. P - QKt3	P - QKt3
13. B - Kt2	B - Kt2
14. Q - Q3	

White has built up the ideal attacking position.

DIAGRAM 364

The immediate threat is *15.* P - Q5.

| *14. . . .* | P - Kt3 |

Unavoidable weakening.

15. QR - K1

Threatening R x KP.

15. . . .   Kt - R4

To reply to 16. R x P with . . . Kt - B5.

16. B - B1 !   K - Kt2

(See Diagram 188)

17. R x P

Anyhow.

17. . . .   Kt - B3

For 17. . . . P x R allows mate in two.

18. Kt - K5   P - B4
19. B x P ch   K x B
20. Kt x P ch   Resigns

Mate or crushing loss of material is the dolorous choice.

In the next game we see the center Pawn used as the basis for a winning ending.

GAME NO. 32
New York, 1940

WHITE: *Reshevsky*   BLACK: *Woliston*

French Defense

1. P - K4, P - K3; 2. P - Q4, P - Q4; 3. Kt - QB3, P x P; 4. Kt x P, Kt - Q2; 5. Kt - KB3, KKt - B3; 6. Kt x Kt ch, Kt x Kt; 7. B - Q3, P - B4; 8. P x P, B x P; 9. O - O, O - O; 10. B - KKt5, P - QKt3; 11. Q - K2, B - Kt2; 12. QR - Q1, Q - B2; 13. B x Kt, P x B.

DIAGRAM 365

Here White has the choice of a K-side attack or an end game; he chooses the latter.

14. B - K4, QR - Q1; *15.* B x B, Q x B; *16.* Kt - Q2, B - K2; *17.* Kt - K4, R x R (better *17. . . . * P - B4 and *18. . . . * B - B3 to hit at the White Pawns); *18.* R x R, R - Q1; *19.* R x R ch, B x R; *20.* Q - Q3, B - K2; *21.* P - KR3, Q - B2 ? (the exchange of Queens is a serious positional blunder; Black should still try . . . P - B4 and . . . B - B3, to mobilize his own advantage—see the comments in the last chapter on even positions that are unbalanced); *22.* Q - Kt3 ch, Q x Q; *23.* Kt x Q, K - B1; *24.* K - B1, K - K1; *25.* K - K2, K - Q2; *26.* K - Q3, K - B3; *27.* Kt - K2, B - B4; *28.* P - KB4, P - Kt4 (facilitating White's plan. The side with the minority of Pawns does best not to move them at all); *29.* P - KKt4, P - QR3; *30.* K - K4 (strong centralization), B - B1; *31.* Kt - Q4 ch, K - Q3; *32.* Kt - Kt3, B - K2; *33.* Kt - Q2, B - B1; *34.* P - B4, K - B4; *35.* P x P, P x P.

White has achieved the ideal end-game position—Black's Pawn majority is immobilized, White's King is well centralized, and he has a good Knight against a poor Bishop. The rest merely involves setting up an outside passed Pawn on the Q-side and forcing a decisive gain of material on the other wing.

DIAGRAM 366

36. Kt - Kt3 ch, K - Q3; *37.* Kt - Q4, K - B4; *38.* P - B5, P - K4; *39.* Kt - B3 (threatening P - Kt5), P - R3; *40.* P - KR4, B - K2; *41.* P - R5 ! (fixing the Black KRP, which makes the plight of Black's Bishop even worse), B - Q3; *42.* P - R3, P - Kt5; *43.* P - R4, P - Kt6; *44.* Kt - Q2, K - Kt5; *45.* P - R5, K x P (on other moves the Knight wins the KtP and enters the K-side); *46.* Kt - B4 ch, resigns.

It should be remembered that with the P at Q4, when Black plays . . . P - QB4, he may be able to exchange White's QP and set up an isolani at Q4; this has been discussed in Chapter VIII.

2. Pawn at K4 vs. Pawn at Q3

HERE there is in general only one good continuation, the attack against the King. The natural question arises, why the difference between this case and the previous one? The answer is that the majority of Pawns is set up on the same side as the King, which is not ordinarily an end-game advantage. The attack usually involves pressure along the long diagonal QR1 to KR8 and occupation of the outposts Q5 or KB5. Here is a model game.

GAME NO. 33
Match, New York, 1942

WHITE: *Kashdan*   BLACK: *Reshevsky*

Ruy Lopez

1. P - K4, P - K4; *2.* Kt - KB3, Kt - QB3; *3.* B - Kt5, P - QR3; *4.* B - R4, P - Q3; *5.* P - B4, B - Q2; *6.* Kt - B3, Kt - B3; *7.* P - Q4, P x P; *8.* Kt x P, Kt x Kt; *9.* B x B ch, Q x B; *10.* Q x Kt, B - K2; *11.* O - O, O - O.

DIAGRAM 367

In this position White has an ideal setup. The plan is to use the advantage in space conferred by his KP to build up an attack.

12. P - QKt3

First the long diagonal is occupied.

12. . . .	KR - K1
13. B - Kt2	B - B1
14. QR - Q1	R - K3
15. KR - K1	QR - K1
16. P - B3	K - R1 ?

Black for his part plays too passively, forgetting that the Pawns are not balanced. To get counterplay 'he should try

... P - QKt4 followed by ... P - QB3, ... Q - Kt2 and pressure against the center and Q-side.

17. Kt - K2	Q - B1
18. Q - B2	Kt - Q2
19. Kt - Q4	R(K3) - K2
20. Q - Kt3	P - KB3
21. Kt - B5	R - K3
22. P - KR4	

White consistently increases the pressure.

22. . . .	P - QKt4

Too late now—the White pieces are too strongly posted.

23. P x P	P x P
24. P - R5	Q - R3
25. P - R3	P - B4
26. R - Q5	Kt - K4
27. R(K1) - Q1	Kt - B2
28. Q - R4	Kt - K4
29. P - B4	Kt - B2

DIAGRAM 368

30. P - R6 !

The decisive break.

30. . . .	P - Kt3
31. B x P ch	K - Kt1
32. Kt - Kt3	B x P
33. B - Kt2	B - Kt2
34. P - B5 !	B x B
35. P x R	R x P
36. Q - Kt4	

After this the remainder is easy. The concluding moves were:

36. . . . R - K1; *37.* Q - Q7, R - Q1; *38.* Q - K7, R - KB1; *39.* R - KB1, B - K4; *40.* R - Q3, Q - B1; *41.* R(Q3) - KB3, Q - K1; *42.* R x Kt, Q x Q; *43.* R x Q, B x Kt; *44.* R x R ch, K x R; *45.* R - QKt7, P - B5; *46.* P x P, resigns.

As we have indicated, Black's defensive play against the Pawn setup should have been to exert pressure against White's center at an early stage. He could try to liberate himself with . . . P - KB4, or under certain circumstances with . . . P - Q4.

3. Pawn at Q4 vs. Pawn at Q4

THIS is the basic structure of the Queen's Gambit and Queen's Pawn Game. White's first objective is to get back to Case 1, this can be done by P - K4 if Black exchanges. From a purely theoretical point of view there are then two possibilities. If the Pawns are balanced, Pawns at Q4 and K4 vs. Pawns at Q4 and K3, White will continue with P - K5, setting up a Pawn chain with Black's base at K3, which is then taken under attack; Pawn-chain play has already been discussed. If the Pawns are unbalanced, White by advancing gets a steamroller attack that is almost impossible to meet. Here is a model game that illustrates this second possibility.

GAME NO. 34
Groningen, 1946

WHITE: *Euwe*   BLACK: *Steiner*

Nimzoindian Defense

1. P - Q4, Kt - KB3; *2.* P - QB4, P - K3; *3.* Kt - QB3, B - Kt5; *4.* P - K3, O - O; *5.* B - Q3, P - Q4; *6.* P - QR3, B x Kt ch; *7.* P x B, QKt - Q2 (a weak rejoinder); *8.* P x P, P x P.

DIAGRAM 369

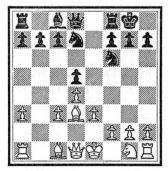

White has achieved his first goal: solidification of the center with an unbalanced Pawn structure, which calls for the steamroller advance P - K4 - K5. In what follows Black defends poorly, but it is likely that this position is already strategically won for White.

9. Kt - K2

The Knight must not go to B3, where it would merely impede the Pawn advance.

9. . . .	R - K1
10. O - O	Kt - B1

11.	P - B3	P - B4
12.	Kt - Kt3	P x P
13.	BP x P	P - QR3

For the moment P - K4 is impossible because the QP is en prise.

14. Q - Q2

Preparing B - Kt2 and P - K4.

14. . . .   B - Q2

To reply to P - K4 with the combination that follows.

15.	P - K4	P x P
16.	P x P	B - B3
17.	P - Q5	

Forced. Black now thinks that he has some compensation because of the hole at K4, but he is taken by surprise by a neat combination.

17. . . .   B - Kt4

DIAGRAM 370

18.	B - Kt2	Q - Kt3 ch
19.	K - R1	B x B

Apparently winning a piece.

$20.$ **R x Kt !**

This was the idea.

$20.$ . . .	**P x R**
$21.$ **Kt - R5**	**R - K4**

Forced—on $21.$ . . . Kt - Q2; $22.$ Q - R6 mates.

$22.$ **B x R**	**P x B**
$23.$ **Q x B**	

Although the material is still even, Black's King is badly exposed, which makes his game positionally hopeless. The conclusion was:

$23.$ . . . Q - R3; $24.$ Q - R3, R - Q1; $25.$ R - KB1, Q - Kt4; $26.$ Q - KB3, Q - Kt3; $27.$ Kt - Kt3, R - Q2; $28.$ Q - B3, Q - Q3; $29.$ Kt - B5, Q - B2; $30.$ Q - Kt3 ch, Kt - Kt3; $31.$ Q - Kt5, Q - Q1; $32.$ Kt - R6 ch, K - Kt2; $33.$ R - B6, Q - R4; $34.$ R - B1, Q x RP (if $34.$ . . . Q - Q1; $35.$ Kt x P wins); $35.$ Kt - B5 ch, K - Kt1; $36.$ Q - B6, Q - B1; $37.$ R - B1 (threatening R - B8), R - Q1; $38.$ R - B7, and Black resigned.

4. Pawn at K4 vs. Pawn at K4

THIS runs parallel to the situation with the Pawns at Q4, yet again curiously with the difference that the steam-roller attack via P - Q4 is not quite so strong. These differences explain why the KP openings with $1.$ P - K4, P - K4 are more suitable for open play, the QP for closed play.

In many instances of the KP openings White secures the setup Pawns at K4 and Q4 vs. Pawns at K4 and Q3. The exchange of Pawns with . . . KP x QP would then lead to Case 3. Black usually does better not to exchange, in which event White retains some slight pressure, but generally one that is hard to exploit further in a positional manner. The advance P - Q5 can set up a Pawn chain with Black's base at Q3. Or at times he can exchange and use the open Q file.

With the Pawns set up at K4, the advance P - KB4, where it cannot be countered by . . . P - Q4, is often even stronger for White than P - Q4.

5. One Side Has No Pawns in the Center

THESE situations can come about in one of two ways. Either one side plays badly, in which case the opponent occupies the center and gets a tremendous positional advantage. E.g., the Irregular Opening 1. P - K4, P - Q3; 2. P - Q4, P - K3. White then gets command of much more terrain and proceeds accordingly. Or one side deliberately refrains from occupying the center with Pawns. As we have said, this can be done for one of two reasons: either he will occupy the center later, or he will attack the enemy Pawns.

Delayed Occupation of the Center

The delayed occupation is the maneuver introduced by the hypermoderns. It can be exceedingly effective, yet it must be played with great skill. Here is a model game that shows how strong it can be.

GAME NO. 35

New York, 1931

WHITE: *Capablanca*   BLACK: *Santasiere*

Reti's Opening

1. Kt - KB3, Kt - KB3; 2. P - QKt3, P - Q4; 3. B - Kt2, B - B4; 4. P - Kt3, P - K3; 5. B - Kt2, QKt - Q2; 6. O - O, B - Q3; 7. P - Q3, P - KR3; 8. QKt - Q2, Q - K2; 9. R - K1 (White is already threatening to win a piece with P - K4 - K5), P - K4; 10. P - B4, P - B3 (better 10. . . . P - Q5); 11. P x P, P x P.

The strength of Black's position is only apparent, as the sequel shows.

12. P - K4	P x P
13. P x P	B - K3
14. Kt - R4	

Equilibrium in the center Pawns has now been established, but White has an advantage first because his Bishops are in potentially more commanding positions, and second because his Knights can get to the vital squares Q5 and KB5 more quickly.

14. . . .	P - KKt3
15. Kt - B1	O - O
16. Kt - K3	

Threatening Kt - Q5, uncovering an attack on the KP after . . . B x Kt; P x B.

16. . . .	KR - B1 ?

Allows a pretty combination; 16. . . . Kt - Kt3 was better.

17. Kt(R4) - B5	P x Kt
18. P x P	

And White's Bishop has come into his own.

                    18. . . .   **P - K5**

Blocking the KB but freeing the QB.

                    19. P x B   **Q x P**
                    20. B - KR3 !   **Q x B**
                    21. Q x B

With weak Pawns and the powerful long diagonal in White's unchallengeable possession the win was an easy matter. The remaining moves were:

21. . . . R - B3; *22.* Q - B4, R - K1; *23.* QR - B1, Kt - R4; *24.* Q - B5, Q x Q; *25.* Kt x Q, R(K1) - K3 (weaknesses can no longer be avoided); *26.* R x R, P x R; *27.* R - Q1, Kt - K4; *28.* Kt x P ch, K - Kt2; *29.* Kt - Kt4, P - B3; *30.* B x Kt, P x B; *31.* R - K1, K - Kt3; *32.* R x P, K - B4; *33.* P - B3, Kt - Kt2; *34.* Kt - K3 ch, K - B3; *35.* R - QR4, R - Q3; *36.* R x P, R - Q7; *37.* Kt - Kt4 ch, and Black resigned.

Counterattack on the Center Pawns

This was also one of the favorite maneuvers of the hypermoderns. It was Breyer who said: "After *1.* P - K4 White's game is in its last throes," by which he meant that the exposed center Pawns would be taken under attack and captured. In openings where one side is given an opportunity to occupy the center with Pawns he must be careful lest they become too weak.

Here is the model game which refuted an apparent powerhouse setup for White in the K - Indian Defense.

GAME NO. 36
Wiesbaden, 1925

WHITE: *Saemisch*   BLACK: *Euwe*

King's Indian Defense

1. P - Q4, Kt - KB3; *2.* P - QB4, P - KKt3; *3.* Kt - QB3, B - Kt2; *4.* P - K4, P - Q3; *5.* P - B4, O - O; *6.* Kt - B3.

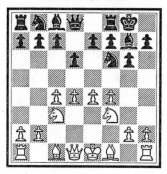

Up to the time this game was played the four Pawns abreast had been considered so powerful that Black's opening strategy was felt to be refuted. Instead Black demonstrates that White's Pawns are a serious weakness.

6. . . .	P - B4
7. P - Q5	

If instead 7. P x P, Q - R4; 8. B - Q2, Q x BP with strong pressure.

7. . . .	P - K3
8. B - Q3	P·x P
9. BP x P	

To hold on to his Pawn center. If 9. KP x P, R - K1 ch; 10. Kt - K2, P - QKt4 gives Black the needed counterplay.

9. . . .	Q - Kt3

Prevents castling because of the discovered check. And if 10. B - B2, P - B5 becomes too strong, e.g., 11. Q - Q4, Q x Q; 12. Kt x Q, Kt x KP. Note how White's center Pawns are a continual target.

10. Kt - Q2

Intending Kt - B4 and O - O.

10. . . .   **Kt - Kt5**

Threatening . . . P.- B5, even if White plays *11.* P - KR3.

11. Kt - B4   **Q - Q1**

Again White can not castle because of . . . B - Q5 ch and . . . Kt - B7 ch winning the exchange, or play P - KR3 because of . . . Q - R5 ch. Meanwhile Black threatens . . . P - B4, which will rip White's position open.

12. B - K2   **P - KR4**

Best for White now is *13.* B x Kt, B x B; *14.* Q - B2, Q - R5 ch; *15.* P - Kt3, Q - K2; *16.* O - O, P - R5 but Black has a strong attack. Instead he played:

13. Kt - Kt5

and lost a piece and the game as follows:

13. . . . P - QR3; *14.* Kt(Kt5) x P, P - QKt4; *15.* Kt x B, P x Kt; *16.* P - K5 (hoping to get some compensation through his center Pawns), Q x Kt; *17.* P - KR3, Kt - R3; *18.* P - KKt4, Kt - Q2; *19.* P x P, Q - Q1; *20.* O - O, Q - R5 (with White's Pawns so weak the Black counterattack crashes through); *21.* R - B3, P x P; *22.* R - B3, QR - K1; *23.* B - Q2, Kt x P (returns the piece for the attack); *24.* P x Kt, R x P; *25.* B - K1, Q - K2; *26.* P - Q6, Q - K3; *27.* B - B1, R - Kt4 ch; *28.* R - Kt3, Q - K6 ch; *29.* K - Kt2, B - Q5; *30.* R x R ch, Q x R ch, and White resigned.

There is still a third method available for meeting the Pawn center, which really cuts across the previous two. In the event that one side has, say, two Pawns at K4 and Q4, with an unbalanced Pawn structure, the opponent will have a majority of Pawns on one wing. If they are on the Q-side, he has a potential passed Pawn there, and thus an end-game advantage.

His plan would then be to take the sting out of the enemy center Pawns by suitable simplifications and heading for the ending. This has already been discussed in the chapter on Pawn structure (see pp. 261–63).

These five cases cover the basic Pawn skeletons found in every chess game. Naturally the plans described here are of a general character and cannot be applied mechanically to the actual game; due attention must always be paid to the tactical situation.

XIV. *Entering the End Game*

A T V A R I O U S   P O I N T S throughout the previous chapters we have indicated the situations where transition to an end game is favorable and where it is unfavorable. In this chapter we shall pull this material together in a more systematic manner.

The exact point where the middle game ends and the end game begins is difficult to define. For all practical purposes, however, we may take it to be the exchange of Queens. Then the question is: When should the Queens be exchanged, and when not?

In general, we can say that it is desirable to head for the end game under any one of four conditions:

1. Material advantage
2. Superior Pawn structure
3. To break an attack (the end game as a defensive weapon)
4. When the enemy Queen is the most mobile piece (superior end-game mobility)

Conversely, it would be undesirable to go into an end game when there is a material disadvantage, when the Pawn structure is inferior, when one is on the offensive, and when one's own Queen is the most mobile piece. Let us look at these in more detail.

Material Advantage

W E   K N O W that with an advantage of two Pawns or more, the only possible compensation the defender can have is an attack.

Nothing breaks the back of an attack under way or nips in the bud any potential attack so effectively as the exchange of Queens. Hence with a large material plus the end game is the shortest road to victory.

With one Pawn to the good, a counterattack is still in many cases the strongest possible defense. Again the end game removes any such possibility. E.g., in *Diagram 373,* from Euwe-

DIAGRAM 373

Alekhine, Zurich, 1934, White concluded as follows:

> *1.* R - K3   Q - Q7
> *2.* R - K8

Since one Pawn is in and of itself not sufficient to win, it must be used to gain more material. Hence the transition to the end game is deferred until a more suitable date.

> *2.* . . .   Q - Q6

On *3.* R - Q8 (threatening an eventual P - Q6) Black has . . . Q - K5 ch with counterplay. The time is now ripe for exchanges.

> *3.* Q - Q4   Q - B5

Hoping to get some counterplay through the passed Pawn. The alternative 3. . . . Q x Q; 4. Kt x Q, R - B5; 5. Kt - B6, Kt - Q3; 6. R - R8, R - B7; 7. R x P, Kt - K5; 8. R - R8 is hopeless; White's RP advances to R7, then the Rook moves and wins a Rook.

4. Q - K4 ch

Simpler than 4. Q x Q.

4. . . .	Q x Q ch

Forced, for if 4. . . . P - Kt3; 5. Q - K6 with mates in the offing.

5. R x Q	K - Kt1

Black sees that he cannot avoid the loss of a second Pawn: if 5. . . . R - Q2; 6. R - K8, R - B2; 7. Kt - Kt8, etc.

6. Kt - Kt8	K - B2
7. Kt x P	R - Q2
8. R - Q4	Kt - K2
9. P - Q6	Kt - B4
10. R - Q5	Kt x QP
11. Kt - B5	R - Q1
12. Kt - K4	Kt - Kt2
13. P - R6 !	

Naturally 13. R x P also wins.

13. . . .	K - K3

Or 13. . . . R x R; 14. P x Kt, R - Q1; 15. Kt - Q6 ch, K - K3; 16. Kt - B8 and queens.

14. R x R

and Black resigned.

On the other hand, a mechanical exchange of Queens just

because one is a Pawn ahead is not to be recommended. E.g., in *Diagram 374*, from Treysman-Fine, New York, 1936, White should play *1.* Q - B3 followed by Kt - Q2, etc. and Black's compensation for the Pawn is largely a matter of hope. Instead White played:

1. Q - Q5 ?	Q x Q
2. B x Q	R - Q1

DIAGRAM 374

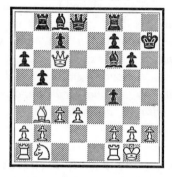

3. B - K4	P - B4

And suddenly White is in trouble. If *4.* R - Q1, B - KKt2, and White's development remains backward, for if *5.* Kt - Q2, P - B4, and if *5.* Kt - R3, P - Kt5; in both cases regaining the Pawn with a better game. White tried:

4. Kt - Q2	B - KKt2
5. Kt - Kt3	P - B4
6. B - B3	P - B5
7. P x P	P x P
8. Kt - R5	R x P
9. Kt x P	R - B7
10. KR - B1	R x QBP
11. R x R	B x R

Black has regained his Pawn and with the two Bishops has the better end-game prospects. The remaining moves were:

12. R - QB1, B - KKt2; *13.* K - B1, B - K3; *14.* B - Kt7, P - R4; *15.* P - QR4, R - Q5; *16.* B - R6, B - KB1; *17.* B - Kt5, B - Kt5; *18.* Kt - K5, K - Kt2; *19.* P - R4, K - B3; *20.* Kt - B3, R - Q3; *21.* Kt - Kt5, B - Kt6; *22.* Kt - B3, R - Q8 ch; *23.* R x R, B x R; *24.* B - B6, B - B6; *25.* B - K8, K - K2; *26.* B - Kt5, K - Q3; *27.* Kt - K1, B - B3; *28.* Kt - Q3, P - B6; *29.* P x P, B x KRP; *30.* Kt - Kt2, QB x P; *31.* Kt - B4 ch, K - B4; *32.* Kt x P, B - Q4; *33.* B - R6, B - Q1; *34.* Kt - Kt7 ch, K - Kt3, and White resigned because the Kt is lost.

These two examples illustrate the most important principle involved in transposition to an end game with one Pawn ahead: *The player with the extra Pawn should not go into an end game until he is reasonably sure that in the resulting position he will be able to win another Pawn, or reach one of the elementary wins with one Pawn ahead.*

Superior Pawn Structure

WE HAVE already in Chapter VIII discussed the various types of Pawn structure. Those favorable for the end game are the ones in which the Pawn weakness is of a permanent character —doubled, isolated, or badly blocked; in other positions, such as a Pawn at K4 vs. a Pawn at Q3, a middle-game advantage may actually become a disadvantage in the end game.

One example will suffice here; the fuller discussion is in Chapter VIII.

In *Diagram 375,* from Bernstein-Reshevsky, New York, 1940, White's Pawns are badly blocked, so that Black has a potential end-game advantage. He must be careful, however, not to let the agile Kt get into too good a position. The game continued:

1. Q - B1   Q - Kt4

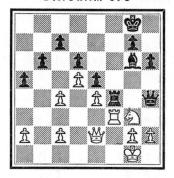

Avoids the trap. On *1. . . .* B x P; 2. Kt x B, R x Kt; 3. R - B8 ch leads to mate.

2. Q - B1	Q - Kt5
3. P - KR3	Q - R5
4. K - R2	P - R4

To drive the Kt away from its excellent post.

5. P - R3	Q - B3
6. Q - B1	Q - Kt4

On *6. . . .* P - R5; 7. Kt - K2 Black does not have time to take the KP. And if *7. . . .* R x R ?; 8. Q x R, Q x Q; 9. P x Q, White's KP is reinforced, and the resulting ending is no longer lost for him.

7. Q - B1	Q - R3

Threatening . . . P - KR5, for if then Kt - B5, B x Kt; R x R, Q x R ch; Q x Q, P x Q; P x B, K - B2 winning a Pawn—for this variation Black's Queen had to be defended.

8. K - Kt1	P - KR5
9. R x R	Q x R
10. Q x Q	P x Q

11. Kt - K2	B x P
12. Kt - Q4	

To get at the BP. On the alternative *12.* Kt x P Black wins with *12.* . . . B x BP; *13.* Kt - K6, B - Kt6; *14.* Kt x BP, B x P; *15.* Kt - R8, P - QKt4.

12. . . .	K - B2
13. Kt - Kt5	B x BP
14. Kt x BP	B - Q6
15. Kt - R8	P - QKt4
16. P x P	B x P
17. K - B2	K - B3

The remainder is easy because Black wins another P:
18. Kt - Kt6, B - R3; *19.* K - B3, K - B4; *20.* Kt - R8, B - Q6; *21.* Kt - Kt6, P - Kt4; *22.* P - R4, B - R3; *23.* Kt - R8, B - B5; *24.* Kt - Kt6, B - Kt6 (White is now in *zugzwang*); *25.* K - B2, K - K5, and White resigned.

Breaking an Attack

TRANSPOSITION to an end game is one of the most effective of defensive weapons. An attack is often conducted at the expense of a sacrifice of material or a disruption of the position, both end-game disadvantages. Besides, the Queen is the strongest piece for the offensive; after she is exchanged the attack often collapses.

Diagram 376 is an illustration from a world championship match, Alekhine-Euwe, 1935. Both sides here have a strong attack, but White has fewer pieces developed. Alekhine later showed that the strongest continuation for Black is *1.* . . . Q - B7, and then best play for both is *2.* Q - B6 ch, R - Kt2; *3.* R - KKt1, Q x KtP; *4.* P - K6 !, Q x R ch; *5.* B - Q1, Kt - Q5; *6.* Q x R ch, K x Q; *7.* B - R4 dis ch, K - R3; *8.* B - Kt5 ch, K any;

9. B - R4 dis ch with a draw by perpetual check. Instead, Black played:

1. . . .	Q - K5 ?
2. Q x Q	P x Q
3. B - R4	

And White has a won ending because he gets command of the Queen file.

3. . . .	P - KR3
4. O - O - O	QR - K1
5. B - B6 ch	K - R2
6. P - KB4 !	P x P e.p.
7. B x P	

Stronger than the win of the exchange with 7. B - Q3 ch.

7.	Kt - R4
8. B x B	Kt x B
9. R - Q7	

After this Black loses at least two Pawns. The remaining moves were:

9. . . . Kt - B4; *10.* R x P ch, K - Kt3; *11.* R x P, Kt - Q6 ch; *12.* K - Kt1, K - B4; *13.* R - Q1, Kt x KP; *14.* R - B1 ch, K - K5; *15.*

R x P (*15.* B x Kt wins too), Kt - B5; *16.* R - Q7, K - K6; *17.* R - K1 ch, K - B6; *18.* R x R, R x R; *19.* R - Q4, Kt - K6; *20.* R - KR4, Kt - B4; *21.* R - QKt4, and Black resigned. Another Pawn goes after *21.* . . . R - K3; *22.* B - Q8.

Often the exchange of Queens, while it does not force a won ending, leads to one that is favorable for the defender and immediately removes any attacking possibilities. Such a situation is seen in *Diagram 377* from Alekhine-Fine, AVRO

DIAGRAM 377

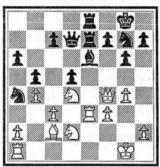

Tournament, 1938. Here if White can get in Q - B6, followed by QR - K1, his attack would be quite strong. Black nips this in the bud with:

1. . . .   Q - Q3 !

If now *2.* Q - B6, B - Q2, and if *2.* Q - R6, P - QB4; *3.* P x P, Kt x P(B4); *4.* QR - K1, B - Q2, and Black's defensive task is not difficult.

2. Q x Q   P x Q
3. QR - K1   R - B2

As a result of the Queen exchange, Black has the better end-game prospects, though he won only because of a later oversight by White.

⌐Superior End-Game Mobility

THIS applies to those positions where the Queen is the most aggressive piece. Often enough the Queen supports the position in such a way that when she is exchanged the other pieces are completely disunited. *Diagram 378*, from Reshevsky-Steiner, New York, 1942, is an illustration.

DIAGRAM 378

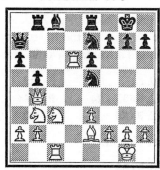

White has an obviously superior position but cannot make further headway because of the Black Queen. So:

> *1.* Q - B5 !   Q x Q

Black must of course exchange.

> *2.* Kt x Q   Kt - B4
> *3.* R(Q6) - Q1

A temporary retreat.

> *3.* . . .   B - Kt2
> *4.* P - K4   Kt - K2
> *5.* P - B4   Kt(K4) - B3
> *6.* R - Q7

Re-entry with redoubled force.

6. . . .	B - B1
7. R - Q6	

Now the Rook cannot be driven away from here.

7. . . .	P - KR3
8. K - B2	R - Q1
9. R(B1) - Q1	R x R
10. R x R	

Because of the strong Rook Black is almost paralyzed. Note that if there were Queens on the board, say Black's at QB2, White's at Q2, White's advantage would amount to very little.

10. . . .	P - Kt5
11. Kt(B3) - R4	P - QR4
12. P - K5	B - Kt2

To free his other Knight.

13. B - B3

Not so soon, he says!

13. . . .	B - R1
14. Kt - Q7	R - Q1
15. Kt(R4) - Kt6	

A curious position: Black cannot avoid the loss of a piece.

15. . . .	Kt - B1
16. Kt x Kt	R x Kt
17. Kt - Kt6	

Black now loses a piece, and therefore resigned.

Index of Players

Index of Openings and Variations